Other Books and Series by Jeff Bowen

Applications for Enrollment of Chickasaw Newborn Act of 1905
Volumes I, II, III, IV & V,

Visit our website at **www.nativestudy.com** to learn more about these and other books and series by Jeff Bowen

APPLICATIONS FOR ENROLLMENT OF CHICKASAW NEWBORN ACT OF 1905 VOLUME VI

TRANSCRIBED BY
JEFF BOWEN

NATIVE STUDY
Gallipolis, Ohio
USA

Other Books and Series by Jeff Bowen

1901-1907 Native American Census Seneca, Eastern Shawnee, Miami, Modoc, Ottawa, Peoria, Quapaw, and Wyandotte Indians (Under Seneca School, Indian Territory)

1932 Census of The Standing Rock Sioux Reservation with Births And Deaths 1924-1932

Census of The Blackfeet, Montana, 1897- 1901 Expanded Edition

Eastern Cherokee by Blood, 1906-1910, Volumes I thru XIII

Choctaw of Mississippi Indian Census 1929-1932 with Births and Deaths 1924-1931 Volume I
Choctaw of Mississippi Indian Census 1933, 1934 & 1937, Supplemental Rolls to 1934 & 1935 with Births and Deaths 1932-1938, and Marriages 1936-1938 Volume II

Eastern Cherokee Census Cherokee, North Carolina 1930-1939 Census 1930-1931 with Births And Deaths 1924-1931 Taken By Agent L. W. Page Volume I
Eastern Cherokee Census Cherokee, North Carolina 1930-1939 Census 1932-1933 with Births And Deaths 1930-1932 Taken By Agent R. L. Spalsbury Volume II
Eastern Cherokee Census Cherokee, North Carolina 1930-1939 Census 1934-1937 with Births and Deaths 1925-1938 and Marriages 1936 & 1938 Taken by Agents R. L. Spalsbury And Harold W. Foght Volume III

Seminole of Florida Indian Census, 1930-1940 with Birth and Death Records, 1930-1938

Texas Cherokees 1820-1839 A Document For Litigation 1921

Choctaw By Blood Enrollment Cards 1898-1914 Volumes I thru XVII

Starr Roll 1894 (Cherokee Payment Rolls) Districts: Canadian, Cooweescoowee, and Delaware Volume One
Starr Roll 1894 (Cherokee Payment Rolls) Districts: Flint, Going Snake, and Illinois Volume Two
Starr Roll 1894 (Cherokee Payment Rolls) Districts: Saline, Sequoyah, and Tahlequah; Including Orphan Roll Volume Three

Cherokee Intruder Cases Dockets of Hearings 1901-1909 Volumes I & II

Indian Wills, 1911-1921 Records of the Bureau of Indian Affairs Books One thru Seven;
Native American Wills & Probate Records 1911-1921

Other Books and Series by Jeff Bowen

Turtle Mountain Reservation Chippewa Indians 1932 Census with Births & Deaths, 1924-1932

Chickasaw By Blood Enrollment Cards 1898-1914 Volume I thru V

Cherokee Descendants East An Index to the Guion Miller Applications Volume I
Cherokee Descendants West An Index to the Guion Miller Applications Volume II (A-M)
Cherokee Descendants West An Index to the Guion Miller Applications Volume III (N-Z)

Applications for Enrollment of Seminole Newborn Freedmen, Act of 1905

Eastern Cherokee Census, Cherokee, North Carolina, 1915-1922, Taken by Agent James E. Henderson   Volume I (1915-1916)
Volume II (1917-1918)
Volume III (1919-1920)
Volume IV (1921-1922)

Complete Delaware Roll of 1898

Eastern Cherokee Census, Cherokee, North Carolina, 1923-1929, Taken by Agent James E. Henderson   Volume I (1923-1924)
Volume II (1925-1926)
Volume III (1927-1929)

Applications for Enrollment of Seminole Newborn Act of 1905 Volumes I & II

North Carolina Eastern Cherokee Indian Census 1898-1899, 1904, 1906, 1909-1912, 1914 Revised and Expanded Edition

1932 Hopi and Navajo Native American Census with Birth & Death Rolls (1925-1931) Volume 1 - Hopi
1932 Hopi and Navajo Native American Census with Birth & Death Rolls (1930-1932) Volume 2 - Navajo

Western Navajo Reservation Navajo, Hopi and Paiute 1933 Census with Birth & Death Rolls 1925-1933

Cherokee Citizenship Commission Dockets 1880-1884 and 1887-1889 Volumes I thru V

Copyright © 2013
by Jeff Bowen

ALL RIGHTS RESERVED
No part of this publication may be reproduced
or used in any form or manner whatsoever
without previous written permission from the
copyright holder or publisher.

Originally published:
Baltimore, Maryland
2013

Reprinted by:

Native Study LLC
Gallipolis, OH
www.nativestudy.com
2020

Library of Congress Control Number: 2020917160

ISBN: 978-1-64968-068-6

Made in the United States of America.

This series is dedicated to the descendants of the Chickasaw newborn listed in these applications.

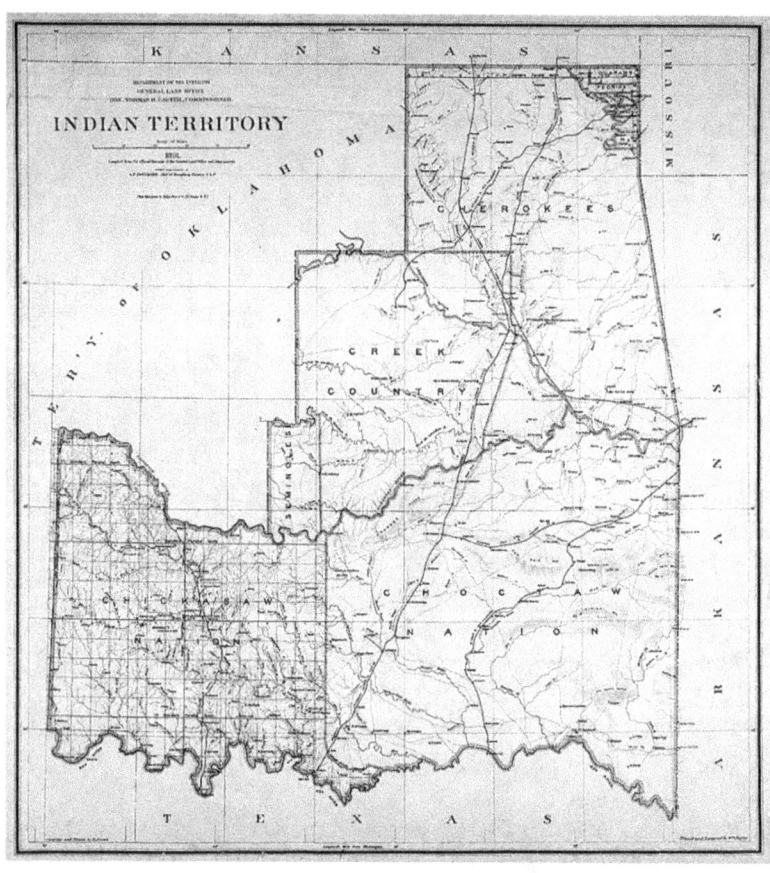

This map of Indian Territory shows how large the Choctaw and Chickasaw Nations' land base was that contained huge deposits of asphalt and coal. Just the size and territory involved was flooded with the "Grafters".

DEPARTMENT OF THE INTERIOR,
Commission to the Five Civilized Tribes.

Rules and Regulations Governing the Selection of Allotments and the Designation of Homesteads in the Choctaw and Chickasaw Nations.

1. Selections of allotments and designations of homesteads for adult citizens and selections of allotments for adult freedmen must be made in person except as herein otherwise provided.

2. Applications to have land set apart and homesteads designated for duly identified Mississippi Choctaws must be made personally before the Commission to the Five Civilized Tribes. Fathers may apply for their minor children and if the father be dead the mother may apply. Husbands may apply for wives. Applications for orphans, insane persons and persons of unsound mind may be made by duly appointed guardian or curator, and for aged and infirm persons and prisoners by agents duly authorized thereunto by power of attorney, in the discretion of said Commission.

3. At the time of the selection of allotment each citizen and duly identified Mississippi Choctaw shall designate as a homestead out of said selection land equal in value to one hundred and sixty acres of the average allottable land of the Choctaw and Chickasaw Nations, as nearly as may be.

4. Each Choctaw and Chickasaw freedman, at the time of selection shall designate as his or her allotment of the lands of the Choctaw and Chickasaw Nations, land equal in value to forty acres of the average allottable land of the Choctaw and Chickasaw Nations.

5. Citizens, freedmen and identified Mississippi Choctaws who are married, whether they have attained their majority or not, will be regarded as of age for the purpose of making selections.

6. Selections may be made by citizen and freedman parents for unmarried male children under twenty-one years of age and for unmarried female children under eighteen years of age, and a male citizen or freedman may make selection for his wife, if she is entitled to make selection, unless she shall, at the time or previously thereto, protest in writing.

7. Where the father of an unmarried minor citizen, freedman or identified Mississippi Choctaw is a non-citizen, the citizen, freedman or identified Mississippi Choctaw mother of such children must make selection in person in behalf of said children.

8. Selections of allotments and designations of homesteads for minor citizens and selections of allotments for minor freedmen may be made by the citizen father or mother or freedman father or mother, as the case may be, or by a guardian, curator, or an administrator having charge of their estate, in the order named.

9. Selections of allotments and designations of homesteads for citizen, and selections of allotment for freedmen, prisoners, convicts, aged and infirm persons and soldiers and sailors of the United States on duty outside of Indian Territory, may be made by duly appointed agents under power of attorney, and for incompetents by guardians, curators, or other suitable person akin to them.

10. Selections may be made and homesteads designated by duly identified Mississippi Choctaws, who have, within one year after the date of their identification as such, made satisfactory proof of bona fide settlement within the Choctaw-Chickasaw country, at any time within six months after the date of their said identification.

11. Persons authorized to make selections by power of attorney, as provided in rules 2 and 9 hereof, must be the husband or wife, or a relative not further removed than a cousin of the first degree of the person for whom such selection is made.

12. It shall be the duty of the Commission to the Five Civilized Tribes to see that selections of allotments and designations of homesteads for the classes of persons mentioned in rules 2, 6, 7, 8 and 9 hereof, are made for the best interests of such persons.

13. Selections of allotments for citizens, freedmen and identified Mississippi Choctaws who have died subsequent to September 25, 1902, and before making a selection of allotment, shall be made by a duly appointed administrator or executor. If, however, such administrator or executor be not duly and expeditiously appointed, or fails to act promptly when appointed, or for any other cause such selections be not so made within a reasonable and practicable time, the Commission to the Five Civilized Tribes shall designate the lands thus to be allotted.

14. In determining the value of a selection the appraised value of the land selected shall be increased by the appraised value of such pine timber on such land as has heretofore been estimated by the Commission to the Five Civilized Tribes.

15. Selections of allotments may be made only by citizens and freedmen whose enrollment has been approved by the Secretary of the Interior, and by persons duly identified by the Commission to the Five Civilized Tribes as Mississippi Choctaws, and by none others.

16. When a selection of land has been made by a citizen, freedman or identified Mississippi Choctaw, and the land so selected is claimed by a person whose rights as a citizen or freedman have not been finally determined, contest for the land so selected may be instituted by the person claiming the land, formal application for the land being first made as is required by the Rules of Practice in Choctaw and Chickasaw allotment contest cases.

THE COMMISSION TO THE FIVE CIVILIZED TRIBES.
TAMS BIXBY, Chairman.

Muskogee, Indian Territory, March 24, 1903.

The above statement published prior to 1905, was established for what was supposed to be a set of guidelines when it came to allotments. But with supplemental agreements and Congressional legislation, time frames as well as rules and regulations often changed and were not the same for every tribe.

INTRODUCTION

The *Applications for Enrollment of Chickasaw Newborn Act of 1905*, National Archive film M-1301, Rolls 455-458, are found under the heading of Applications for Enrollment of the Commission to the Five Civilized Tribes. For this series, I have transcribed the application forms filled out by individuals applying for enrollment in the Five Civilized Tribes under the Dawes Commission. These applications contain considerably more information than stated on the census cards found in series M-1186. M-1301 possesses its own numerical sequence, separate from M-1186. To find each party's roll number you would have to reference M-1186.

The Chickasaw as well as the Choctaw allotments were likely some of the most sought after properties in Indian Territory. There was supposed to be a 25-year restriction on the sale or lease of any Indian lands so as to insure that the owners wouldn't be swindled, but that isn't what happened. This fact is borne out in the Dawes Commission General Allotment Act, of February 8, 1887, Section 5, which "Provides that after an Indian person is allotted land, the United States will hold the land 'in trust [1] for the sole use and benefit of the Indian' (or his heirs if the Indian landowner dies) for a period of 25 years. (Land held in trust by the United States government cannot be sold or in anyway alienated by the Indian landowner, since the United States government considers the underlying ownership of the land held by itself and not the tribe. After the period of trust ends, the Indian landowner is free to sell the land and is free from any encumbrance from the United States.)"[1] Instead, Native Americans were exploited by the devious. The Chickasaw and Choctaw Districts both had huge asphalt and coal deposits, so there was pressure from outsiders to acquire them from the minute they were discovered. After repeated attacks throughout the years and many legislative changes, President "Roosevelt finally signed the Five Tribes Bill at noon on April 26, 1906, the forces seeking to end all restrictions were disappointed. Section 19 removed restrictions from the sale of all inherited land but directed that no full-bloods could sell their land for twenty-five years. The Act also prohibited leases for more than one year without the approval of the Secretary of the Interior."[2]

Angie Debo described the opportunists that wanted these Native American allotments as, "Grafters". The parents of the newborns enumerated within this series would no sooner receive the approval for their child's allotment than there would be someone there with cash in hand holding a new deed or lease for the parents to sign their child's birthright away. Angie Debo said it best, "As the business incapacity of the allottees became apparent, a horde of despoilers fastened themselves upon their property." According to Debo, "The term 'grafter' was applied as a matter of course to dealers in Indian land, and was frankly accepted by them. The speculative fever also affected Government employees so that it was almost impossible to prevent them from making personal investments."[3]

---

[1] General Allotment Act, Act of Feb. 8, 1887 (24 Stat. 388, ch. 119, 25 USCA 331)
[2] The Dawes Commission and the Allotment of the Five Civilized Tribes, 1893-1914 by Kent Carter, pg. 173
[3] And Still the Waters Run, Angie Debo, p. 92.

INTRODUCTION

According to the Department of Interior in 1905, "It is estimated that there will be added to the final rolls of the citizens and freedmen of the Choctaw and Chickasaw nations the names of 2,000 persons, including 1,500 new-born children to be enrolled under the provisions of the act of Congress approved March 3, 1905."[4]

The quote below explains, in detail, the requirements for qualifying as a newborn Chickasaw, "By the act of Congress approved March 3, 1905 (H.R. 17474), entitled 'An act making appropriations for the current and contingent expenses of the Indian Department and for fulfilling treaty stipulations with various Indian tribes for the fiscal year ending June 30, 1906, and for other purposes,' it was provided as follows:

'That the Commission to the Five Civilized Tribes is hereby authorized for sixty days after the date of the approval of this act to receive and consider applications for enrollment of infant children born prior to September twenty-fifth, nineteen hundred and two, and who were living on said date, to citizens by blood of the Choctaw and Chickasaw tribes of Indians whose enrollment has been approved by the Secretary of the Interior prior to the date of the approval of this act; and to enroll and make allotments to such children.'

'That the Commission to the Five Civilized Tribes is authorized for sixty days after the date of the approval of this act to receive and consider applications for enrollment of children born subsequent to September twenty-fifth, nineteen hundred and two, and prior to March fourth, nineteen hundred and five, and who were living on said latter date, to citizens by blood of the Choctaw and Chickasaw tribes of Indians whose enrollment has been approved by the Secretary of the Interior prior to the date of the approval of this act; and to enroll and make allotments to such children.'

"Notice is hereby given that the Commission to the Five Civilized Tribes will, up to and inclusive of midnight, May 2, 1905, receive applications for the enrollment of infant children born prior to September 25, 1902, and who were living on said date, to citizens by blood of the Choctaw and Chickasaw tribes of Indians whose enrollment has been approved by the Secretary of the Interior prior to March 3, 1905."[5]

Following is the scope of these transcriptions: Besides the applications themselves, researchers will find the identities of other individuals within these applications -- doctors, lawyers, mid-wives, and other relatives -- that may help with you genealogical research.

Jeff Bowen
Gallipolis, Ohio
NativeStudy.com

---

[4] Annual Reports of the Department of the Interior For the Fiscal Year Ended June 30, 1905, p. 609.
[5] Annual Reports of the Department of the Interior For the Fiscal Year Ended June 30, 1905, p. 593.

Applications for Enrollment of Chickasaw Newborn
Act of 1905   Volume VI

Chic. N.B - 438
(Mandy Filmore
Born November 8, 1904)

BIRTH AFFIDAVIT.

DEPARTMENT OF THE INTERIOR.
COMMISSION TO THE FIVE CIVILIZED TRIBES.

IN RE APPLICATION FOR ENROLLMENT, as a citizen of the Chickasaw Nation of Mandy Fillmore, born on the 8 day of November, 1905[sic]

Name of Father: Benjamin Franklin Fillmore   a citizen of the ~~Choctaw~~ Chickasaw Nation.
Name of Mother: Sallie Fillmore   a citizen of the Chickasaw Nation.

Postoffice   Ninnekah, I.T.

AFFIDAVIT OF MOTHER.

UNITED STATES OF AMERICA, INDIAN TERRITORY,
Southern   DISTRICT.

I, Sallie Fillmore, on oath state that I am 26 years of age and a citizen by intermarraige[sic], of the Chickasaw Nation; that I am the lawful wife of Benjamin Franklin Filmore[sic], who is a citizen, by Blood of the Chickasha[sic] Nation; that a Female child was born to me on 8 day of November, 190 5, that said child has been named Mandy Filmore, and is now living.

Mrs Sallie Fillmore

WITNESSES TO MARK:
Sallie Hunnicutt
Mrs Hattie Patterson

Subscribed and sworn to before me this 30 day of March, 1905.

W.H. Ater
Notary Public.

Applications for Enrollment of Chickasaw Newborn
Act of 1905 Volume VI

AFFIDAVIT OF ATTENDING PHYSICIAN OR MID-WIFE.

UNITED STATES OF AMERICA, INDIAN TERRITORY, }
Southern DISTRICT.

I, P.W. Waltrep M.D. , a Physician , on oath state that I attended on Mrs. Sallie Filmore , wife of Benjamin Franklin Filmore on the 8 day of Nov , 190 5; that there was born to her on said date a female child; that said child is now living and is said to have been named Mandy Filmore[sic]

P.M. Waltrep M.D.

WITNESSES TO MARK:
{ Geo R Beeler
Fred G. Beeler

Subscribed and sworn to before me this 30 day of March , 1905.

W.H. Ater
Notary Public.

BIRTH AFFIDAVIT.

DEPARTMENT OF THE INTERIOR.
COMMISSION TO THE FIVE CIVILIZED TRIBES.

IN RE APPLICATION FOR ENROLLMENT, as a citizen of the Chicasaw[sic] Nation, of Mandy Filmore , born on the 8 day of November , 1904

Name of Father: Benjamin Franklin Filmore a citizen of the Chicasaw Nation.
Name of Mother: Sallie Filmore a citizen of the Chicasaw Nation.

Postoffice Ninnekah Ind Ter

AFFIDAVIT OF MOTHER.

UNITED STATES OF AMERICA, Indian Territory, }
Southern DISTRICT.

I, Sallie Filmore , on oath state that I am 26 years of age and a citizen by marriage , of the Chickasha[sic] Nation; that I am the lawful wife of Benjamin Franklin Filmore , who is a citizen, by Blood of the Chicasaw Nation; that a Female child was born to me on 8 day of November , 1904; that said child has been named Mandy Filmore , and was living March 4, 1905.

Mrs. Sallie Fillmore[sic]

2

Applications for Enrollment of Chickasaw Newborn
Act of 1905   Volume VI

Witnesses To Mark:
{ Ollie Waltrip
Florence Madison

Subscribed and sworn to before me this 21 day of   April   , 1905

W.H. Ater
Notary Public.

AFFIDAVIT OF ATTENDING PHYSICIAN OR MID-WIFE.

UNITED STATES OF AMERICA, Indian Territory,
Southern   DISTRICT.

I,   P.M. Woltrep[sic]   , a Phifissan[sic]   , on oath state that I attended on Mrs.   Sallie Filmore   , wife of Benjamin Franklin Filmore   on the 8 day of November   , 1904; that there was born to her on said date a   Female child; that said child was living March 4, 1905, and is said to have been named mndy Filmore

P.M. Waltrep M.D.

Witnesses To Mark:
{

Subscribed and sworn to before me this 22 day of   April   , 1905

W.H. Ater
Notary Public.

9-1322

Muskogee, Indian Territory, April 6, 1905.

Benjamin Franklin Fillmore,
    Ninnekah, Indian Territory.

Dear Sir:

Receipt is hereby acknowledged of the affidavits of Mrs. Sallie Fillmore and P. M. Waltrip to the birth of Mandy Fillmore, daughter of Benjamin Franklin and Sallie Fillmore, November 8, 1905.

It appears from the affidavits heretofore forwarded that this child was born November 8, 1905, and as this is evidently an error you are requested to have the enclosed blank executed showing the correct date of the birth of your child Mandy Fillmore.

Applications for Enrollment of Chickasaw Newborn
Act of 1905   Volume VI

Respectfully,

Commissioner in Charge.

Chickasaw 1322.

Muskogee, Indian Territory, April 26, 1905.

Benjamin Franklin Fillmore,
  Ninnekah, Indian Territory.

Dear Sir:

Receipt is hereby acknowledged of the affidavits of Mrs. Sallie Fillmore and P. M. Waltrep to the birth of Mandy Fillmore, daughter of Benjamin Franklin and Sallie Fillmore, November 8, 1904, and the same have been filed with our records as an application for the enrollment of said child.

Respectfully,

Chairman.

Chic. N.B - 439
  (Vernon Collins
  Born January 21, 1903)

BIRTH AFFIDAVIT.

Department of the Interior,
COMMISSION TO THE FIVE CIVILIZED TRIBES.

IN RE APPLICATION FOR ENROLLMENT, as a citizen of the   Chickasaw   Nation, of   Vernon Collins   , born on the   21   day of   January   , 190 3

Name of Father: Ben C. Collins   a citizen of the Chickasaw Nation.
Name of Mother: Hettie H. Collins   a citizen of the Chickasaw Nation.

Post-Office: Emet, Ind Tery

Applications for Enrollment of Chickasaw Newborn
Act of 1905   Volume VI

AFFIDAVIT OF MOTHER.

UNITED STATES OF AMERICA,
    INDIAN TERRITORY,
Southern   District.

I,   Hettie H Collins   , on oath state that I am   27th[sic]   years of age and a citizen by   Blood , of the   Chickasaw   Nation; that I am the lawful wife of Ben C. Collins , who is a citizen, by blood   of the   Chickasaw   Nation; that a   boy   child was born to me on 21 day of   January , 190 3, that said child has been named   Vernon Collins   , and is now living.

                                Hettie H. Collins

WITNESSES TO MARK:
   { Janice Heald Hardy
     Maude Collins

Subscribed and sworn to before me this 15 day of   April , 190

                                A J McKinney
                                  Notary Public.
            Emet I T

AFFIDAVIT OF ATTENDING PHYSICIAN OR MID-WIFE.

UNITED STATES OF AMERICA,
    INDIAN TERRITORY,
Southern   District.

I,   Mollie H. Ingram   , a   Midwife , on oath state that I attended on Mrs. Hettie H. Collins , wife of Ben C. Collins   on the 21 day of   January , 190 3; that there was born to her on said date a   Boy   child; that said child is now living and is said to have been named Vernon Collins

                                Mollie H. Ingram

WITNESSES TO MARK:
   { Janice Heald Hardy
     Maude Collins

Subscribed and sworn to before me this 15 day of   April , 190

                                A J McKinney
                                  Notary Public.

Applications for Enrollment of Chickasaw Newborn
Act of 1905   Volume VI

Chickasaw 714.

Muskogee, Indian Territory, April 26, 1905.

Ben C. Collins,
  Emet, Indian Territory.

Dear Sir:

    Receipt is hereby acknowledged of the affidavits of Hettie H. Collins and Mollie H. Ingram to the birth of Vernon Collins, son of Ben C. and Hettie H. Collins, January 21, 1903, and the same have been filed with our records as an application for the enrollment of said child.

Respectfully,

Chairman.

Chic. N.B - 440
  (Clarence R. Hancock
  Born December 11, 1903)

BIRTH AFFIDAVIT.

DEPARTMENT OF THE INTERIOR.
COMMISSION TO THE FIVE CIVILIZED TRIBES.

    IN RE APPLICATION FOR ENROLLMENT, as a citizen of the   Chicasaw[sic]   Nation, of   Clarence R. Hancock   , born on the   11   day of   December   , 1903

Name of Father: Robert Hancock   a citizen of the   Chicasaw   Nation.
Name of Mother: Katie Hancock   a citizen of the   Chickasaw   Nation.

Postoffice   Russellville, Ind. T.

AFFIDAVIT OF MOTHER.

UNITED STATES OF AMERICA, Indian Territory,
  Western   DISTRICT.

    I,   Katie Hancock   , on oath state that I am   23   years of age and a citizen by   In=termarriage[sic]   , of the   Chickasaw   Nation; that I am the lawful wife of   Robert Hancock   , who is a citizen, by Blood   of the   Chickasaw   Nation; that a   Male   child was born to me on   11   day of   December   , 1903;

Applications for Enrollment of Chickasaw Newborn
Act of 1905 Volume VI

that said child has been named   Clarence R. Hancock   , and was living March 4, 1905.

                                        Katie Hancock

Witnesses To Mark:
{

    Subscribed and sworn to before me this   22   day of   April   , 1905

                                        J. M. White
                                        Notary Public.

AFFIDAVIT OF ATTENDING PHYSICIAN OR MID-WIFE.

UNITED STATES OF AMERICA, Indian Territory, }
    Western   DISTRICT.

    I,   Jane Davis   , a   Midwife   , on oath state that I attended on Mrs.   Katie Hancock   , wife of   Robert Hancock   on the   11 day of December   , 1903; that there was born to her on said date a   Male   child; that said child was living March 4, 1905, and is said to have been named   Clarence R. Hancock

                                          Jane Davis

Witnesses To Mark:
{

    Subscribed and sworn to before me this   22   day of   April   , 1905

                                        J. M. White
                                        Notary Public.

                                                        9-1041.

                       Muskogee, Indian Territory, April 26, 1905.

Robert Hancock,
    Russellville, Indian Territory.

Dear Sir:

    Receipt is hereby acknowledged of the affidavits of Katie Hancock and Jane Davis to the birth of Clarence R. Hancock, son of Robert and Katie Hancock, December 11, 1903, and the same have been filed with our records as an application for the enrollment of said child.

                                Respectfully,

                                                   Chairman.

Applications for Enrollment of Chickasaw Newborn
Act of 1905 Volume VI

Chic. N.B - 441
  (Junetta Youngblood
  Born January 21, 1904)

BIRTH AFFIDAVIT.

  IN RE-APPLICATION FOR ENROLLMENT, as a citizen of the Chickasaw Nation, of Junetta Youngblood , born on the 21st day of Jan , 190 4

Name of Father: L. C. Youngblood a citizen of the .... Nation.
Name of Mother: Edna Youngblood a citizen of the Chickasaw Nation.

  Postoffice Troy I.T.

AFFIDAVIT OF MOTHER.

UNITED STATES OF AMERICA, INDIAN TERRITORY,
  Southern District District.

  I, Edna Youngblood , on oath state that I am 19 years of age and a citizen by blood , of the Chickasaw Nation; that I am the lawful wife of L. C. Youngblood , who is a citizen, by Marriage of the Chickasaw Nation; that a Female child was born to me on 21st day of January , 1904 , that said child has been named Juneta[sic] Youngblood , and is now living.

  Edna Youngblood

Witnesses To Mark:
  Tommie Pickens
  J.B. Pittman

  Subscribed and sworn to before me this 6th day of April , 1905.

  W.H. Pittman
  Notary Public.

AFFIDAVIT OF ATTENDING PHYSICIAN OR MID-WIFE.

UNITED STATES OF AMERICA, INDIAN TERRITORY,
  Southern District District.

  I, Elsie Norton , a Midwife , on oath state that I attended on Mrs. Edna Youngblood , wife of L. C. Youngblood on the 21st day

Applications for Enrollment of Chickasaw Newborn
Act of 1905   Volume VI

of   January , 190 4; that there was born to her on said date a   Female   child; that said child is now living and is said to have been named Juneta[sic] Youngblood

her
Elsie x Norton
mark

Witnesses To Mark:
{ Tommie Pickens
{ J.B. Pittman

Subscribed and sworn to before me this   6th   day of   April   , 1905.

W.H. Pittman
Notary Public.

Muskogee, Indian Territory, April 15, 1905.

L. C. Youngblood,
Troy, Indian Territory.

Dear Sir:

Receipt is hereby acknowledged of the affidavits of Edna Youngblood and Elsie Norton to the birth of Juneta Youngblood daughter of L. C. and Edna Youngblood, January 21, 1904.

It is stated in the affidavits of the mother that she is a citizen by blood of the Chickasaw Nation. If this is correct you are requested to state under what name she was enrolled, the names of her parents and if she has selected an allotment of the lands of the Choctaw or Chickasaw Nation please give her roll number as it appears on her allotment certificate.

Respectfully,

Chairman.

---

9 731

Muskogee, Indian Territory, April 28, 1905.

Edna Youngblood,
Troy, Indian Territory.

Dear Madam:

Receipt is hereby acknowledged of your letter of April 21, 1905, stating that you were enrolled under your maiden name, Edna Brown. This information has enabled us to identify you as an enrolled citizen by blood of the Chickasaw Nation and the affidavits

Applications for Enrollment of Chickasaw Newborn
Act of 1905   Volume VI

heretofore forwarded to the birth of Juneta Youngblood, have been filed with our records as an application for the enrollment of said child.

Respectfully,

Chairman.

Chic. N.B - 442
  (Essie May Perry
  Born July 24, 1903)

BIRTH AFFIDAVIT.

IN RE-APPLICATION FOR ENROLLMENT, as a citizen of the   Chickasaw   Nation, of   Essie May Perry   , born on the   24   day of   July   , 190 3

Name of Father: Thomas J. Perry   a citizen of the Chickasaw   Nation.
Name of Mother: Kittie Peddycoat Perry   a citizen of the Chickasaw   Nation.

Postoffice   Duncan I.T.

AFFIDAVIT OF MOTHER.

UNITED STATES OF AMERICA, INDIAN TERRITORY,
  Southern District   District.

I,   Kittie Peddycoart Perry   , on oath state that I am   24   years of age and a citizen by   Intermarriage   , of the   Chickasaw   Nation; that I am the lawful wife of Thomas J. Perry   , who is a citizen, by   Blood   of the   Chickasaw   Nation; that a Female   child was born to me on   24   day of   July   , 1903 , that said child has been named Essie May Perry   , and is now living.

Kittie Peddycoart Perry

Witnesses To Mark:

Subscribed and sworn to before me this   17th day of   March   , 1905.

John Vaughn
  Notary Public.

Applications for Enrollment of Chickasaw Newborn
Act of 1905 Volume VI

AFFIDAVIT OF ATTENDING PHYSICIAN OR MID-WIFE.

UNITED STATES OF AMERICA, INDIAN TERRITORY, }
Southern District.

I, M. E. Peddycoart, a ——————, on oath state that I attended on Mrs. Kittie Peddycoart Perry, wife of Thomas J. Perry on the 24 day of July, 190 3; that there was born to her on said date a Female child; that said child is now living and is said to have been named Essie May Perry

M E Peddycoart

Witnesses To Mark:

Subscribed and sworn to before me this 18th day of March, 1905.

John Vaughn
Notary Public.

BIRTH AFFIDAVIT.

DEPARTMENT OF THE INTERIOR.
COMMISSION TO THE FIVE CIVILIZED TRIBES.

IN RE APPLICATION FOR ENROLLMENT, as a citizen of the Chickasaw Nation, of Essie May Perry, born on the 24 day of July, 1903

Name of Father: Thomas J Perry   a citizen of the Chickasaw Nation.
                                        by intermarriage
Name of Mother: Kittie Peddycoart Perry a citizen of the Chickasaw Nation.

Postoffice Duncan I.T.

AFFIDAVIT OF MOTHER.

UNITED STATES OF AMERICA, Indian Territory, }
Southern DISTRICT.

I, Kittie Peddycoart Perry, on oath state that I am 24 years of age and a citizen by intermarrige[sic], of the Chickasaw Nation; that I am the lawful wife of Thomas J Perry, who is a citizen, by blood of the Chickasaw Nation; that a female child was born to me on 24 day of July, 1903; that said child has been named Essie May Perry, and was living March 4, 1905.

Kittie Peddycoart Perry

Applications for Enrollment of Chickasaw Newborn
Act of 1905   Volume VI

Witnesses To Mark:
{

    Subscribed and sworn to before me this   22   day of   April   , 1905

                        John Vaughn
                          Notary Public.

AFFIDAVIT OF ATTENDING PHYSICIAN OR MID-WIFE.

UNITED STATES OF AMERICA, Indian Territory, }
   Southern   DISTRICT.

    I,   Mary E Peddycoart   , a ...., on oath state that I attended on Mrs.   Kittie Peddycoart Perry   , wife of   Thomas J Perry   on the   24   day of   July   , 1903; that there was born to her on said date a   female   child; that said child was living March 4, 1905, and is said to have been named   Essie May Perry

                       M E Peddycoart

Witnesses To Mark:
{

    Subscribed and sworn to before me this   22   day of   April   , 1905

                        John Vaughn
                          Notary Public.

                              9-222.

            Muskogee, Indian Territory, April 27, 1905.

Thomas J. Perry,
    Duncan, Indian Territory.

Dear Sir:

    Receipt is hereby acknowledged of your letter of April 22, 1905 transmitting affidavits of Kittie Peddycoart Perry and Mary E. Peddycoart to the birth of Essie May Perry, daughter of Thomas and Kittie Peddycoart Perry, July 24, 1903, and the same have been filed with our records as an application for the enrollment of said child.

                Respectfully,

                              Chairman.

Applications for Enrollment of Chickasaw Newborn
Act of 1905 Volume VI

Chic. N.B - 443
    (Clarance Cadian Colbert
    Born June 13, 1903)

BIRTH AFFIDAVIT.

DEPARTMENT OF THE INTERIOR.
COMMISSION TO THE FIVE CIVILIZED TRIBES.

IN RE APPLICATION FOR ENROLLMENT, as a citizen of the Chickasaw Nation, of Clarance Cadian Colbert , born on the 13 day of June , 1903

Name of Father: James Beldon Colbert   a citizen of the Chickasaw Nation.
Name of Mother: Ida Colbert   a citizen of the Chickasaw Nation.

        Postoffice   Kosoma I.T

AFFIDAVIT OF MOTHER.

UNITED STATES OF AMERICA, Indian Territory,
                              DISTRICT.

    I, Ida Colbert , on oath state that I am 29 years of age and a citizen by Marrage[sic] , of the Chickasaw Nation; that I am the lawful wife of James Beldon Colbert , who is a citizen, by Blood of the Chickasaw Nation; that a male child was born to me on 13 day of June , 1903; that said child has been named Clarane[sic] Cadian Colbert , and was living March 4, 1905.

                              Ida Colbert

Witnesses To Mark:
    Isaac J Impson
    A B Impson

    Subscribed and sworn to before me this 21st day of April , 1905

                            W.m.[sic] Harrison
                              Notary Public.

Applications for Enrollment of Chickasaw Newborn
Act of 1905   Volume VI

AFFIDAVIT OF ATTENDING PHYSICIAN OR MID-WIFE.

UNITED STATES OF AMERICA, ~~Indian Territory~~,
Territory of
Gila Land   DISTRICT.

I, Mrs Minnie Holderman, a Midwife, on oath state that I attended on Mrs. Ida Colbert, wife of James Beldon Colbert on the 13 day of June, 1903; that there was born to her on said date a male child; that said child was living March 4, 1905, and is said to have been named Clarance Cadian Colbert

Mrs Minnie Holderman

Witnesses To Mark:
- C.W. Holderman
- *(Name Illegible)*

Subscribed and sworn to before me this 13th day of April, 1905

NOTARY PUBLIC   Cora E Smith
In and for the County of Cochise, Territory of Arizona
My Commission Expires March 21, 1908.   Notary Public.

9-1285.

Muskogee, Indian Territory, April 27, 1905.

James B. Colbert,
   Kosoma, Indian Territory.

Dear Sir:

Receipt is hereby acknowledged of the affidavits of Ida Colbert and Mrs. Minnie Holderman to the birth of Clarance Cadian Colbert, son of James B. and Ida Colbert, June 13, 1903, and the same has been filed with our records as an application for the enrollment of said child.

Respectfully,

Chairman.

Chic. N.B - 444
   (Daisy Lee Owens
   Born September 4, 1904)

Applications for Enrollment of Chickasaw Newborn
Act of 1905 Volume VI

BIRTH AFFIDAVIT.

DEPARTMENT OF THE INTERIOR.
COMMISSION TO THE FIVE CIVILIZED TRIBES.

IN RE APPLICATION FOR ENROLLMENT, as a citizen of the Chickasaw Nation, of Daisy Lee Owens, born on the 4th day of Sept, 1904

Name of Father: Solomon Owens   a citizen of the Chickasaw Nation.
Name of Mother: Mary J Owens   a citizen of the U.S. ~~Nation~~.

Postoffice   Viola I.T.

AFFIDAVIT OF MOTHER.

UNITED STATES OF AMERICA, Indian Territory,
Southern   DISTRICT.

I, Mary J Owens, on oath state that I am 25 years of age and a citizen ~~by~~ ———, of the United States ~~Nation~~; that I am the lawful wife of Solomon Owens, who is a citizen, by blood of the Chickasaw Nation; that a female child was born to me on the 4th day of September, 1904; that said child has been named Daisy Lee Owens, and was living March 4, 1905.

                             Mary J Owens

Witnesses To Mark:
{

Subscribed and sworn to before me this 17 day of April, 1905

                     ~~Mary J Owens~~   JE Williams
                                     Notary Public.

AFFIDAVIT OF ATTENDING PHYSICIAN OR MID-WIFE.

UNITED STATES OF AMERICA, Indian Territory,
Southern   DISTRICT.

I, Cromer Logan, a Midwife, on oath state that I attended on Mrs. Mary J Owens, wife of Solomon Owens on the 4th day of September, 1904; that there was born to her on said date a female child; that said child was living March 4, 1905, and is said to have been named Daisy Lee Owens

                             Cromer Logan

Witnesses To Mark:
{

Applications for Enrollment of Chickasaw Newborn
Act of 1905 Volume VI

Subscribed and sworn to before me this 22 day of   April   , 1905

                         E. J. Ball
                              Notary Public.

NB 444

DEPARTMENT OF THE INTERIOR,
Commission to the Five Civilized Tribes.
FILED
APR 27 1905
Tams Bixby CHAIRMAN.

No. 1524

Certificate of Record of Marriages.

UNITED STATES OF AMERICA,
  INDIAN TERRITORY, } SCT:
  Central   DISTRICT.

    I,   E.J. Fannin   , Clerk of the United States Court in the Indian Territory and District aforesaid, do hereby CERTIFY, that the License for and Certificate of the Marriage of

Mr.   S. L. Owens   and

M rs Mary Camron   was

filed in my office in said Territory and District the   2   day of   July   A.D., 190 2 and duly recorded in Book 2   of Marriage Record, Page   144

    WITNESS my hand and seal of said Court, at   Atoka   , this 2 day of   July   , A.D. 190 2

             E.J. Fannin
                     Clerk.

By   JD Catlin   *Deputy.*

Applications for Enrollment of Chickasaw Newborn
Act of 1905 Volume VI

No. 1524

FORM NO. 598.

MARRIAGE LICENSE.

UNITES STATES OF AMERICA,
THE INDIAN TERRITORY,   } ss:
Central   DISTRICT.

To any Person Authorized by Law to Solemnize Marriage—Greeting:

You are hereby commanded to solemnize the Rite and publish the **Banns of Matrimony** *between* Mr. S.L. Owens *of* Byrne *in the Indian Territory, aged* 29 *years, and* Mrs Mary Camron *of* Byrne *in the Indian Territory, aged* 23 *years, according to law, and do you officially sign and return this License to the parties therein named.*

WITNESS my hand and official seal, this 13 day of June A. D. 190 2

E. J. Fannin
Clerk of the United States Court.

J D Catlin
Deputy

CERTIFICATE OF MARRIAGE.

UNITES STATES OF AMERICA,
THE INDIAN TERRITORY,   } ss: I,   H. P. Hook
DISTRICT.   a   minister of the Gospel

do hereby CERTIFY, that on the 15 day of June A, D. 190 2 ; I did duly and according to law, as commanded in the foregoing License, solemnize the Rite and publish the BANNS OF MATRIMONY between the parties therein named.

Witness my hand this 16 day of June , A. D. 190 2

My credentials are recorded in the office of the Clerk of the United States Court in the Indian Territory, Central District, Book B   Page   166

H.P. Hook
a   M of the Gos.

Applications for Enrollment of Chickasaw Newborn
Act of 1905 Volume VI

Chickasaw 753.

Muskogee, Indian Territory, April 28, 1905.

Solomon Owens,
    Wapanucka, Indian Territory.

Dear Sir:

    Receipt is hereby acknowledged of your letter of April 22, enclosing affidavits of Mary J. Owens and Cromer Logan to the birth of Daisy Lee Owens, daughter of Solomon and Mary J. Owens, September 4, 1904, and the same have been filed with our records as an application for the enrollment of said child.

    Receipt is also acknowledged of the marriage license and certificate between S. L. Owen and Mrs. Mary Camron, and the same have been filed with the records in the matter of the enrollment of the above named child.

                    Respectfully,

                              Chairman.

Chic. N.B - 445
    (Florence M. Walner
    Born October 17, 1903)

BIRTH AFFIDAVIT.

DEPARTMENT OF THE INTERIOR.
COMMISSION TO THE FIVE CIVILIZED TRIBES.

    IN RE APPLICATION FOR ENROLLMENT, as a citizen of the Chickasaw Nation, of Florence M. Walner, born on the 17th day of October, 1903

Name of Father: Robert Walner   a citizen of the Chickasaw Nation.
Name of Mother: May Walner   a citizen of the Chickasaw Nation.

                    Postoffice

Applications for Enrollment of Chickasaw Newborn
Act of 1905   Volume VI

AFFIDAVIT OF MOTHER.

UNITED STATES OF AMERICA, Indian Territory,
Southern   DISTRICT.

I,   May Walner , on oath state that I am Twenty one   years of age and a citizen ~~by~~   of the United States —— Nation; that I am the lawful wife of   Robert Walner , who is a citizen, by blood   of the   Chickasaw   Nation; that a Female   child was born to me on   17th   day of   October , 1903; that said child has been named   Florence M Walner , and was living March 4, 1905.

Mrs May Walner

Witnesses To Mark:
{ Frank L Robinson

Subscribed and sworn to before me this 22nd day of April , 1905

Frank L Robinson
Notary Public.

AFFIDAVIT OF ATTENDING PHYSICIAN OR MID-WIFE.

UNITED STATES OF AMERICA, Indian Territory,
Southern   DISTRICT.

I,   W.E. Settle , a Physician , on oath state that I attended on Mrs. May Walner , wife of   Robert Walner   on the 17th day of October , 1903; that there was born to her on said date a   Female   child; that said child was living March 4, 1905, and is said to have been named Florence M Walner

W.E. Settle M.D.

Witnesses To Mark:
{ Frank L Robinson

Subscribed and sworn to before me this 22nd day of April , 1905

Frank L Robinson
Notary Public.

Applications for Enrollment of Chickasaw Newborn
Act of 1905   Volume VI

BIRTH AFFIDAVIT.

DEPARTMENT OF THE INTERIOR.
COMMISSION TO THE FIVE CIVILIZED TRIBES.

IN RE APPLICATION FOR ENROLLMENT, as a citizen of the Chickasaw Nation, of Florence M. Walner, born on the 17 day of Oct, 1903

Name of Father: Robert Walner   a citizen of the Chickasaw Nation.
Name of Mother: Cornelia M Walner   a citizen of the non citizen Nation.

Postoffice   Wynnewood I.T.

AFFIDAVIT OF MOTHER.

UNITED STATES OF AMERICA, Indian Territory, } DISTRICT.

I, Cornelia M Walner, on oath state that I am 21 years of age and a citizen by ——, of the United States ~~Nation~~; that I am the lawful wife of Robert Walner, who is a citizen, by blood of the Chickasaw Nation; that a female child was born to me on 17 day of October, 1903; that said child has been named Florence M Walner, and was living March 4, 1905.

Cornelia M Walner

Witnesses To Mark:
{ W.W. Craig
{ C. Boswell

Subscribed and sworn to before me this 12th day of July, 1905

(Name Illegible)
Notary Public.

AFFIDAVIT OF ATTENDING PHYSICIAN OR MID-WIFE.

UNITED STATES OF AMERICA, Indian Territory, } DISTRICT.

I, W.E. Settle, a Physician, on oath state that I attended on Mrs. Cornelia M Walner, wife of Robert Walner on the 17 day of October, 1903; that there was born to her on said date a female child; that said child was living March 4, 1905, and is said to have been named Florence M Walner

Dr W.E. Settle

Applications for Enrollment of Chickasaw Newborn
Act of 1905   Volume VI

Witnesses To Mark:
{ W.B. Camp
  MG Norvell

Subscribed and sworn to before me this 10th day of   July   , 1905

(Name Illegible)
Notary Public.

Pauls Valley   #2128

Certificate of Record of Marriage

United States of America, ⎫
   Indian Territory,   ⎬ sct.
     Southern District. ⎭

DEPARTMENT OF THE INTERIOR,
COMMISSION TO THE FIVE CIVILIZED TRIBES.

FILED

MAY 2*6* 1905

Tams Bixby   CHAIRMAN.

I, C. M. CAMPBELL, Clerk of the United States Court, in the Territory and District aforesaid DO HEREBY CERTIFY, that the License for and Certificate of Marriage of

MR   W. R. Walner   and

M   Cornelia M. Chiek

were filed in my office in said Territory and District the   2   day of   January   A.D., 190 3   and duly recorded in Book   G   of Marriage Record, Page   108

F I L E D

(Illegible)
C. M. CAMPBELL, Clerk.
Southern Dist. Ind. Ter.

WITNESS my hand and Seal of said Court, at Ardmore,
this   2   day of
January   A.D. 190 3

C. M. Campbell
CLERK.

Applications for Enrollment of Chickasaw Newborn
Act of 1905   Volume VI

MARRIAGE LICENSE

Nº.

UNITED STATES OF AMERICA,
INDIAN TERRITORY,   ss: To Any Person Authorized by Law to Solemnize Marriage, Greeting:
SOUTHERN DISTRICT.

You are hereby commanded to solemnize the Rite and publish the Banns of Matrimony between Mr. W. R. Walner of Wynnewood in the Indian Territory, aged 23 years, and M Cornelia M. Chiek of Wynnewood in the Indian Territory, aged 19 years, according to law; and do you officially sign and return this License to the parties therein named.

Witness my hand and official Seal, this 31" day of December A. D. 190 2

C. M. CAMPBELL
Clerk of the United States Court.

(Name Illegible) Dy

Certificate of Marriage.

UNITED STATES OF AMERICA,
INDIAN TERRITORY,   ss:
SOUTHERN DISTRICT.   I,   J. M. Martin

_____ do hereby certify that on the 31 day of December , A. D. 190 2 , I did duly according to law, as commanded in the foregoing License, solemnize the Rite and publish the Banns of Matrimony between the parties therein named.

Witness my hand this 1 day of Jan A. D. 190 2

My credentials are recorded in the office of the Clerk of the United States Court, Indian Territory, Southern District, at Ardmore, Book A , Page 302

(NOTE-The person officiating should fill in the spaces for book and page and sign here.)

J. M. Martin
a Minister

Applications for Enrollment of Chickasaw Newborn
Act of 1905   Volume VI

9-459.

Muskogee, Indian Territory, April 27, 1905.

Robert Walner,
    Wynnewood, Indian Territory.

Dear Sir:

    Receipt is hereby acknowledged of your letter of April 22, 1905 transmitting affidavits of May Walner and W. E. Settle to the birth of Florence M. Walner, daughter of Robert and May Walner, October 17, 1903, and the same have been filed with our records as an application for the enrollment of said child.

    Respectfully,

    Chairman.

9-NB-445.

Muskogee, Indian Territory, May 18, 1905.

Robert Walner,
    Wynnewood, Indian Territory.

Dear Sir:

    Referring to the application for the enrollment of your infant child, Florence Walner, born October 17, 1903, it is noted that the applicant claims through you.

    In this event it will be necessary for you to file with the Commission either the original or a certified copy of the license and certificate of your marriage to the mother of the applicant, May[sic] Walner.

    Respectfully,

    Chairman.

Applications for Enrollment of Chickasaw Newborn
Act of 1905   Volume VI

9 N. B. 445.

Muskogee, Indian Territory, May 26, 1905.

Robert Walmer[sic],
    Wynnewood, Indian Territory.

Dear Sir:

    Receipt is hereby acknowledged of your letter of May 23, enclosing the marriage license and certificate between W. R. Walner and Carnelia[sic] M. Chick[sic], which you offer in support of the application for the enrollment of your child, Florence M. Walner, and the same have been filed with the records in this case.

Respectfully,

Chairman.

9-NB-445

Muskogee, Indian Territory, July 6, 1905.

Robert Walner,
    Wynnewood, Indian Territory.

Dear Sir:

    There is inclosed you herewith for execution application for the enrollment of your infant child, Florence M. Walner, born October 17, 1903.

    In the marriage license and certificate filed with the application heretofore made for the enrollment of your child, you name is given as W. R. Walner, and that of your wife as Cornelia M. Chiek. The affidavits executed by your wife April 22, 1905, is signed May Walner and it appears from the records of this office that you are enrolled under the name of Robert Walner. In the inclosed affidavits the names of yourself and wife are made to conform to the name under which you are enrolled and the name of your wife as it appears in the marriage license and certificate. Please have the affidavits properly executed and return to this office.

    This matter should be given your immediate attention as no further action can be taken relative to the enrollment of your child until the evidence requested is supplied.

Respectfully,

LM 6-1

Commissioner.

Applications for Enrollment of Chickasaw Newborn
Act of 1905   Volume VI

9-NB-445

Muskogee, Indian Territory, July 18, 1905.

Robert Walner,
    Wynnewood, Indian Territory.

Dear Sir:

    Receipt is hereby acknowledged of the affidavits of Cornelia M. Walner and W. E. Settle to the birth of Florence M. Walner, daughter of Robert and Cornelia M. Walner, October 17, 1903, and the same have been filed with the records of this office in the matter of the enrollment of said child.

    Respectfully,

    Commissioner.

9-NB-445

Muskogee, Indian Territory, September 8, 1905.

Robert Walmer[sic],
    Wynnewood, Indian Territory.

Dear Sir:

    Replying to your letter of September 1st, you are advised that the name of your child, Florence M. Walmer[sic], was included in a schedule of the new-born citizens by blood of the Chickasaw Nation which was submitted to the Secretary of the Interior for his approval on August 26, 1905, and when this office has been advised of the approval of the said schedule by the Secretary of the Interior, you will be notified thereof.

    Until the final approval by the Secretary of the Interior of the enrollment of your child, no allotment can be selected for her.

    Respectfully,

    Acting Commissioner.

Applications for Enrollment of Chickasaw Newborn
Act of 1905   Volume VI

Chic. N.B - 446
    (Joseph Overton Massey
    Born September 19, 1903)
    (Mildred Marine Massey
    Born March 3, 1905)

BIRTH AFFIDAVIT.

DEPARTMENT OF THE INTERIOR.
COMMISSION TO THE FIVE CIVILIZED TRIBES.

IN RE APPLICATION FOR ENROLLMENT, as a citizen of the   Chickasaw   Nation, of   Joeph[sic] Overton Massey   , born on the   19   day of   September   , 1903

Name of Father: Guss[sic] R. Massey   a citizen of the   Chickasaw   Nation.
Name of Mother: Nancy Elizibeth Massey   a citizen of the   Chickasaw   Nation.

        Postoffice   Sterrett

AFFIDAVIT OF MOTHER.

UNITED STATES OF AMERICA, Indian Territory,
    Central   DISTRICT.

    I,   Nancy Elizibeth Massey   , on oath state that I am   23   years of age and a citizen by   blood   , of the   Chickasaw   Nation; that I am the lawful wife of   Guss R Massey   , who is a citizen, by   Intermarriage   of the   Chickasaw   Nation; that a   male   child was born to me on   19   day of   September   , 1903, that said child has been named   Joeph Overton   , and is now living.

Witnesses To Mark:
    L. L. Mead
    Mrs F. E. Mead

    Subscribed and sworn to before me this   28   day of   February   , 1905.

                          Notary Public.

Applications for Enrollment of Chickasaw Newborn
Act of 1905 Volume VI

AFFIDAVIT OF ATTENDING PHYSICIAN OR MID-WIFE.

UNITED STATES OF AMERICA, Indian Territory, } Central DISTRICT.

I, D C McCalib , a M.D. , on oath state that I attended on Mrs. Nancy Elizabeth Massey , wife of Gus R Massey on the 19th day of Sept, 1903; that there was born to her on said date a male child; that said child is now living and is said to have been named Joeph Overton Massey

DC McCalib

Witnesses To Mark:
{ L. L. Mead
{ Mrs F. E. Mead

Subscribed and sworn to before me this 28th day of Feb , 1905.

(Name Illegible)
Notary Public.

BIRTH AFFIDAVIT.

DEPARTMENT OF THE INTERIOR.
COMMISSION TO THE FIVE CIVILIZED TRIBES.

IN RE APPLICATION FOR ENROLLMENT, as a citizen of the Chickasaw Nation, of Joseph Overton Massey , born on the 19th day of September , 1903

Name of Father: Gus R. Massey a *non* citizen of the Choctaw Nation.
Name of Mother: Nancy Elizabeth Massey a citizen of the Chickasaw Nation.

Postoffice Sterrett I.T.

AFFIDAVIT OF MOTHER.

UNITED STATES OF AMERICA, Indian Territory, } Central DISTRICT.

I, Nancy Elizabeth Massey , on oath state that I am 23 years of age and a citizen by Blood , of the Chickasaw Nation; that I am the lawful wife of Gus R Massey , who is a ~~citizen~~ *non*, by .... of the Choctaw Nation; that a male child was born to me on 19th day of September , 1903; that said child has been named Joseph Overton Massey , and was living March 4, 1905.

Nancy Elizabeth Massey

Applications for Enrollment of Chickasaw Newborn
Act of 1905 Volume VI

Witnesses To Mark:
{

Subscribed and sworn to before me this 24 day of April , 1905

G W Goodwin
Notary Public.

AFFIDAVIT OF ATTENDING PHYSICIAN OR MID-WIFE.

UNITED STATES OF AMERICA, Indian Territory, }
Central Judicial DISTRICT. }

I, D C McCalib , a Phycian[sic] , on oath state that I attended on Mrs. Nancy Elizabeth Massey , wife of G. R. Massey on the 19th day of September , 1905[sic]; that there was born to her on said date a male child; that said child was living March 4, 1905, and is said to have been named Joseph Overton Massey

D C McCalib MD

Witnesses To Mark:
{

Subscribed and sworn to before me this 24 day of April , 1905

G W Goodwin
Notary Public.

BIRTH AFFIDAVIT.

DEPARTMENT OF THE INTERIOR.
COMMISSION TO THE FIVE CIVILIZED TRIBES.

IN RE APPLICATION FOR ENROLLMENT, as a citizen of the Chickasaw Nation, of Mildred Marine Massey , born on the Third day of March , 1905

non

Name of Father: Gus R. Massey   a citizen of the Choctaw Nation.
Name of Mother: Nancy Elizabeth Massey   a citizen of the Chickasaw Nation.

Postoffice Sterrett I.T.

Applications for Enrollment of Chickasaw Newborn
Act of 1905 Volume VI

AFFIDAVIT OF MOTHER.

UNITED STATES OF AMERICA, Indian Territory, ⎫
   Central Dist   DISTRICT. ⎬

    I, Nancy Elizabeth Massey , on oath state that I am 23 years of age and a citizen by Blood , of the Chickasaw Nation; that I am the lawful wife of Gus R Massey , who is a citizen, by ....of the Choctaw Nation; that a Female child was born to me on 3rd day of March , 1905; that said child has been named Mildred Marine Massey , and was living March 4, 1905.

                                  Nancy Elizabeth Massey

Witnesses To Mark:
{

    Subscribed and sworn to before me this 24th day of April , 1905

                          G W Goodwin
                          Notary Public.

AFFIDAVIT OF ATTENDING PHYSICIAN OR MID-WIFE.

UNITED STATES OF AMERICA, Indian Territory, ⎫
   Central Jud   DISTRICT. ⎬

    I, D C McCalib , a Phycian[sic] , on oath state that I attended on Mrs. Nancy Elizabeth Massey , wife of Gus R. Massey on the 3rd day of March , 1905; that there was born to her on said date a Female child; that said child was living March 4, 1905, and is said to have been named Mildred Marine Massey

                                D C McCalib MD

Witnesses To Mark:
{

    Subscribed and sworn to before me this 24 day of April , 1905

                          G W Goodwin
                        Notary Public.

Applications for Enrollment of Chickasaw Newborn
Act of 1905 Volume VI

BIRTH AFFIDAVIT.

DEPARTMENT OF THE INTERIOR.
COMMISSION TO THE FIVE CIVILIZED TRIBES.

IN RE APPLICATION FOR ENROLLMENT, as a citizen of the Chickasaw Nation, of Joseph Overton Massey, born on the 19th day of Sept, 1903

Name of Father: Gus R. Massey   a citizen of the non citizen Nation.
Name of Mother: Nancy Elizabeth Massey   a citizen of the Chickasaw Nation.

Postoffice   Sterrett I.T.

AFFIDAVIT OF MOTHER.

UNITED STATES OF AMERICA, Indian Territory, }
.... DISTRICT. }

I, Nancy Elizabeth Massey, on oath state that I am 23 years of age and a citizen by blood, of the Chickasaw Nation; that I am the lawful wife of Gus R Massey, who is a citizen, by ——— of the U.S. Nation; that a male child was born to me on 19th day of September, 1903; that said child has been named Joseph Overton Massey, and was living March 4, 1905.

                            Nancy Elizabeth Massey

Witnesses To Mark:
{

Subscribed and sworn to before me this 12th day of July, 1905

                            G W Goodwin
                                 Notary Public.

AFFIDAVIT OF ATTENDING PHYSICIAN OR MID-WIFE.

UNITED STATES OF AMERICA, Indian Territory, }
Central   DISTRICT. }

I, D C McCalib, a Physician, on oath state that I attended on Mrs. Nancy Elizabeth Massey, wife of Gus R. Massey on the 19th day of September, 1903; that there was born to her on said date a male child; that said child was living March 4, 1905, and is said to have been named Joseph Overton Massey

                            D C McCalib MD

Witnesses To Mark:
{

Applications for Enrollment of Chickasaw Newborn
Act of 1905   Volume VI

Subscribed and sworn to before me this   12th   day of   July   , 1905

G W Goodwin
Notary Public.

9-NB-446

Muskogee, Indian Territory, July 6, 1905.

Gus R. Massey,
    Sterrett, Indian Territory.

Dear Sir:

    There is inclosed you herewith for execution application for the enrollment of your infant child, Joseph Overton Massey.

    In the affidavits heretofore filed with the Commission to the Five Civilized Tribes the affidavit of the mother gives date of birth of said child as September 19, 1903, and the affidavit of the physician gives date of birth as September 19, 1905. In the inclosed affidavit the date of birth is left blank. Please insert the correct date and when affidavits are properly executed forward same to this office.

    This matter should receive your immediate attention as no further action can be taken relative to the enrollment of said child until the evidence requested is supplied.

Respectfully,

LM 6-2   Commissioner.

9-NB-446

Muskogee, Indian Territory, July 19, 1905.

N. B. Massey,
    Sterritt[sic], Indian Territory.

Dear Sir:

    Receipt is hereby acknowledged of your letter of July 12, 1905, transmitting affidavits of Nancy Elizabeth Massey and D. C. McCalib to the birth of Joseph Overton Massey, son of Gus R. and Nancy Elizabeth Massey, September 19, 1903, and the same have been filed with the records of this office in the matter of the enrollment of said child.

Applications for Enrollment of Chickasaw Newborn
Act of 1905   Volume VI

Respectfully,

Commissioner.

9-NB-446

Muskogee, Indian Territory, November 9, 1905.

G. R. Massey,
Sterritt[sic], Indian Territory.

Dear Sir:

Receipt is hereby acknowledged of your letter of November 7, 1905, asking if your son Joseph Overton Massey has been approved.

In reply to your letter you are advised that the name of your son Joseph Overton Massey has been placed upon a schedule of citizens by blood of the Chickasaw Nation which has been forwarded the Secretary of the Interior.

Respectfully,

Commissioner.

99-NB-446

Muskogee, Indian Territory, March 12, 1906.

Nancy E. Massey,
Sterrett, Indian Territory.

Dear Madam:

Receipt is hereby acknowledged of your letter of March 5, 1906, in which you state that you have two children for whom you desire to make selection of allotments, Joseph Overton Massey and Mildred Marine Massey who are both on the Chickasaw roll and that you desire to select for your child Joseph Overton Massey certain land described in your previous letter as having been filed upon by a Mississippi Choctaw.

In reply to your letter you are advised that if your desire to make application for certain land upon which another citizen has already filed, you will be permitted to do so upon your personal appearance at the land office for the nation in which the land is situated at any time within nine months after the original selection, and will be permitted to institute contest proceedings therefor.

Applications for Enrollment of Chickasaw Newborn
Act of 1905   Volume VI

Respectfully,

Acting Commissioner.

Chic. N.B - 447
(Thomas Colville Hamm
Born December 3, 1903)

BIRTH AFFIDAVIT.   #117

DEPARTMENT OF THE INTERIOR.
COMMISSION TO THE FIVE CIVILIZED TRIBES.

IN RE APPLICATION FOR ENROLLMENT, as a citizen of the   Chickasaw   Nation, of   Thomas Colville Hamm   , born on the   3"   day of   Dec   , 1903

Name of Father: C.S. Hamm   a citizen of the United States Nation.
Name of Mother: Mattie L. Hamm   a citizen of the   Chickasaw   Nation.

Postoffice   Purdy, Ind. Ter.

AFFIDAVIT OF MOTHER.

UNITED STATES OF AMERICA, Indian Territory,
       Southern   DISTRICT.

I, Mattie L. Hamm , on oath state that I am 20 years of age and a citizen by blood , of the Chickasaw Nation; that I am the lawful wife of C. S. Hamm , who is a citizen, by .... of the   United States ~~Nation~~; that a Male child was born to me on third day of December , 1903, that said child has been named Thomas Colville Hamm , and is now living.

Mattie L. Hamm

Witnesses To Mark:
{

Subscribed and sworn to before me this 23 day of Feb , 1905.

V. Smith
Notary Public.

Applications for Enrollment of Chickasaw Newborn
Act of 1905   Volume VI

AFFIDAVIT OF ATTENDING PHYSICIAN OR MID-WIFE.

UNITED STATES OF AMERICA, Indian Territory, }
Southern   DISTRICT.

I,   T. C. Branum   , a   Physician   , on oath state that I attended on Mrs.   Mattie L. Hamm   , wife of   C S. Hamm   on the   3"   day of Dec   , 1903; that there was born to her on said date a   male   child; that said child is now living and is said to have been named   Thomas Colville Hamm

T.C. Branum, M.D.

Witnesses To Mark:
{

Subscribed and sworn to before me this   17"   day of   January   , 1905.

C.H. Thomason
Notary Public.

BIRTH AFFIDAVIT.

DEPARTMENT OF THE INTERIOR,
COMMISSION TO THE FIVE CIVILIZED TRIBES.

IN RE APPLICATION FOR ENROLLMENT, as a citizen of the   Chickasaw   Nation, of   Thomas Colville Hamm   , born on the   3rd   day of   December   , 1903

Name of Father: C.S. Hamm   a citizen of the   U.S.   ~~Nation~~.
Name of Mother: Mattie Love Hamm   a citizen of the   Chickasaw   Nation.

Postoffice   Purdy I.T.

AFFIDAVIT OF MOTHER.

UNITED STATES OF AMERICA, Indian Territory, }
So   District.

I,   Mattie Love Hamm   , on oath state that I am   20   years of age and a citizen by   Blood   , of the   Chickasaw   Nation; that I am the lawful wife of   CS Hamm   , who is a citizen, ~~by~~   US   of the   ———   ~~Nation~~; that a   male   child was born to me on   3rd   day of   December   , 1903 , that said child has been named Thomas Colville Hamm   , and was living March 4, 1905.

Mattie Love Hamm

Witness to Mark:
{

Applications for Enrollment of Chickasaw Newborn
Act of 1905   Volume VI

Subscribed and sworn to before me this   19   day of   April   , 1905.

J.D. Wagner
Notary Public.

AFFIDAVIT OF ATTENDING PHYSICIAN OR MID-WIFE.

UNITED STATES OF AMERICA, Indian Territory,
So   District.

Branum Callaway
We,   (Name Illegible)   , a   M.D.   , on oath state that I attended on Mrs. Mattie L. Hamm   , wife of   C.S. Hamm   on the 3rd day of December , 1903 ; that there was born to her on said date a   Male   child; that said child was living March 4, 1905, and is said to have been named   Thomas Colville Hamm

Branum Callaway
Witness to Mark: per James R. Callaway, M.D.
{

Subscribed and sworn to before me this   21st day of   April   , 1905.

C.H. Thomason
Notary Public.

9-473.

Muskogee, Indian Territory, April 27, 1905.

C. S. Hamm,
   Purdy, Indian Territory.

Dear Sir:

Receipt is hereby acknowledged of the affidavits of Mattie Love Hamm and Branum Callaway to the birth of Thomas Colville Hamm, son of C. S. and Mattie Love Hamm, December 3, 1903, and the same have been filed with our records as an application for the enrollment of said child.

Respectfully,

Chairman.

Applications for Enrollment of Chickasaw Newborn
Act of 1905 Volume VI

Chic. N.B - 448
(Burnie C. Hampton
Born September 14, 1903)

BIRTH AFFIDAVIT.

DEPARTMENT OF THE INTERIOR,
COMMISSION TO THE FIVE CIVILIZED TRIBES.

IN RE APPLICATION FOR ENROLLMENT, as a citizen of the Chickasaw Nation, of Burnie C. Hampton , born on the 14th day of Sept , 1903

Name of Father: J. W. Hampton a citizen of the ———— Nation.
Name of Mother: Mary C. Hampton a citizen of the Chickasaw Nation.

Postoffice Albany I.T.

AFFIDAVIT OF MOTHER.

UNITED STATES OF AMERICA, Indian Territory, }
Central District. }

I, Mary C. Hampton , on oath state that I am 26 years of age and a citizen by Blood , of the Chickasaw Nation; that I am the lawful wife of J.W. Hampton , who is a citizen, by ———— of the ———— Nation; that a Male child was born to me on 14th day of September , 1903 , that said child has been named Burnie C. Hampton , and was living March 4, 1905.

Mary C. Hampton
Witness to Mark:
{

Subscribed and sworn to before me this 22nd day of April , 1905.

W.J. O'Donby
Notary Public.

AFFIDAVIT OF ATTENDING PHYSICIAN OR MID-WIFE.

UNITED STATES OF AMERICA, Indian Territory, }
Central District. }

I, Sallie Collie , a Midwife , on oath state that I attended on Mrs. Mary C. Hampton , wife of J.W. Hampton on the 14th day of September , 1903 ; that there was born to her on said date a Male child; that said child was living March 4, 1905, and is said to have been named Burnie C. Hampton

Applications for Enrollment of Chickasaw Newborn
Act of 1905   Volume VI

                                                her
                                    Sallie x Callie

Witness to Mark: mark
  { C C Pruitt
    (Name Illegible)

Subscribed and sworn to before me this 22nd day of April , 1905.

                                                  W.J. O'Donby
                                                        Notary Public.

                                                                                        9-1188.

                              Muskogee, Indian Territory, April 27, 1905.

J.W. Hampton,
       Albany, Indian Territory.

Dear Sir:

      Receipt is hereby acknowledged of the affidavits of Mary C. Hampton and Sallie Collie to the birth of Burnie C. Hampton, son of J. W. and Mary C. Hampton, September 14, 1903, and the same has been filed with our records as an application for the enrollment of said child.

                                     Respectfully,

                                                    Chairman.

Chic. N.B - 449
       (James Hardiman Kennedy
       Born October 21, 1902)
       (Ida May Kennedy
       Born February 4, 1905)

Applications for Enrollment of Chickasaw Newborn
Act of 1905   Volume VI

BIRTH AFFIDAVIT.

DEPARTMENT OF THE INTERIOR.
COMMISSION TO THE FIVE CIVILIZED TRIBES.

IN RE APPLICATION FOR ENROLLMENT, as a citizen of the Chickasaw Nation, of James Hardiman Kennedy, born on the 21 day of October, 1902

Name of Father: John W Kennedy   a citizen of the Chickasaw Nation.
Name of Mother: Mary C I Kennedy   a citizen of the Chickasaw Nation.

Postoffice   Fitzhugh Ind. T.

AFFIDAVIT OF MOTHER.

UNITED STATES OF AMERICA, Indian Territory,
Southern   DISTRICT.

I, Mary C I Kennedy, on oath state that I am 24 years of age and a citizen by blood, of the Chickasaw Nation; that I am the lawful wife of John W Kennedy, who is a citizen, by Inter Marriage of the Chickasaw Nation; that a male child was born to me on 21 day of October, 1902; that said child has been named James Hardiman Kennedy, and was living March 4, 1905.

Mary C.I. Kennedy

Witnesses To Mark:

Subscribed and sworn to before me this 15" day of April, 1905

JE White NP
My Commission Expires Mar 26" 07   Notary Public.

AFFIDAVIT OF ATTENDING PHYSICIAN OR MID-WIFE.

UNITED STATES OF AMERICA, Indian Territory,
Southern   DISTRICT.

I, Elizabeth A Kennedy, a Midwife, on oath state that I attended on Mrs. Mary C I Kennedy, wife of John W Kennedy on the 21 day of October, 1902; that there was born to her on said date a male child; that said child was living March 4, 1905, and is said to have been named James Hardiman Kennedy

her
Elizabeth x A Kennedy
mark

Applications for Enrollment of Chickasaw Newborn
Act of 1905 Volume VI

Witnesses To Mark:
- C.E. Talley Stonewall I.T.
- A.C. Ellis   Fitzhugh, I.T.

Subscribed and sworn to before me this 15 day of April , 1905

My Commission Expires Mar 26" 07

JE White NP
Notary Public.

BIRTH AFFIDAVIT.

DEPARTMENT OF THE INTERIOR.
COMMISSION TO THE FIVE CIVILIZED TRIBES.

IN RE APPLICATION FOR ENROLLMENT, as a citizen of the Chickasaw Nation, of Ida May Kennedy , born on the 4th day of Feby' , 1905

Name of Father: John W. Kennedy   a citizen of the Chickasaw Nation.
Name of Mother: Mary C. I. Kennedy   a citizen of the Chickasaw Nation.

Postoffice   FITZHUGH I.T.

AFFIDAVIT OF MOTHER.

UNITED STATES OF AMERICA, Indian Territory,
Southern   DISTRICT.

I, Mary C. I. Kennedy , on oath state that I am 24 years of age and a citizen by Blood , of the Chickasaw Nation; that I am the lawful wife of John W. Kennedy , who is a citizen, by Intermarriage of the Chickasaw Nation; that a Female child was born to me on 4th day of February , 1905; that said child has been named Ida May Kennedy , and was living March 4, 1905.

Mary C.I. Kennedy

Witnesses To Mark:

Subscribed and sworn to before me this 15 day of April , 1905

JE White NP
My Commission Expires March 26" 07   Notary Public.

Applications for Enrollment of Chickasaw Newborn
Act of 1905 Volume VI

AFFIDAVIT OF ATTENDING PHYSICIAN OR MID-WIFE.

UNITED STATES OF AMERICA, Indian Territory,
Southern DISTRICT.

I, Elizabeth A Kennedy , a midwife , on oath state that I attended on Mrs. Mary C. I. Kennedy , wife of John W. Kennedy on the 4th day of Feby' , 1905; that there was born to her on said date a Female child; that said child was living March 4, 1905, and is said to have been named Ida May Kennedy

                              her
                  Elizabeth A x Kennedy
                          mark

Witnesses To Mark:
- C.E. Talley Stonewall I.T.
- A.C. Ellis   Fitzhugh, I.T.

Subscribed and sworn to before me this 15" day of April , 1905

                        JE White NP
My Commission Expires March 26" 07   Notary Public.

BIRTH AFFIDAVIT.   No 59

DEPARTMENT OF THE INTERIOR.
COMMISSION TO THE FIVE CIVILIZED TRIBES.

IN RE APPLICATION FOR ENROLLMENT, as a citizen of the Chickasaw Nation, of James Hardiman Kennedy , born on the 21" day of October , 1902

Name of Father: John W Kennedy   a citizen of the Chicasaw[sic] Nation.
Name of Mother: Mary C.I. Kennedy   a citizen of the Chicasaw Nation.

                Postoffice   Fitzhugh I.T.

AFFIDAVIT OF MOTHER.

UNITED STATES OF AMERICA, Indian Territory,
Sou DISTRICT.

I, Mary C.I. Kennedy , on oath state that I am 24 years of age and a citizen by blood , of the Chicasaw Nation; that I am the lawful wife of John W. Kennedy , who is a citizen, by Inter-marriage of the Chicasaw Nation; that a male child was born to me on 21st day of October , 1902, that said child has been named James Hardiman , and is now living.

Applications for Enrollment of Chickasaw Newborn
Act of 1905 Volume VI

Witnesses To Mark:
{

Mary C.I. Kennedy

Subscribed and sworn to before me this 28th day of December, 1904

My Commission Expires
26th day March 1907

JE White
Sou Dist Notary Public.

AFFIDAVIT OF ATTENDING PHYSICIAN OR MID-WIFE.

UNITED STATES OF AMERICA, Indian Territory,
Southern   DISTRICT. }

I, Elizabeth Kennedy, a Mid wife, on oath state that I attended on Mrs. Mary C I Kennedy, wife of John W Kennedy on the 21" day of October, 1902; that there was born to her on said date a male child; that said child is now living and is said to have been named James Hardiman

Witnesses To Mark:
{

Elizabeth Kennedy

Subscribed and sworn to before me this 28th day of December, 1904

My Commission Expires Mar 26" 1907

JE White
Sou Dist Notary Public.

9-105.

Muskogee, Indian Territory, Aprl 27, 1905.

John W. Kennedy,
   Fitzhugh, Indian Territory.

Dear Sir:

Receipt is hereby acknowledged of the affidavits of Mary C. I. Kennedy and Elizabeth A. Kennedy to the birth of James Hardiman Kennedy and Ida May Kennedy children of John W. and Mary C. I. Kennedy, October 21, 1902 and February 4, 1905, respectively, and the same have been filed with our records as applications for the enrollment of said children.

Respectfully,

Chairman.

Applications for Enrollment of Chickasaw Newborn
Act of 1905   Volume VI

9-NB-449

Muskogee, Indian Territory, June 7, 1905.

John W. Kennedy,
    Fitzhugh, Indian Territory.

Dear Sir:

    Receipt is hereby acknowledged of your letter of June 1, 1905, asking if the enrollment of your children James Hardiman and Ida May Kennedy have been approved.

    In reply to your letter you are advised that the names of your children James Hardiman and Ida May Kennedy have been placed upon a schedule of citizens by blood of the Chickasaw Nation which has been prepared for forwarding to the Secretary of the Interior forwarding to the Department, but their enrollment has not yet been approved by the Secretary of the Interior.

                                                Respectfully,

                                                         Chairman.

Chic. N.B - 450
    (Helen Rennie
    Born December 4, 1903)

BIRTH AFFIDAVIT.
DEPARTMENT OF THE INTERIOR.
COMMISSION TO THE FIVE CIVILIZED TRIBES.

    IN RE APPLICATION FOR ENROLLMENT, as a citizen of the _____ Nation, of _____, born on the _____ day of _____, 1_____

Name of Father: _____ a citizen of the _____ Nation.
Name of Mother _____ a citizen of the _____ Nation.

                    Postoffice _____

Applications for Enrollment of Chickasaw Newborn
Act of 1905   Volume VI

AFFIDAVIT OF MOTHER.

UNITED STATES OF AMERICA, Indian Territory, }
.... DISTRICT. }

    I, ..., on oath state that I am .... years of age and a citizen by ...., of the .... Nation; that I am the lawful wife of ...., who is a citizen, by .... of the .... Nation; that a .... child was born to me on .... day of ...., 1........, that said child has been named ...., and was living March 4, 1905.

                                                     Lula D. Renner

Witnesses To Mark:
{ ....
  .... }

    Subscribed and sworn to before me this .... day of ...., 1905.

                                                   Geo. W. Burris
                                                    Notary Public.

AFFIDAVIT OF ATTENDING PHYSICIAN OR MID-WIFE.

UNITED STATES OF AMERICA, Indian Territory, }
    Southern   DISTRICT. }

    I, W. W. Vannoy , a Doctor , on oath state that I attended on Mrs. Lula D. Rennie , wife of Alexander Rennie Jr on the 4th day of December , 1903; that there was born to her on said date a Female child; that said child was living March 4, 1905, and is said to have been named Helen Rennie

                                                W.W. Vannoy M.D.

Witnesses To Mark:
{

    Subscribed and sworn to before me this 2nd day of May , 1905

                                                   Geo W Burris
                                                   Notary Public.

Applications for Enrollment of Chickasaw Newborn
Act of 1905   Volume VI

BIRTH AFFIDAVIT.   No 24

DEPARTMENT OF THE INTERIOR.
COMMISSION TO THE FIVE CIVILIZED TRIBES.

IN RE APPLICATION FOR ENROLLMENT, as a citizen of the   Chickasaw   Nation, of   Helen Rennie   , born on the 4th day of   December   , 1903

Name of Father: Alexander Rennie Jr   a citizen of the   Chickasaw   Nation.
Name of Mother: Lula Burris Rennie   a citizen of the   Chickasaw   Nation.

Postoffice   Tishomingo I.T.

AFFIDAVIT OF MOTHER.

UNITED STATES OF AMERICA, Indian Territory, }
    So   DISTRICT. }

I,   Lula Burris Rennie   , on oath state that I am   23   years of age and a citizen by   blood   , of the   Chickasaw   Nation; that I am the lawful wife of Alexander Rennie Jr   , who is a citizen, by   blood   of the   Chickasaw   Nation; that a   female   child was born to me on   4   day of   Dec   , 1903, that said child has been named   Helen Rennie   , and is now living.

Lula Burris Rennie

Witnesses To Mark:

Subscribed and sworn to before me this   7   day of   May   , 1905.

Cornelius Hardy
Notary Public.

AFFIDAVIT OF ATTENDING PHYSICIAN OR MID-WIFE.

UNITED STATES OF AMERICA, Indian Territory, }
    So   DISTRICT. }

I,   W.W. Vannoy   , a   Physician   , on oath state that I attended on Mrs.   Lula Burris Rennie   , wife of   Alexander Rennie Jr   on the   4   day of Dec , 1903; that there was born to her on said date a   female   child; that said child is now living and is said to have been named   Helen Rennie

W.W. Vannoy

Applications for Enrollment of Chickasaw Newborn
Act of 1905   Volume VI

Witnesses To Mark:

{

Subscribed and sworn to before me this 7 day of May , 1905.

Cornelius Hardy
Notary Public.

BIRTH AFFIDAVIT.

DEPARTMENT OF THE INTERIOR.
COMMISSION TO THE FIVE CIVILIZED TRIBES.

IN RE APPLICATION FOR ENROLLMENT, as a citizen of the Chickasaw Nation, of Helen Rennie , born on the 4th day of December , 1903

Name of Father: Alexander Rennie Jr   a citizen of the Chickasaw Nation.
Name of Mother: Lula Rennie   a citizen of the Chickasaw Nation.

Postoffice   Ardmore, I.T.

AFFIDAVIT OF MOTHER.

UNITED STATES OF AMERICA, Indian Territory,
Southern   **DISTRICT.**

I, Lula Rennie , on oath state that I am 23 years of age and a citizen by blood , of the Chickasaw Nation; that I am the lawful wife of Alexander Rennie Jr , who is a citizen, by blood of the Chickasaw Nation; that a female child was born to me on the 4th day of December , 1903; that said child has been named Helen Rennie , and was living March 4, 1905.

Lula Rennie

Witnesses To Mark:

{

Subscribed and sworn to before me this 15th day of April , 1905

JE Williams
Notary Public.

Applications for Enrollment of Chickasaw Newborn
Act of 1905   Volume VI

AFFIDAVIT OF ATTENDING PHYSICIAN OR MID-WIFE.

UNITED STATES OF AMERICA, Indian Territory, }
.... DISTRICT. }

I, ..., a ...., on oath state that I attended on Mrs. ...., wife of .... on the .... day of ...., 1........; that there was born to her on said date a .... child; that said child was living March 4, 1905, and is said to have been named ....

Witnesses To Mark:
{ ....
{ ....

Subscribed and sworn to before me this .... day of ...., 1905.

....
Notary Public.

(The Birth Affidavit above given again.)

9-44.

Muskogee, Indian Territory, April 27, 1905.

Alexander Rennie,
    Ardmore, Indian Territory.

Dear Sir:

Receipt is hereby acknowledged of the affidavit of Lula Rennie to the birth of Helen Rennie, daughter of Alexander and Lula Rennie, December 4, 1903, and the same has been filed with our records as an application for the enrollment of said child.

Respectfully,

Chairman.

Applications for Enrollment of Chickasaw Newborn
Act of 1905   Volume VI

9 NB 450

Muskogee, Indian Territory, May 13, 1905.

Alexander Rennie,
Ardmore, Indian Territory.

Dear Sir:

Receipt is hereby acknowledged of the affidavit of W. W. Vannoy to the birth of Helen Rennie, daughter of Lula D. and Alexander Rennie, Jr., December 4, 1903, and the same has been filed with our records in the matter of the application for the enrollment of said child.

Respectfully,

Chairman.

Chic. N.B - 451
(Burris Donaven Duffy
Born April 10, 1904)

DEPARTMENT OF THE INTERIOR
COMMISSION TO THE FIVE CIVILIZED TRIBES.
BIRTH AFFIDAVIT.

IN RE-APPLICATION FOR ENROLLMENT, as a citizen of the   Chickasaw   Nation, of   Burris Donaven Duffy   , born on the   10   day of   April   , 190 4

Name of Father: Patrick Duffy   a citizen of the   Chickasaw   Nation.
Name of Mother: Edith Ethel Duffy   a citizen of the   Chickasaw   Nation.

Postoffice   Center Ind Ter

AFFIDAVIT OF MOTHER.

UNITED STATES OF AMERICA, INDIAN TERRITORY, }
Southern   District. }

I,   Edith Ethel Duffy   , on oath state that I am   26   years of age and a citizen by Blood   , of the   Chickasaw   Nation; that I am the lawful wife of   Patrick Duffy   , who is a citizen, by   Marriage   of the   Chickasaw   Nation; that a   male   child was

Applications for Enrollment of Chickasaw Newborn
Act of 1905   Volume VI

born to me on   10   day of   April   , 1904 , that said child has been named   Burris Donaven Duffy   , and is now living.

Edith E Duffy

Witnesses To Mark:

{

Subscribed and sworn to before me this   24   day of   Apr   , 1905.

J.M. Stanfield
Notary Public.

AFFIDAVIT OF ATTENDING PHYSICIAN OR MID-WIFE.

UNITED STATES OF AMERICA, INDIAN TERRITORY, }
Southern   District.

I,   J. R. Craig   , a   Physician   , on oath state that I attended on Mrs.   Edith Ethel Duffy   , wife of   Patrick Duffy   on the   10   day of   April   , 190 4; that there was born to her on said date a   male   child; that said child is now living and is said to have been named   Burris Donaven Duffy

J.R. Craig M.D.

Witnesses To Mark:

{

Subscribed and sworn to before me this   24   day of   Apr   , 1905.

J.M. Stanfield
Notary Public.

9-307.

Muskogee, Indian Territory, April 27, 1905.

Patrick Duffy,
    Center, Indian Territory.

Dear Sir:

Receipt is hereby acknowledged of the affidavits of Edith E. Duffy and J. R. Craig to the birth of Burris Donaven Duffy, son of Patrick and Edith E. Duffy, April 10, 1904, and the same have been filed with our records as an application for the enrollment of said child.

Respectfully,

Chairman.

Applications for Enrollment of Chickasaw Newborn
Act of 1905   Volume VI

9 NB 451

Muskogee, Indian Territory, July 3, 1905.

Patrick Duffy,
    Center, Indian Territory.

Dear Sir:

    Receipt is hereby acknowledged of your letter of June 26, 1905, in which you ask if you will be permitted to institute a contest against certain land and file on it for your baby.

    In reply to your letter you are advised that the name of your child Burris Donaven Duffy has been placed upon a schedule of citizens by blood of the Chickasaw Nation prepared for forwarding to the Secretary of the Interior and you will be notified when his enrollment is approved. You are advised, however, that no selection of allotment can be permitted nor can a contest be instituted for children enrolled under the provisions of the act of Congress approved March 3, 1905, until their enrollment has been approved by the Secretary of the Interior.

Respectfully,

Commissioner.

Chic. N.B - 452
    (Richard Perry Wade
    Born January 10, 1904)
    (George Wade, Jr.
    Born February 19, 1905)

DEPARTMENT OF THE INTERIOR
COMMISSION TO THE FIVE CIVILIZED TRIBES.
BIRTH AFFIDAVIT.

    IN RE-APPLICATION FOR ENROLLMENT, as a citizen of the   Chicasaw[sic]   Nation, of   Richard Perry Wade   , born on the 10   day of Jan   , 190 4

Name of Father: Geo. Wade   a citizen of the   Chicasaw   Nation.
Name of Mother: Minnie M Wade   *not* a citizen of the   Chicasaw   Nation.

Postoffice   Francis I.T.

Applications for Enrollment of Chickasaw Newborn
Act of 1905 Volume VI

AFFIDAVIT OF MOTHER.

UNITED STATES OF AMERICA, INDIAN TERRITORY,
Southern District.

I, Minnie May Wade, on oath state that I am 28 years of age and ^not a citizen by Marriage, of the Chicasaw Nation; that I am the lawful wife of George Wade, who is a citizen, by Birth of the Chicasaw Nation; that a Male child was born to me on 10 day of Jan, 1904, that said child was named Richard Perry Wade, and ~~is now living~~. Died on Mar 25 - 1904

Minnie May Wade

Witnesses To Mark:

Subscribed and sworn to before me this 22 day of April, 1905.

John I McCoole
Notary Public.

MY COMMISSION EXPIRES FEBY. 11TH, 1907.

AFFIDAVIT OF ATTENDING PHYSICIAN OR MID-WIFE.

UNITED STATES OF AMERICA, INDIAN TERRITORY,
Southern District.

I, S. M. Richey, a Physician, on oath state that I attended on Mrs. Geo Wade, wife of Geo Wade on the 10 day of Jan, 1904; that there was born to her on said date a male child; that said child is now Dead and is said to have been named Richard Perry Wade

S.M. Richey M.D.

Witnesses To Mark:

Subscribed and sworn to before me this 22 day of April, 1905.

John I McCoole
Notary Public.

MY COMMISSION EXPIRES FEBY. 11TH, 1907.

Applications for Enrollment of Chickasaw Newborn
Act of 1905 Volume VI

DEPARTMENT OF THE INTERIOR
COMMISSION TO THE FIVE CIVILIZED TRIBES.
BIRTH AFFIDAVIT.

IN RE-APPLICATION FOR ENROLLMENT, as a citizen of the Chicasaw[sic] Nation, of George Wade Jr, born on the 19 day of February, 1905

Name of Father: George Wade   a citizen of the Chicasaw Nation.
Name of Mother: Minnie M Wade   ~~not~~ a citizen of the Chicasaw Nation.

Postoffice   Francis I.T.

AFFIDAVIT OF MOTHER.

UNITED STATES OF AMERICA, INDIAN TERRITORY,
Southern District.

I, Minnie May Wade, on oath state that I am 28 years of age and ^not^ a citizen by Marriage, of the Chicasaw Nation; that I am the lawful wife of Geo Wade, who is a citizen, by Birth of the Chicasaw Nation; that a Male child was born to me on 19 day of Feb., 1905, that said child has been named Geo Wade Jr, and is now living.

               Minnie May Wade

Witnesses To Mark:

Subscribed and sworn to before me this 22 day of April, 1905.

               John I McCoole
               Notary Public.

MY COMMISSION EXPIRES FEBY. 11TH, 1907.

AFFIDAVIT OF ATTENDING PHYSICIAN OR MID-WIFE.

UNITED STATES OF AMERICA, INDIAN TERRITORY,
Southern District.

I, S. M. Richey, a Physician, on oath state that I attended on Mrs. Minnie Wade, wife of Geo Wade on the 19 day of Feb., 1905; that there was born to her on said date a male child; that said child is now ~~living~~ Dead and is said to have been named Geo Wade Jr

               S.M. Richey M.D.

Witnesses To Mark:

Applications for Enrollment of Chickasaw Newborn
Act of 1905   Volume VI

Subscribed and sworn to before me this   22   day of   April   , 1905.

John I McCoole
Notary Public.

MY COMMISSION EXPIRES FEBY. 11TH, 1907.

It appearing from within affidavits that Richard Perry Wade born January 10, 1904, for whose enrollment as a citizen by blood of the Chickasaw Nation application was made under the provisions of the Act of Congress approved March 3, 1905, (33 Stat. 1071), died March 25, 1904, it is hereby ordered that the application for the enrollment of Richard Perry Wade as a citizen by blood of the Chickasaw Nation be dismissed.

Tams Bixby Commissioner.

Muskogee, Indian Territory.
AUG 26 1905

DEPARTMENT OF THE INTERIOR.
COMMISSION TO THE FIVE CIVILIZED TRIBES.

In the matter of the death of   Richard Perry Wade   a citizen of the   Chickasaw   Nation, who formerly resided at or near   Francis   , Ind. Ter., and died on the   25   day of   Mch   , 1904

AFFIDAVIT OF RELATIVE.

UNITED STATES OF AMERICA, Indian Territory,
Southern   DISTRICT.

they
We,   George & Minnie Wade   , on oath state that I am   48 and 28   years of age and a citizen by   blood and Intermarriage   , of the   Chickasaw   Nation; that my postoffice address is   Francis   , Ind. Ter.; that I am   Father and Mother   of   Richard Perry Wade   who was a citizen, by   blood   , of the Chickasaw   Nation and that said   Richard Perry Wade   died on the   25   day of   March   , 1904

George Wade
Minnie Wade

Witnesses To Mark:

Subscribed and sworn to before me this   23   day of   Aug   , 1905.

MY COMMISSION EXPIRES FEBY. 11TH, 1907.

John I McCoole
Notary Public.

Applications for Enrollment of Chickasaw Newborn
Act of 1905   Volume VI

AFFIDAVIT OF ACQUAINTANCE.

UNITED STATES OF AMERICA, Indian Territory,
Southern   DISTRICT.

I, We, Simon Shield and Lucy Harjoe, on oath state that we am 31 and 45 years of age, and a citizen by blood of the Chickasaw Nation; that my postoffice address is Allen, Ind. Ter.; that I was personally acquainted with Richard Perry Wade who was a citizen, by blood, of the Chickasaw Nation; and that said Richard Perry Wade died on the 25 day of March, 1904

Witnesses To Mark:
  Simon Shield
  Nannie Wade

Simon Shield
her
Lucy x Harjoe
mark

Subscribed and sworn to before me this 23 day of Aug, 1905.

John I McCoole
Notary Public.

MY COMMISSION EXPIRES FEBY. 11TH, 1907.

DEPARTMENT OF THE INTERIOR,
Commission to the Five Civilized Tribes.
FILED
JUN - 1905 *Tams Bixby* CHAIRMAN.

No. 1799

Certificate of Record of Marriages.

UNITED STATES OF AMERICA,
INDIAN TERRITORY,   SCT:
Central   DISTRICT.

I, E.J. Fannin, Clerk of the United States Court in the Indian Territory and District aforesaid, do hereby CERTIFY, that the License for and Certificate of the Marriage of

Mr. Geo Wade   and

Miss Minnie Waldren   was

filed in my office in said Territory and District the 21 day of January A.D., 190 1 and duly recorded in Book 9 of Marriage Record, Page ....

WITNESS my hand and seal of said Court, at South McAlester, this 9th day of FEB, A.D. 190 1

E. J. FANNIN.
Clerk.

By *(Name Illegible)* Deputy.

53

Applications for Enrollment of Chickasaw Newborn
Act of 1905 Volume VI

No. 1799

FORM NO. 598.

MARRIAGE LICENSE.

UNITES STATES OF AMERICA, ⎫
   THE INDIAN TERRITORY,   ⎬ ss:
   Central   DISTRICT. ⎭

To any Person Authorized by Law to Solemnize Marriage—Greeting:

You are hereby commanded to solemnize the Rite and publish the **Banns of Matrimony** *between* Mr. George Wade *of* Allen *in the Indian Territory, aged* 45 *years, and* Miss Minnie Waldren *of* Allen *in the Indian Territory, aged* 23 *years, according to law, and do you officially sign and return this License to the parties therein named.*

WITNESS my hand and official seal, this   8   day of   January   A. D. 190 1

(Name Illegible)
Clerk of the United States Court.

Deputy

CERTIFICATE OF MARRIAGE.

UNITES STATES OF AMERICA, ⎫
   THE INDIAN TERRITORY,   ⎬ ss: I,   Richard Williams
   ....DISTRICT. ⎭   a   Gospel Minister

do hereby CERTIFY, that on the   16   day of   Jan   A, D. 190 1 ; I did duly and according to law, as commanded in the foregoing License, solemnize the Rite and publish the BANNS OF MATRIMONY between the parties therein named.

Witness my hand this   16   day of   January , A. D. 190 1

My credentials are recorded in the office of the Clerk of the United States Court in the Indian Territory, Central District, Book   A   Page   249

Richard Williams
a Gospel Minister

Applications for Enrollment of Chickasaw Newborn
Act of 1905   Volume VI

9-196.

Muskogee, Indian Territory, April 27, 1905.

George Wade,
    Francis, Indian Territory.

Dear Sir:

    Receipt is hereby acknowledged of the affidavits of Minnie May Wade and S.M. Richey to the birth of George Wade Jr., and Richard Perry Wade, children of George and Minnie May Wade, January 10, 1904 and February 19, 1905, respectively, and the same have been filed with our records as an application for the enrollment of said children.

    Respectfully,

    Chairman.

9-NB-452.

Muskogee, Indian Territory, May 19, 1905.

George Wade,
    Francis, Indian Territory.

Dear Sir:

    Referring to the application for the enrollment of your infant children, Richard Perry Wade and George Wade, Jr., born January 10, 1904, and February 19, 1905, respectively, it is noted that the applicants claim through you.

    If this is correct it will be necessary for you to file with the Commission either the original or a certified copy of the license and certificate of your marriage to the applicants' mother, Minnie May Wade.

    Respectfully,

    Chairman.

Applications for Enrollment of Chickasaw Newborn
Act of 1905   Volume VI

9-N.B. 452.

Muskogee, Indian Territory, June 5, 1905.

George Wade,
    Francis, Indian Territory.

Dear Sir:

    Receipt is hereby acknowledged of your letter of May 28, transmitting marriage license and certificate between yourself and Minnie Waldren which you offer in support of the application for the enrollment of your children, Richard Perry Wade and George Wade, Jr., and the same have been filed with the records in this case.

        Respectfully,

                Commissioner in Charge.

9-NB-452

Muskogee, Indian Territory, August 17, 1905.

George Wade,
    Francis, Indian Territory.

Dear Sir:

    It appears that your son, Richard Perry Wade, who was born January 10, 1904, died March 25, 1904, and for the purpose of making his death a matter of record there is inclosed herewith blank form for proof of death which please have executed and returned to this office at once in order that disposition may be made of the application for the enrollment of Richard Perry Wade as a citizen of the Chickasaw Nation.

        Respectfully,

D. C.   Acting Commissioner.

Applications for Enrollment of Chickasaw Newborn
Act of 1905   Volume VI

9-NB-452

Muskogee, Indian Territory, August 2, 1905.

George Wade,
    Francis, Indian Territory.

Dear Sir:

    Receipt is hereby acknowledged of your letter of July 25, 1905, asking if your children George Wade, Jr., and Richard Perry Wade have been enrolled.

    In reply to your letter you are advised that the name of your child, George Wade, Jr., has been placed upon a schedule of citizens by blood of the Chickasaw Nation which has been forwarded the Secretary of the Interior and you will be notified when his enrollment is approved by the Department.

    You are further advised that it appears from the records that your child Richard Perry Wade, died March 25, 1904, and under the provisions of the act of Congress approved March 3, 1905, he would not be entitled to enrollment.

    The matter of the land referred to in your letter has been made the subject of another communication.

                      Respectfully,

                                Commissioner.

9-NB-452

Muskogee, Indian Territory, August 26, 1905.

George Wade,
    Francis, Indian Territory.

Dear Sir:

    Receipt is hereby acknowledged of the affidavit of Minnie Wade and the joint affidavit of Simon Shield and Lucy Harjoe to the death of your child, Richard Perry Wade, which occurred March 25, 1904, and the same have been filed as evidence of death of the above named child.

                      Respectfully,

                                Commissioner.

Applications for Enrollment of Chickasaw Newborn
Act of 1905   Volume VI

9-NB-452

Muskogee, Indian Territory, August 26, 1905.

George Wade,
    Francis, Indian Territory.

Dear Sir:

You are hereby advised that it appearing from the records of this office that your child, Richard Perry Wade, died prior to March 4, 1905, the Commissioner to the Five Civilized Tribes on August 26, 1905, dismissed the application for his enrollment as a citizen by blood of the Chickasaw Nation.

Respectfully,

Commissioner.

Chic. N.B - 453
    (William Jesse Bacon
    Birthdate not given)

453

Chickasaw
(Act March 3 1905)

William Jesse Bacon

Transferred to 25 - 463
March 12, 1907

Chic. N.B - 454
    (Newton Melville
    Born November 13, 1903)

Applications for Enrollment of Chickasaw Newborn
Act of 1905   Volume VI

BIRTH AFFIDAVIT.   99

    IN RE-APPLICATION FOR ENROLLMENT, as a citizen of the   Chickasaw   Nation, of   Newton Melville   , born on the   13th   day of   November   , 190 4[sic]

Name of Father: Samuel C. Melville   a citizen of the Chickasaw Nation.
Name of Mother: Francis Melville   a citizen of the Chickasaw Nation.

        Postoffice   Ada, Indian Territory.

AFFIDAVIT OF MOTHER.

UNITED STATES OF AMERICA, INDIAN TERRITORY, }
    Sothern[sic]   District.

    I,   Francis Melville   , on oath state that I am   18   years of age and a citizen by Blood   , of the   Chickasaw   Nation; that I am the lawful wife of   Samuel C. Melville   , who is a citizen, by   Blood   of the   Chickasaw   Nation; that a   boy   child was born to me on   13th   day of   November   , 1904 , that said child has been named   Newton Melville   , and is now living.

                  Francis Melville

Witnesses To Mark:
{

    Subscribed and sworn to before me this   25th   day of   February   , 1905.

                  Notary Public.

AFFIDAVIT OF ATTENDING PHYSICIAN OR MID-WIFE.

UNITED STATES OF AMERICA, INDIAN TERRITORY, }
    Southern   District.

    I,   Bettie Hays[sic]   , a   Midwife   , on oath state that I attended on Mrs.   Francis Melville   , wife of   Samuel C. Melville   on the   13th day of   November   , 190 4; that there was born to her on said date a   male   child; that said child is now living and is said to have been named   Newton Melville

                  Bettie Hayes

Witnesses To Mark:
{

    Subscribed and sworn to before me this   25th   day of   February   , 1905.

                  Notary Public.

Applications for Enrollment of Chickasaw Newborn
Act of 1905   Volume VI

BIRTH AFFIDAVIT.

DEPARTMENT OF THE INTERIOR.
COMMISSION TO THE FIVE CIVILIZED TRIBES.

IN RE APPLICATION FOR ENROLLMENT, as a citizen of the Chickasaw Nation, of Newton Melville, born on the 13th day of Nov, 1903

Name of Father: Samuel C. Melville   a citizen of the Chickasaw Nation.
Name of Mother: Frances[sic] Melville   a citizen of the Chickasaw Nation.

Postoffice   Stonewall I.T.

AFFIDAVIT OF MOTHER.

UNITED STATES OF AMERICA, Indian Territory,
Southern DISTRICT.

I, Frances Melville, on oath state that I am 18 years of age and a citizen by blood, of the Chickasaw Nation; that I am the lawful wife of Samuel C. Melville, who is a citizen, by blood of the Chickasaw Nation; that a male child was born to me on 13th day of November, 1903; that said child has been named Newton Melville, and was living March 4, 1905.

~~James E Webb~~
Witnesses To Mark: Frances Melville

Subscribed and sworn to before me this 24 day of April, 1905.

James E Webb
Notary Public.

AFFIDAVIT OF ATTENDING PHYSICIAN OR MID-WIFE.

UNITED STATES OF AMERICA, Indian Territory,
Southern DISTRICT.

I, Bettie Hayes, a midwife, on oath state that I attended on Mrs. Frances Melville, wife of Samuel C. Melville on the 13th day of Nov., 1903; that there was born to her on said date a male child; that said child was living March 4, 1905, and is said to have been named Newton Melville

Bettie Hayes
Witnesses To Mark:

Applications for Enrollment of Chickasaw Newborn
Act of 1905 Volume VI

Subscribed and sworn to before me this 25 day of April , 1905

James E Webb
Notary Public.

Chickasaw 142.

Muskogee, Indian Territory, April 15, 1905.

Sam C. Melville,
    Stonewall, Indian Territory.

Dear Sir:

    Receipt is hereby acknowledged of your letter of April 8, asking if application for the enrollment of your son, Newton Melville, has been received.

    In reply to your letter you are informed that it does not appear from our records that affidavits to the birth of your son, Newton Melville, has been received at this office, and for your convenience there is enclosed herewith a blank for the enrollment of an infant child, which you should have executed and returned to this office within sixty days from March 3, 1905.

                                Respectfully,

1 B.C.   Chairman.

9-142.

Muskogee, Indian Territory, April 28, 1905.

Samuel C. Melville,
    Stonewall, Indian Territory.

Dear Sir:

    Receipt is hereby acknowledged of the affidavits of Frances Melville and Bettie Hayes to the birth of Newton Melville, son of Samuel C. and Frances Melville, November 13, 1903, and the same have been filed with our records as an application for the enrollment of said child.

                                Respectfully,

                                                                       Chairman.

Applications for Enrollment of Chickasaw Newborn
Act of 1905   Volume VI

Chic. N.B - 455
   (Albert Perry
   Born June 10, 1903)

BIRTH AFFIDAVIT.

DEPARTMENT OF THE INTERIOR.
COMMISSION TO THE FIVE CIVILIZED TRIBES.

   IN RE APPLICATION FOR ENROLLMENT, as a citizen of the   Chickasaw   Nation, of   Albert Perry   , born on the   10   day of   June   , 1903

Name of Father: Simon Perry   a citizen of the   Chickasaw   Nation.
Name of Mother: Cicen Perry   a citizen of the   Chickasaw   Nation.

                    Postoffice   Ada I.T.

AFFIDAVIT OF MOTHER.

UNITED STATES OF AMERICA, Indian Territory, }
   Southern   DISTRICT. }

   I,   Cicen Perry   , on oath state that I am   20   years of age and a citizen by blood , of the   Chickasaw   Nation; that I am the lawful wife of   Simon Perry , who is a citizen, by blood   of the   Chickasaw   Nation; that a   male   child was born to me on   10   day of   June   , 1903; that said child has been named   Albert Perry   , and was living March 4, 1905.

                                  her
                         Cicen x Perry
Witnesses To Mark: mark
   { Simon Perry
   { JE Williams

   Subscribed and sworn to before me this 25   day of   April   , 1905

                         JE Williams
                               Notary Public.

Applications for Enrollment of Chickasaw Newborn
Act of 1905 Volume VI

AFFIDAVIT OF ATTENDING PHYSICIAN OR MID-WIFE.

UNITED STATES OF AMERICA, Indian Territory,
Southern DISTRICT.

I, Stamfioke Factor, a mid-wife, on oath state that I attended on Mrs. Cicen Perry, wife of Simon Perry on the 10 day of June, 1903; that there was born to her on said date a male child; that said child was living March 4, 1905, and is said to have been named Albert Perry

                                        her
                              Stamfioke x Factor
Witnesses To Mark: mark
   Simon Perry
   JE Williams

Subscribed and sworn to before me this 25 day of April, 1905

                              JE Williams
                              Notary Public.

No 39

Birth Affidavit.

DEPARTMENT OF THE INTERIOR
COMMISSION TO THE FIVE CIVILIZED TRIBES.

IN RE THE APPLICATION FOR ENROLLMENT, as a citizen of the Chickasaw Nation, of Albert Perry born on the 10th day of June 1903

Name of Father Simon Perry Citizen of the Chickasaw Nation
Name of Mother Cicen Perry a citizen of the Chickasaw Nation.

                            Postoffice Ada I.T.

AFFIDAVIT OF MOTHER.

United States of America
Southern District.

I, Cicen Perry, on oath state that I am 25 years of age and a citizen of the Chickasaw Nation, by blood; that I am the lawful wife of Simon Perry, who is a citizen of the Chickasaw Nation; that a male child was born on the 10th day of June 190 3., that said child has been named Albert Perry and is now living.

                                      her
                                Cicen x Perry
                                  mark

Applications for Enrollment of Chickasaw Newborn
Act of 1905 Volume VI

Witnesses to mark:
　D B Smith
　Tom D McKeown

Subscribed and sworn to before me this 3rd day of January 1905.

　　　　　　　　　　　　　　　　Tom D. McKeown
　　　　　　　　　　　　　　　　　　Notary Public.

AFFIDAVIT OF ATTENDING PHYSICIAN OR MID-WIFE.

United States of America
Southern District.

　　　　　I, Ishtuky Factor a Mid-wife on oath state that I attended Mrs. Cicen Perry, wife of Simon Perry on the 10th day of June, 1903 that there was born to her on the said date a male child; that said child is now living and is said to have been named Albert Perry　　　　　her
　　　　　　　　　　　　　　　　Ishtuky x Factor
　　　　　　　　　　　　　　　　　　mark

Witnesses to mark:
　D B Smith
　W.H. Ebey

Subscribed and sworn to before me this 3rd day of January 1905.

　　　　　　　　　　　　　　　　Tom D. McKeown
　　　　　　　　　　　　　　　　　　Notary Public.

　　　　　　　　　　　　　　　　　　　　　　9-223.

　　　　　　　Muskogee, Indian Territory, April 28, 1905.

Simon Perry,
　Ada, Indian Territory.

Dear Sir:

　　Receipt is hereby acknowledged of the affidavits of Cicen Perry and Stamfioke Factor to the birth of Albert Perry, son of Simon and Cicen Perry, June 10, 1903, and the same have been filed with our records as an application for the enrollment of said child.

　　　　　　　Respectfully,

　　　　　　　　　　　　　　　Chairman.

Applications for Enrollment of Chickasaw Newborn
Act of 1905   Volume VI

Chic. N.B - 456
*(Miller Woodson Grayson
Born March 29, 1904)*

BIRTH AFFIDAVIT.

DEPARTMENT OF THE INTERIOR.
COMMISSION TO THE FIVE CIVILIZED TRIBES.

IN RE APPLICATION FOR ENROLLMENT, as a citizen of the   Chickasaw   Nation, of   Miller Woodson Grayson   , born on the   29   day of   March   , 1904

Name of Father: Felix Grayson   a citizen of the   Chickasaw   Nation.
Name of Mother: Elsie Grayson   a citizen of the   Chickasaw   Nation.
            (Nee Burris)
                    Postoffice   Ada, I.T.

AFFIDAVIT OF MOTHER.

UNITED STATES OF AMERICA, Indian Territory, }
    Southern   DISTRICT.

I,   Elsie Grayson   , on oath state that I am   22   years of age and a citizen by blood   , of the   Chickasaw   Nation; that I am the lawful wife of   Felix Grayson , who is a citizen, by blood   of the   Chickasaw   Nation; that a   male   child was born to me on   the 29th day of   March   , 1904; that said child has been named   Miller Woodson Grayson   , and was living March 4, 1905.

                        Elsie Grayson
Witnesses To Mark:

{

Subscribed and sworn to before me this   25   day of   April   , 1905

                        JE Williams
                        Notary Public.

AFFIDAVIT OF ATTENDING PHYSICIAN OR MID-WIFE.

UNITED STATES OF AMERICA, Indian Territory, }
    Southern   DISTRICT.

I,   M W Ligon   , a   physician   , on oath state that I attended on Mrs.   Elsie Grayson   , wife of   Felix Grayson   on the   29   day of   March   ,

Applications for Enrollment of Chickasaw Newborn
Act of 1905 Volume VI

1904; that there was born to her on said date a   fmale[sic]   child; that said child was living March 4, 1905, and is said to have been named Miller Woodson Grayson

M W Ligon

Witnesses To Mark:
{

Subscribed and sworn to before me this 25 day of   April   , 1905

JE Williams
Notary Public.

9-111.

Muskogee, Indian Territory, April 28, 1905.

Felix Grayson,
    Ada, Indian Territory.

Dear Sir:

    Receipt is hereby acknowledged of the affidavits of Elsie Grayson and M. W. Ligon to the birth of Miller Woodson Grayson, son of Felix and Elsie Grayson, March 24, 1904, and the same have been filed with our records as an application for the enrollment of said child.

                      Respectfully,

                                   Chairman.

Chic. N.B - 457
    (Leo Curtis Johnston
    Born December 3, 1903)

Applications for Enrollment of Chickasaw Newborn
Act of 1905 Volume VI

BIRTH AFFIDAVIT.

DEPARTMENT OF THE INTERIOR.
COMMISSION TO THE FIVE CIVILIZED TRIBES.

IN RE APPLICATION FOR ENROLLMENT, as a citizen of the Chickasaw Nation, of Leo Curtis Johnston , born on the 3rd day of Dec , 1903

Name of Father: Lem Johnston a citizen of the Chickasaw Nation.
Name of Mother: Etta Johnston a citizen of the Chickasaw Nation.

Postoffice Johnston I.T.

AFFIDAVIT OF MOTHER.

UNITED STATES OF AMERICA, Indian Territory,
Southern DISTRICT.

I, Etta Johnston , on oath state that I am 29 years of age and a citizen by marriage , of the Chickasaw Nation; that I am the lawful wife of Lem Johnston , who is a citizen, by Blood of the Chickasaw Nation; that a Boy child was born to me on 3rd day of December , 1903; that said child has been named Leo Curtis Johnston , and was living March 4, 1905.

Etta Johnston

Witnesses To Mark:
{

Subscribed and sworn to before me this 24 day of April , 1905

C P Hoggard
Notary Public.

AFFIDAVIT OF ATTENDING PHYSICIAN OR MID-WIFE.

UNITED STATES OF AMERICA, Indian Territory,
DISTRICT.

I, G. L. Johnston[sic] , a Physician , on oath state that I attended on Mrs. Etta Johnston , wife of Lem Johnston on the 3rd day of December , 1903; that there was born to her on said date a male child; that said child was living March 4, 1905, and is said to have been named Leo Curtis Johnston

G.L. Johnson M.D.

Witnesses To Mark:
{

Applications for Enrollment of Chickasaw Newborn
Act of 1905   Volume VI

Subscribed and sworn to before me this 24 day of April , 1905

                                                    C P Hoggard
                                                   Notary Public.

BIRTH AFFIDAVIT.

IN RE-APPLICATION FOR ENROLLMENT, AS A CITIZEN of the Chickasaw Nation, of Leo Curtis Johnston   born on the   3   day of   December 190 3

Name of Father   Lem Johnston   a citizen of the   Chickasaw   Nation.
Name of Mother   Etta Johnston   a citizen of the   Chickasaw   Nation.

                                        Postoffice   Byars I.T.

AFFIDAVIT OF MOTHER.

UNITED STATES OF AMERICA, INDIAN TERRITORY,
Southern Judicial   District,

    I, Etta Johnston , on oath state that I am   29   years of age, and a citizen by Marriage   of the   Chickasaw   Nation. that I am the lawful wife of   Lem Johnston who is a citizen by   Blood   of the   Chickasaw   Nation: that a   Male   child was born to me on   3   day of   December   190 3 ; that said child has been named   Leo Curtis Johnston   , and is now living.

                                                  Etta Johnston

WITNESSES TO MARK.

....
....

Subscribed and sworn to before me this   2   day of   March   190 5

                                               J M Nichols
                                                  Notary Public.

AFFIDAVIT OF ATTENDING PHYSICIAN OR MIDWIFE.

UNITED STATES OF AMERICA, INDIAN TERRITORY,
Southern Judicial   District,

    I, G.L. Johnson   a   Physician   on oath state that I attended on Mrs.   Etta Johnston   , wife of   Lem Johnston   on the   3   day of   December   190 3, that there

Applications for Enrollment of Chickasaw Newborn
Act of 1905   Volume VI

was born to her on said date a male child; that said child is now living and is said to have been named Leo Curtis Johnston

G L Johnson M.D.

WITNESSES TO MARK.

....

....

Subscribed and sworn to before me this 2 day of March   190 5

J M Nichols

Notary Public.

9-392.

Muskogee, Indian Territory, April 28, 1905.

Lem Johnston,
    Johnson[sic], Indian Territory.

Dear Sir:

    Receipt is hereby acknowledged of the affidavits of Etta Johnston and G. L. Johnson to the birth of Leo Curtis Johnston, son of Lem and Etta Johnston, December 3, 1903, and the same have been filed with our records as an application for the enrollment of said child.

Respectfully,

Chairman.

Chic. N.B - 458
    (Eva Gaddis
    Born January 27, 1903)
    (Pearl Gaddis
    Born December 28, 1904)

Applications for Enrollment of Chickasaw Newborn
Act of 1905 Volume VI

BIRTH AFFIDAVIT.

DEPARTMENT OF THE INTERIOR.
COMMISSION TO THE FIVE CIVILIZED TRIBES.

IN RE APPLICATION FOR ENROLLMENT, as a citizen of the Chickasaw Nation, of Eva Gaddis, born on the 27 day of Jany, 1903

Name of Father: George L Gaddis   a citizen of the Chickasaw Nation.
Name of Mother: Martha Gaddis   a citizen of the United States Nation.

Postoffice   Loco I.T.

AFFIDAVIT OF MOTHER.

UNITED STATES OF AMERICA, Indian Territory,
Southern DISTRICT.

I, Martha Gaddis, on oath state that I am 23 years of age and a citizen by Marriage, of the United States ~~Nation~~; that I am the lawful wife of George L Gaddis, who is a citizen, by Blood of the Chickasaw Nation; that a female child was born to me on 27" day of Jany, 1903; that said child has been named Eva Gaddis, and was living March 4, 1905.

Martha Gaddis

Witnesses To Mark:
{

Subscribed and sworn to before me this 13" day of April, 1905

M M Hightower
Notary Public.

AFFIDAVIT OF ATTENDING PHYSICIAN OR MID-WIFE.

UNITED STATES OF AMERICA, Indian Territory,
Southern DISTRICT.

I, W.C. Thagard, a M.D., on oath state that I attended on Mrs. Martha Gaddis, wife of George L Gaddis on the 27" day of Jany, 1903; that there was born to her on said date a female child; that said child was living March 4, 1905, and is said to have been named Eva Gaddis

W.C. Thagard M.D.

Witnesses To Mark:
{

Applications for Enrollment of Chickasaw Newborn
Act of 1905   Volume VI

Subscribed and sworn to before me this   13" day of   April   , 1905

M M Hightower
Notary Public.

BIRTH AFFIDAVIT.

DEPARTMENT OF THE INTERIOR.
COMMISSION TO THE FIVE CIVILIZED TRIBES.

IN RE APPLICATION FOR ENROLLMENT, as a citizen of the   Chickasaw   Nation, of   Pearl Gaddis   , born on the   28" day of   Dec , 1904

Name of Father: George L Gaddis   a citizen of the   Chickasaw Nation.
Name of Mother: Martha Gaddis   a citizen of the United States Nation.

Postoffice   Loco I.T.

AFFIDAVIT OF MOTHER.

UNITED STATES OF AMERICA, Indian Territory, }
Southern   DISTRICT.   }

I,   Martha Gaddis   , on oath state that I am   23   years of age and a citizen by   Marriage   , of the   United States   ~~Nation~~; that I am the lawful wife of George L Gaddis   , who is a citizen, by Blood   of the   Chickasaw Nation; that a   female   child was born to me on   28" day of   December   , 1904; that said child has been named   Pearl Gaddis   , and was living March 4, 1905.

Martha Gaddis

Witnesses To Mark:
{

Subscribed and sworn to before me this   13" day of   April   , 1905

M M Hightower
Notary Public.

AFFIDAVIT OF ATTENDING PHYSICIAN OR MID-WIFE.

UNITED STATES OF AMERICA, Indian Territory, }
Southern   DISTRICT.   }

I,   W.C. Thagard   , a   M.D.   , on oath state that I attended on Mrs.   Martha Gaddis   , wife of   George L Gaddis   on the 28" day of

Applications for Enrollment of Chickasaw Newborn
Act of 1905 Volume VI

December , 1904; that there was born to her on said date a female child; that said child was living March 4, 1905, and is said to have been named Pearl Gaddis

W.C. Thagard M.D.

Witnesses To Mark:

{ Subscribed and sworn to before me this 13" day of April , 1905

M M Hightower
Notary Public.

9-1370.

Muskogee, Indian Territory, April 28, 1905.

George L. Gaddis,
    Loco, Indian Territory.

Dear Sir:

    Receipt is hereby acknowledged of the affidavits of Martha Gaddis and W. C. Thagard to the birth of Eva Gaddis and Pearl Gaddis, children of George L. and Martha Gaddis, January 27, 1903, and December 28, 1904, respectively, and the same have been filed with our records as an application for the enrollment of said child.

Respectfully,

Chairman.

---

9 N.B. 458.

Muskogee, Indian Territory, May 15, 1905.

George L. Gaddis,
    Loco, Indian Territory.

Dear Sir:

    Replying to that portion of your letter of April 24, in which you ask if applications have been received for the enrollment of your children, Evie[sic] and Pearl Gaddis, you are advised that the affidavits heretofore forwarded to the birth of your children, Eva and Pearl Gaddis, have been filed with our records as applications for the enrollment of said children.

Respectfully,

Chairman.

Applications for Enrollment of Chickasaw Newborn
Act of 1905 Volume VI

Chic. N.B - 459
(Malita Fay Strickland
Born April 2, 1904)

BIRTH AFFIDAVIT.

DEPARTMENT OF THE INTERIOR.
COMMISSION TO THE FIVE CIVILIZED TRIBES.

IN RE APPLICATION FOR ENROLLMENT, as a citizen of the Chickasaw Nation, of Malita Fay Strickland , born on the 2^{ond} day of April , 1904

Name of Father: Tom Strickland   a citizen of the Chickasaw Nation.
Name of Mother: Jettie Strickland   a citizen of the Chickasaw Nation.

Postoffice Johnston

AFFIDAVIT OF MOTHER.

UNITED STATES OF AMERICA, Indian Territory, }
Southern DISTRICT. }

I, Jettie Strickland , on oath state that I am 21 years of age and a citizen by Marriage , of the Chickasaw Nation; that I am the lawful wife of Tom Strickland , who is a citizen, by Blood of the Chickasaw Nation; that a Girl child was born to me on 2^{ond} day of April , 1904; that said child has been named Malita Fay Strickland , and was living March 4, 1905.

Jettie Strickland

Witnesses To Mark:
{

Subscribed and sworn to before me this 24 day of April , 1905

C.P. Hoggard
Notary Public.

AFFIDAVIT OF ATTENDING PHYSICIAN OR MID-WIFE.

UNITED STATES OF AMERICA, Indian Territory, }
.... DISTRICT. }

I, G. L. Johnson , a Physician , on oath state that I attended on Mrs. Jettie Strickland , wife of Thos Strickland on the 2nd day of April ,

73

Applications for Enrollment of Chickasaw Newborn
Act of 1905 Volume VI

1904; that there was born to her on said date a female child; that said child was living March 4, 1905, and is said to have been named Malita Fay Strickland

G. L. Johnson M.D.

Witnesses To Mark:

{

Subscribed and sworn to before me this 24 day of April , 1905

My Commission expires C P Hoggard
Jan 28 1907 Notary Public.

9-382

Muskogee, Indian Territory, April 17, 1905.

Tom Strickland,
    Johnson, Indian Territory.

Dear Sir:

    Receipt is hereby acknowledged of your letter of March 11, 1905, which was received at this office April 14, 1905, in which you ask if the application for the enrollment of your child Itta[sic] Fay Strickland has been received.

    In reply to your letter you are informed that it does not appear from our records that affidavits have been filed with this office relative to the birth of your child Itta Fay Strickland and for your convenience there is inclosed herewith blank for the enrollment of an infant child which you should have executed and returned to this office within sixty days from March 3, 1905.

                  Respectfully,

                                    Chairman.

B.C.

Applications for Enrollment of Chickasaw Newborn
Act of 1905   Volume VI

Chickasaw 382.

Muskogee, Indian Territory, April 21, 1905.

Tom Strickland,
    Johnson, Indian Territory.

Dear Sir:

    Receipt is hereby acknowledged of your letter of March 13, asking if the application for the enrollment of Malita Fay Strickland, daughter of Tom and Jettie Strickland, born April 2, 1904, has reached this office in proper form.

    In reply to your letter you are informed that it does not appear from our records that affidavits have been filed at this office to the birth of Malita Fay Strickland, daughter of Tom and Jettie Strickland, and for your convenience there is enclosed herewith blank for the enrollment of your child which you should have executed and returned to this office within sixty days from March 3, 1905.

Respectfully,

Chairman.

9-382.

Muskogee, Indian Territory, April 28, 1905.

Tom Strickland,
    Johnson, Indian Territory.

Dear Sir:

    Receipt is hereby acknowledged of the affidavits of Jettie Strickland and G. L. Johnson to the birth of Malita Fay Strickland, daughter of Tom and Jettie Strickland, April 2, 1904, and the same have been filed with our records as an application for the enrollment of said child.

Respectfully,

Chairman.

Applications for Enrollment of Chickasaw Newborn
Act of 1905   Volume VI

Chic. N.B - 460
*(Lutie Mable Keel
Born August 9, 1904)*

BIRTH AFFIDAVIT.

DEPARTMENT OF THE INTERIOR.
COMMISSION TO THE FIVE CIVILIZED TRIBES.

IN RE APPLICATION FOR ENROLLMENT, as a citizen of the   Chickasaw   Nation, of   Lutie Mable Keel   , born on the   9   day of   August   , 1904

Name of Father: Guy Keel   a citizen of the   Chickasaw   Nation.
Name of Mother: Lula Keel   a citizen of the   Chickasaw   Nation.

Postoffice   Madill, Ind Ter

AFFIDAVIT OF MOTHER.

UNITED STATES OF AMERICA, Indian Territory, }
Southern   DISTRICT.

I,   Lula Keel   , on oath state that I am   27   years of age and a citizen by blood   , of the   Chickasaw   Nation; that I am the lawful wife of   Guy Keel   , who is a citizen, by blood   of the   Chickasaw   Nation; that a   female   child was born to me on   9   day of   August   , 1904; that said child has been named Lutie Mable Keel   , and was living March 4, 1905.

Lula Keel

Witnesses To Mark:
{

Subscribed and sworn to before me this   22   day of   April   , 1905

Geo E Rider
Notary Public.

AFFIDAVIT OF ATTENDING PHYSICIAN OR MID-WIFE.

UNITED STATES OF AMERICA, Indian Territory, }
Southern   DISTRICT.

I,   C B Martin   , a   Physician   , on oath state that I attended on Mrs.   Lula Keel   , wife of   Guy Keel   on the   9   day of   August   , 1904;

Applications for Enrollment of Chickasaw Newborn
Act of 1905   Volume VI

that there was born to her on said date a   female   child; that said child was living March 4, 1905, and is said to have been named Lutie Mable Keel

                                      C.B. Martin M.D.

Witnesses To Mark:
{

    Subscribed and sworn to before me this 22 day of   April   , 1905

                                     Geo E Rider
                                         Notary Public.

                                                              9-614.

                          Muskogee, Indian Territory, April 28, 1905.

George E. Rider,
      Attorney at Law,
            Madill, Indian Territory.

Dear Sir:

    Receipt is hereby acknowledged of your two letters of April 25, 1905, enclosing affidavits of Lula Keel and J. S. Welch to the birth of Irene Keel and also the affidavits of Lula Keel and C. B. Martin to the birth of Lutie Mable Keel, children of Guy and Lula Keel, October 2, 1902, and August 9, 1904, respectively, and the same have been filed with our records as an application for the enrollment of said child.

                              Respectfully,

                                          Chairman.

Chic. N.B - 461
        (Gollia Lewis
        Born August 25, 1903)

Applications for Enrollment of Chickasaw Newborn
Act of 1905 Volume VI

McGee IT 3/23/905

Com To The Five Civilized Tribes
  Muskogee I T

Gentlemen:-
  I herewith send you the application of Gollia Lewis, child of Martin Lewis and Nora Lewis for Enrollment as a citizen of the Chickasaw Nation the Chickasaw Nation.
  Please acknowledge receipt of same and advise me if same is in Regular form
Very Respect
  Jos A Edwards

Affidavit of Attending Physician

Territory of Oklahoma
Pottawatomie Co   ss

  I J E Cullum a Physician on oath state that I attended on Mrs. , wife of on the day of , 190 ; that there was born to her on said date a child; that said child was living March 4, 1905, and is said to have been named . on Mrs Nora Lewis wife of Martin Lewis on the 23rd day of August 1903; that there was born to her on said date a Female child; that said child is said to have been named Gollia Lewis and was living the 4 of March 1905

  J E Cullum

Subscribed and sworn to before me this 21st day of March 1905

  A J Grayson
My commission expires Apr 3" 1906   Notary Public

Birth Affidavit

Department of The Interior
  Com To The Five Civilized Tribes

In Re Application for Enrollment as a citizen of The Chickasaw Nation of Gollia Lewis born on the 25 day of Aug. 1903
Name of Father: Martin Lewis   a citizen of The Chickasaw Nation United States
Name of Mother Nora Lewis   a citizen of The ~~Chickasaw Nation~~
  Post Office McGee I T

Affidavit of Mother

United States of America
  Indian Territory
  Southern District

I Nora Lewis on oath state that I am 23 years of age and a citizen by *(blank space)* of The United States ~~Nations~~ that I am the Lawful wife of Martin Lewis who is a citizen by

Applications for Enrollment of Chickasaw Newborn
Act of 1905   Volume VI

blood of the Chickasaw Nation of The Chickasaw Nation That a Femle child was born to me on the 25 day of Aug - 1903 That said child has been named Gollia Lewis and was living March 4th 1905

Nora Lewis

Muskogee, Indian Territory, April 12, 1905.

Joseph A. Edwards,
    McGee, Indian Territory.

Dear Sir:

    Receipt is hereby acknowledged of your letter of March 23, 1905, inclosing application for the enrollment of Gollia Lewis, daughter of Martin and Nora Lewis, as a citizen of the Chickasaw Nation.

    It is stated in the application that the father Martin Lewis is a citizen by blood of the Chickasaw Nation and if this is correct you are requested to state his age, the names of his parents, the time and place application was made for his enrollment and if he has selected an allotment of the lands of the Choctaw or Chickasaw Nation you are requested to give his allotment number as it appears upon the certificate.

Respectfully,

Commissioner in Charge.

9-NB-461

Muskogee, Indian Territory, September 15, 1905.

E. G. Williams,
    c/o Joe A. Edwards,
        McGee, Indian Territory.

Dear Sir:

    This office is in receipt by reference from the Secretary of the Interior for consideration and appropriate action, of your letter of August 31, 1905, in reference to the enrollment of Gollia Lewis as a citizen by blood of the Chickasaw Nation.

    You are advised that on June 21, 1905, the enrollment of Gollia Lewis as a citizen by blood of the Chickasaw Nation was approved by the Secretary of the Interior, and the name of said child appears upon the final roll of new born citizens by blood of the Chickasaw Nation opposite No. 404. You were advised of the approval by the Secretary of the Interior of the enrollment of your child, early in July, 1905. The child is entitled to

Applications for Enrollment of Chickasaw Newborn
Act of 1905 Volume VI

an allotment and selection thereof should be made without delay at the land office for the nation in which the prospective allotment is located.

Respectfully,

Acting Commissioner.

Chic. N.B - 462
(Florence E. Wells
Born October 2, 1903)

BIRTH AFFIDAVIT.

DEPARTMENT OF THE INTERIOR.
COMMISSION TO THE FIVE CIVILIZED TRIBES.

IN RE APPLICATION FOR ENROLLMENT, as a citizen of the Chickasaw Nation, of Florence E. Wells, born on the 2 day of October, 1903

Name of Father: Willard W. Wells   a citizen of the Chickasaw Nation.
Name of Mother: Lula C Wells   a citizen of the U.S. Nation.

Postoffice   Cope Ind. Ty.

AFFIDAVIT OF MOTHER.

UNITED STATES OF AMERICA, Indian Territory, }
22nd Southern   DISTRICT.

I, Lula C. Wells, on oath state that I am 33 years of age and a citizen by birth, of the United States ~~Nation~~; that I am the lawful wife of Willard W. Wells, who is a citizen, by Blood of the Chickasaw Nation; that a Female child was born to me on 2^{ond} day of October, 1903; that said child has been named Florence E. Wells, and was living March 4, 1905.

Lula C. Wells

Witnesses To Mark:

Applications for Enrollment of Chickasaw Newborn
Act of 1905 Volume VI

Subscribed and sworn to before me this 25th day of Aprile[sic] , 1905

T.C. Keller
Notary Public.

AFFIDAVIT OF ATTENDING PHYSICIAN OR MID-WIFE.

UNITED STATES OF AMERICA, Indian Territory, }
22nd Southern   DISTRICT.

I, Lorena M. Gamble , a Mid Wife , on oath state that I attended on Mrs. Lula C. Wells , wife of Willard W Wells on the 2^{ond} day of October , 1903; that there was born to her on said date a Female child; that said child was living March 4, 1905, and is said to have been named Florence E. Wells

her
Lorena x M. Gamble
mark

Witnesses To Mark:
{ *(Name Illegible)*
{ *(Name Illegible)*

Subscribed and sworn to before me this 25th day of Aprile[sic] , 1905

T.C. Keller
Notary Public.

Chic. N.B - 463
(Conchoella B. Gilmore
Born February 19, 1905)

BIRTH AFFIDAVIT.
DEPARTMENT OF THE INTERIOR.
COMMISSION TO THE FIVE CIVILIZED TRIBES.

IN RE APPLICATION FOR ENROLLMENT, as a citizen of the Chickasaw Nation, of Conchoella B. Gilmore , born on the 19th day of February , 1905

Name of Father: Edwin T. Gilmore   a citizen of the United States ~~Nation~~.
Name of Mother: Sarah A. Gilmore   a citizen of the Chickasaw Nation.

Applications for Enrollment of Chickasaw Newborn
Act of 1905   Volume VI

Postoffice   Allen

AFFIDAVIT OF MOTHER.

UNITED STATES OF AMERICA, Indian Territory, }
Central   DISTRICT.

I, Sarah A. Gilmore, on oath state that I am Thirty two years of age and a citizen by Blood, of the Chickasaw Nation; that I am the lawful wife of Edwin T. Gilmore, who is a citizen, by birth of the United States ~~Nation~~; that a Female child was born to me on 19th day of February, 1905; that said child has been named Conchoella B. Gilmore, and was living March 4, 1905.

Sarah A. Gilmore

Witnesses To Mark:
{

Subscribed and sworn to before me this 22 day of April, 1905

Com Exp 1/8/07   W W Jones
                        Notary Public.

AFFIDAVIT OF ATTENDING PHYSICIAN OR MID-WIFE.

UNITED STATES OF AMERICA, Indian Territory, }
Central   DISTRICT.

I, John T. Gilmore M.D., a M.D., on oath state that I attended on Mrs. Sarah A Gilmore, wife of Edwin T Gilmore on the 19th day of February, 1905; that there was born to her on said date a Female child; that said child was living March 4, 1905, and is said to have been named Conchoella B. Gilmore

John T Gilmore

Witnesses To Mark:
{

Subscribed and sworn to before me this 22 day of April, 1905

Com Exp 1/8/07   W W Jones
                        Notary Public.

Applications for Enrollment of Chickasaw Newborn
Act of 1905 Volume VI

9-1683.

Muskogee, Indian Territory, April 29, 1905.

Edwin T. Gilmore,
    Allen, Indian Territory.

Dear Sir:

    Receipt is hereby acknowledged of the affidavits of Sarah A. Gilmore and John T. Gilmore to the birth of Conchoella B. Gilmore, daughter of Edwin T. and Sarah A. Gilmore, February 19, 1905, and the same have been filed with our records as an application for the enrollment of said child.

    Respectfully,

    Chairman.

Chic. N.B - 464
    (Fannie Ford
    Born December 9, 1902)
    (Jewel Ford
    Born December 30, 1904)

BIRTH AFFIDAVIT.   #135

    IN RE-APPLICATION FOR ENROLLMENT, as a citizen of the Chickasaw Nation, of Fannie Ford , born on the 9th day of December , 190 2

Name of Father: Robert P. Ford   a citizen of the Chickasaw Nation.
Name of Mother: Sallie Ford   a citizen of the Chickasaw Nation.

    Postoffice   Ada, Indian Territory

AFFIDAVIT OF MOTHER.

UNITED STATES OF AMERICA, INDIAN TERRITORY,
Southern Judicial District   District.

    I, Sallie Ford , on oath state that I am 28 years of age and a citizen by blood , of the Chickasaw Nation; that I am the lawful wife of Robert P. Ford , who is a citizen, by intermarriage of the Chickasaw Nation; that a female

Applications for Enrollment of Chickasaw Newborn
Act of 1905 Volume VI

child was born to me on 9th day of December , 190 2, that said child has been named Fannie Ford , and is now living.

her
Sallie x Ford
mark

Witnesses To Mark:
- Henry H Ford
- Gorge Ford

Subscribed and sworn to before me this 21st day of February , 1905.

Notary Public.

B.P. Ford

AFFIDAVIT OF ATTENDING PHYSICIAN OR MID-WIFE.

UNITED STATES OF AMERICA, INDIAN TERRITORY,
Southern Judicial District.

I, Alice Jobe , a midwife , on oath state that I attended on Mrs. Sallie Ford , wife of Robert P. Ford on the 9th day of December , 190 2; that there was born to her on said date a female child; that said child is now living and is said to have been named Fannie Ford

Alice Jobe

Witnesses To Mark:
- Henry H Ford
- J.T. Jobe

Subscribed and sworn to before me this 21st day of February , 1905.

B.P. Ford
Notary Public.

BIRTH AFFIDAVIT.

DEPARTMENT OF THE INTERIOR.
COMMISSION TO THE FIVE CIVILIZED TRIBES.

IN RE APPLICATION FOR ENROLLMENT, as a citizen of the Chickasaw Nation, of Fanney[sic] Ford , born on the 11[sic] day of December , 1902

Name of Father: Robert P. Ford a citizen of the Chickasaw Nation.
Name of Mother: Salley Ford a citizen of the Chickasaw Nation.

Postoffice Ada I T

Applications for Enrollment of Chickasaw Newborn
Act of 1905   Volume VI

AFFIDAVIT OF MOTHER.

UNITED STATES OF AMERICA, Indian Territory,
Southern   DISTRICT.

I, Sallie Ford, on oath state that I am 28 years of age and a citizen by Blood, of the Chickasaw Nation; that I am the lawful wife of Robert P. Ford, who is a citizen, by intermared of the Chickasaw Nation; that a girl child was born to me on 11[sic] day of December, 1902; that said child has been named Fanney Ford, and was living March 4, 1905.

             her
            Salley x Ford
Witnesses To Mark: mark
 { Sophey Wright
   Rosey Wright

Subscribed and sworn to before me this 25 day of Aprile, 1905

            B.P. Ford
              Notary Public.

AFFIDAVIT OF ATTENDING PHYSICIAN OR MID-WIFE.

UNITED STATES OF AMERICA, Indian Territory,
Southern   DISTRICT.

I, Allis[sic] Jobe, a mid Wife, on oath state that I attended on Mrs. Sallie Ford, wife of RoBert[sic] Ford on the 11[sic] day of December, 1902; that there was born to her on said date a girl child; that said child was living March 4, 1905, and is said to have been named Fannie Ford

            Alice Jobe
Witnesses To Mark:
 { Lillie Jobe
   Connie Jobe

Subscribed and sworn to before me this 26 day of Aprile, 1905

            B.P. Ford
              Notary Public.

Applications for Enrollment of Chickasaw Newborn
Act of 1905   Volume VI

BIRTH AFFIDAVIT.

DEPARTMENT OF THE INTERIOR.
COMMISSION TO THE FIVE CIVILIZED TRIBES.

IN RE APPLICATION FOR ENROLLMENT, as a citizen of the   Chickasaw   Nation, of   Fannie Ford   , born on the   9   day of   December   , 1902

Name of Father: Robert P. Ford   a citizen of the   Chickasaw   Nation.
Name of Mother: Sallie Ford   a citizen of the   Chickasaw   Nation.

Postoffice   Ada Ind. Ter.

AFFIDAVIT OF MOTHER.

UNITED STATES OF AMERICA, Indian Territory,
Southern Judicial   DISTRICT.

I,   Sallie Ford   , on oath state that I am   28   years of age and a citizen by Blood   , of the   Chickasaw   Nation; that I am the lawful wife of   Robert P. Ford , who is a citizen, by Intermarriage   of the   Chickasaw   Nation; that a   Female   child was born to me on   9th day of   December   , 1902; that said child has been named   Fannie Ford   , and was living March 4, 1905.

                                 her
                        Sallie x Ford
Witnesses To Mark: mark
   Albert Ford
   H. Tomson

Subscribed and sworn to before me this   24   day of   May   , 1905

                        B.P. Ford
                             Notary Public.

AFFIDAVIT OF ATTENDING PHYSICIAN OR MID-WIFE.

UNITED STATES OF AMERICA, Indian Territory,
Southern Judicial   DISTRICT.

I,   Alice Jobe   , a mid-wife   , on oath state that I attended on Mrs.   Sallie Ford   , wife of   Robert P. Ford   on the 9th day of   December , 1902; that there was born to her on said date a   Female   child; that said child was living March 4, 1905, and is said to have been named Fannie Ford

                        Alice Jobe

Applications for Enrollment of Chickasaw Newborn
Act of 1905   Volume VI

Witnesses To Mark:
- Z. Y. Jobe
- Cansada Robinson

Subscribed and sworn to before me this 24 day of May , 1905

B.P. Ford
Notary Public.

BIRTH AFFIDAVIT.   #134

IN RE-APPLICATION FOR ENROLLMENT, as a citizen of the   Chickasaw   Nation, of   Jewell Ford   , born on the 31st[sic] day of December , 1904

Name of Father: Robert P. Ford   a citizen of the Chickasaw Nation.
Name of Mother: Sallie Ford   a citizen of the Chickasaw Nation.

Postoffice   Ada, Indian Territory

AFFIDAVIT OF MOTHER.

UNITED STATES OF AMERICA, INDIAN TERRITORY,
Southern Judicial   District.

I,   Sallie Ford   , on oath state that I am   28   years of age and a citizen by blood , of the   Chickasaw   Nation; that I am the lawful wife of   Robert P. Ford , who is a citizen, by   intermarriage   of the   Chickasaw   Nation; that a   female   child was born to me on 31st[sic] day of   December   , 1904, that said child has been named   Jewell Ford   , and is now living.

her
Sallie x Ford
mark

Witnesses To Mark:
- Henry H Ford
- Gorge Ford

Subscribed and sworn to before me this   21st   day of   February   , 1905.

Notary Public.
B.P. Ford

Applications for Enrollment of Chickasaw Newborn
Act of 1905 Volume VI

AFFIDAVIT OF ATTENDING PHYSICIAN OR MID-WIFE.

UNITED STATES OF AMERICA, INDIAN TERRITORY,
Southern Judicial District District.

I, Maggie Jobe, a midwife, on oath state that I attended on Mrs. Sallie Ford, wife of Robert P. Ford on the 31st[sic] day of December, 1904; that there was born to her on said date a female child; that said child is now living and is said to have been named Jewell Ford

Magie[sic] Jobe

Witnesses To Mark:
- E S Tomas
- L. Wilson

Subscribed and sworn to before me this 21st day of February, 1905.

B.P. Ford
Notary Public.

BIRTH AFFIDAVIT.

DEPARTMENT OF THE INTERIOR.
COMMISSION TO THE FIVE CIVILIZED TRIBES.

IN RE APPLICATION FOR ENROLLMENT, as a citizen of the Chickasaw Nation, of Jewel Ford, born on the 30 day of December, 1904

Name of Father: Robert P. Ford a citizen of the Chickasaw Nation.
Name of Mother: Salley Ford a citizen of the Chickasaw Nation.

Postoffice Ada I T

AFFIDAVIT OF MOTHER.

UNITED STATES OF AMERICA, Indian Territory,
Southern DISTRICT.

I, Salley Ford, on oath state that I am 28 years of age and a citizen by Blood, of the Chickasaw Nation; that I am the lawful wife of Robert P. Ford, who is a citizen, by intermarrige[sic] of the Chickasaw Nation; that a female child was born to me on 30 day of December, 1904; that said child has been named Jewel Ford, and was living March 4, 1905.

her
Salley x Ford
mark

Applications for Enrollment of Chickasaw Newborn
Act of 1905   Volume VI

Witnesses To Mark:
{ Sophey Wright
{ Rosey Wright

Subscribed and sworn to before me this   25 day of   Aprile   , 1905

B.P. Ford
Notary Public.

AFFIDAVIT OF ATTENDING PHYSICIAN OR MID-WIFE.

UNITED STATES OF AMERICA, Indian Territory, }
Southern   DISTRICT.   }

I,   Maggie Ford   , a Mid Wife   , on oath state that I attended on Mrs.   Salley Ford   , wife of   Robert P. Ford   on the 30 day of December , 1904; that there was born to her on said date a   girl   child; that said child was living March 4, 1905, and is said to have been named Jewel Ford

Maggie Ford

Witnesses To Mark:
{ Albert Ford
{ *(Illegible)* Ford

Subscribed and sworn to before me this   26 day of   Aprile   , 1905

B.P. Ford
Notary Public.

BIRTH AFFIDAVIT.
DEPARTMENT OF THE INTERIOR.
COMMISSION TO THE FIVE CIVILIZED TRIBES.

IN RE APPLICATION FOR ENROLLMENT, as a citizen of the   Chickasaw   Nation, of   Jewell Ford   , born on the   30   day of December , 1904

Name of Father: Robert P. Ford   a citizen of the   Chickasaw Nation.
Name of Mother: Sallie Ford   a citizen of the   Chickasaw Nation.

Postoffice   Ada Ind. Ter.

Applications for Enrollment of Chickasaw Newborn
Act of 1905   Volume VI

AFFIDAVIT OF MOTHER.

UNITED STATES OF AMERICA, Indian Territory, ⎫
    Southern Judicial   DISTRICT. ⎭

I, Sallie Ford , on oath state that I am 28 years of age and a citizen by Blood , of the Chickasaw Nation; that I am the lawful wife of Robert P. Ford , who is a citizen, by Intermarriage of the Chickasaw Nation; that a Female child was born to me on 30 day of December , 1904; that said child has been named Jewell Ford , and was living March 4, 1905.

                her
              Sallie x Ford
Witnesses To Mark: mark
 ⎰ Albert Ford
 ⎱ H. Tomson

Subscribed and sworn to before me this 24 day of May , 1905

              B.P. Ford
               Notary Public.

AFFIDAVIT OF ATTENDING PHYSICIAN OR MID-WIFE.

UNITED STATES OF AMERICA, Indian Territory, ⎫
    Southern Judicial   DISTRICT. ⎭

I, Maggie Ford , a mid-wife , on oath state that I attended on Mrs. Sallie Ford , wife of Robert P. Ford on the 30th day of December , 1904; that there was born to her on said date a Female child; that said child was living March 4, 1905, and is said to have been named Jewell Ford

               her
             Maggie x Ford
Witnesses To Mark: mark
 ⎰ *(Illegible)* Ford
 ⎱ B.P. Ford

Subscribed and sworn to before me this 24 day of May , 1905

              B.P. Ford
               Notary Public.

Applications for Enrollment of Chickasaw Newborn
Act of 1905   Volume VI

9-161.

Muskogee, Indian Territory, April 29, 1905.

Robert P. Ford,
    Ada, Indian Territory.

Dear Sir:

    Receipt is hereby acknowledged of the affidavits of Salley Ford and Alice Jobe to the birth of Fanney Ford; also affidavits of Salley Ford and Maggie Ford to the birth of Jewel Ford, children of Robert P. and Salley Ford, December 11, 1902, and December 30, 1904, respectively, and the same have been filed with our records as an application for the enrollment of said children.

                    Respectfully,

                                    Chairman.

9-NB-464.

Muskogee, Indian Territory, May 20, 1905.

Robert P. Ford,
    Ada, Indian Territory.

Dear Sir:

    There is enclosed you herewith for execution application for the enrollment of your infant children, Fannie Ford and Jewell Ford.

    In the affidavits of February 21, 1905, heretofore filed in this office, the date of birth of Fannie Ford is given as December 9, 1902; that of Jewell Ford is given as December 31, 1904, while in the affidavits of April 25, and 26, 1905, the dates of their births are given as December 11, 1902, and December 30, 1904, respectively. In the enclosed applications the dates have been left blank, which you will please insert before executing.

    In having these affidavits executed care should be exercised to see that all names are written in full, as they appear in the body of the affidavit, and in the event that either of the persons signing the affidavit are unable to write, signatures by mark must be attested by two witnesses. Each affidavit must be executed before a Notary Public and the notarial seal and signature of the officer must be attached to each separate affidavit.

                    Respectfully,

VR 20-6.   Chairman.

Applications for Enrollment of Chickasaw Newborn
Act of 1905   Volume VI

9-NB-464.

Muskogee, Indian Territory, June 1, 1905.

Robert P. Ford,
Ada, Indian Territory.

Dear Sir:

Receipt is hereby acknowledged of your letter of May 24, enclosing the affidavits of Sallie Ford and Alice Jobe to the birth of Fannie Ford; also the affidavits of Sallie Ford and Maggie Ford to the birth of Jewell Ford, children of Robert P. and Sallie Ford, December 9, 1902, and December 30, 1904, respectively, and the same have been filed with our records in the matter of the enrollment of said children.

Respectfully,

[sic]

Chic. N.B - 465
  *(Johnson Perry
  Born January 2, 1905)*

BIRTH AFFIDAVIT.

IN RE-APPLICATION FOR ENROLLMENT, as a citizen of the Chickasaw Nation, of Johnson Perry, born on the 2nd day of Jan, 1905

Name of Father: Jeff Perry   a citizen of the Chickasaw Nation.
Name of Mother: Josiphine Kuctchubby Perry   a citizen of the Chickasaw Nation.

Postoffice   Stonewall IT

AFFIDAVIT OF MOTHER.

UNITED STATES OF AMERICA, INDIAN TERRITORY,
Southern District.

I, Josiphine Kuctchubby Perry, on oath state that I am 20 years of age and a citizen by blood, of the Chickasaw Nation; that I am the lawful wife of Jeff Perry, who is a citizen, by blood of the Chickasaw Nation; that a male child was born to me on 2nd day of Jan, 1905, that said child has been named Johnson Perry, and is now living.

Josiphine Kuctchubby Perry

Applications for Enrollment of Chickasaw Newborn
Act of 1905 Volume VI

Witnesses To Mark:
- Katie Stick
- WE Mooney

Subscribed and sworn to before me this 26 day of Apr, 1905.

J.W. Fuller
Notary Public.

AFFIDAVIT OF ATTENDING PHYSICIAN OR MID-WIFE.

UNITED STATES OF AMERICA, INDIAN TERRITORY,
Southern District.

I, Annie Blue, a mid wife, on oath state that I attended on Mrs. Jeff Perry, wife of Jeff Perry on the 2nd day of Jan, 190 5; that there was born to her on said date a male child; that said child is now living and is said to have been named Johnson Perry

her
Annie x Blue
mark

Witnesses To Mark:
- Katie Stick
- WE Mooney

Subscribed and sworn to before me this 26 day of Apr, 1905.

J.W. Fuller
Notary Public.

9-274.

Muskogee, Indian Territory, April 29, 1905.

Jeff Perry,
Stonewall, Indian Territory.

Dear Sir:

Receipt is hereby acknowledged of the affidavits of Josiphine Kuctchubby Perry and Annie Blue to the birth of Johnson Perry, son of Jeff and Josiphine Kuctchubby Perry, January 2, 1905, and the same have been filed with our records as an application for the enrollment of said child.

Respectfully,

Chairman.

Applications for Enrollment of Chickasaw Newborn
Act of 1905 Volume VI

Chickasaw N B 465

Muskogee, Indian Territory, May 18, 1905.

H. O. Newman,
    Attorney at Law,
        Tishomingo, Indian Territory.

Dear Sir:

    Receipt is hereby acknowledged of your letter of May 13, asking if the application for the enrollment of Johnson Perry, infant child of Jeff and Josephine[sic] Perry, born January 2, 1905, has been approved or if anything else is necessary to be done in the matter.

    I reply you are advised that the affidavits heretofore forwarded to the birth of Johnson Perry have been filed with our records as an application for the enrollment of said child and if further evidence is necessary to enable us to pass upon the application for his enrollment Mr. Perry will be notified.

                  Respectfully,

                          Chairman.

Chic. N.B - 466
    (Kirkland B. Johnston
    Born July 31, 1903)

BIRTH AFFIDAVIT.

    IN RE-APPLICATION FOR ENROLLMENT, as a citizen of the Chickasaw Nation, of Kirkland B. Johnston, born on the 31 day of July, 190 3

Name of Father: Joseph E Johnston   a citizen of the Chickasaw Nation.
Name of Mother: Mary Catherine Johnston   a citizen of the Chickasaw Nation.

                Postoffice   Johnson Ind T

Applications for Enrollment of Chickasaw Newborn
Act of 1905   Volume VI

AFFIDAVIT OF MOTHER.

UNITED STATES OF AMERICA, INDIAN TERRITORY, }
Southern   District.

   I, Mary Catherine Johnston, on oath state that I am 42 years of age and a citizen by Marriage, of the Chickasaw Nation; that I am the lawful wife of Joseph E. Johnston, who is a citizen, by Blood of the Chickasaw Nation; that a male child was born to me on 31st day of July, 1903, that said child has been named Kirkland B. Johnston, and is now living.

                             Mary Catherine Johnston
Witnesses To Mark:
{

   Subscribed and sworn to before me this 2 day of March, 1905.

                             W L Barr
                                Notary Public.

AFFIDAVIT OF ATTENDING PHYSICIAN OR MID-WIFE.

UNITED STATES OF AMERICA, INDIAN TERRITORY, }
Southern   District.

   I, E Burfield, a Physician, on oath state that I attended on Mrs. Mary Catherine Johnston, wife of Joseph E. Johnston on the 31st day of July, 190 3; that there was born to her on said date a male child; that said child is now living and is said to have been named Kirkland B Johnston

                             E Burfield M.D.
Witnesses To Mark:
{

   Subscribed and sworn to before me this 2 day of March, 1905.

                             W L Barr
                                Notary Public.

Applications for Enrollment of Chickasaw Newborn
Act of 1905   Volume VI

BIRTH AFFIDAVIT.

DEPARTMENT OF THE INTERIOR.
COMMISSION TO THE FIVE CIVILIZED TRIBES.

IN RE APPLICATION FOR ENROLLMENT, as a citizen of the Chickasaw Nation, of Kirkland B. Johnston, born on the 31 day of July, 1903

Name of Father: Joseph E Johnston   a citizen of the Chickasaw Nation.
Name of Mother: Mary Catherine Johnston   a citizen of the Chickasaw Nation.

Postoffice   Johnson Ind Ter

AFFIDAVIT OF MOTHER.

UNITED STATES OF AMERICA, Indian Territory, } DISTRICT.

I, Mary Catherine Johnston, on oath state that I am 42 years of age and a citizen by marriage, of the Chickasaw Nation; that I am the lawful wife of Joseph E Johnston, who is a citizen, by Blood of the Chickasaw Nation; that a male child was born to me on 31 day of July, 1903; that said child has been named Kirkland B Johnston, and was living March 4, 1905.

Mary Catherine Johnston

Witnesses To Mark:

Subscribed and sworn to before me this 24 day of April, 1905

W A Smith
Notary Public.

AFFIDAVIT OF ATTENDING PHYSICIAN OR MID-WIFE.

UNITED STATES OF AMERICA, Indian Territory, } DISTRICT.

I, E Burfield, a Pysician[sic], on oath state that I attended on Mrs. Mary Catherine Johnston, wife of Joseph E Johnston on the 31 day of July, 1903; that there was born to her on said date a male child; that said child was living March 4, 1905, and is said to have been named Kirkland B Johnston

E Burfield M.D.

Witnesses To Mark:

Applications for Enrollment of Chickasaw Newborn
Act of 1905   Volume VI

Subscribed and sworn to before me this 24 day of April , 1905

W A Smith
Notary Public.

9-304

Muskogee, Indian Territory, April 19, 1905.

Joseph E. Johnston,
    Johnston[sic], Indian Territory.

Dear Sir:

    Receipt is hereby acknowledged of your letter of April 13, 1905, in which you ask if affidavits you had filled out and mailed to T. C. Walker to the birth of your child Kirkland B. Johnston have been received.

    In reply to your letter you are informed that it does not appear from our records that affidavits have been received relative to a child born to you since September 25, 1902, and for your convenience there is inclosed herewith blank for the enrollment of an infant child which you should have executed and returned to this office within sixty days from March 3, 1905.

Respectfully,

B.C.   Chairman.

9-304

Muskogee, Indian Territory, May 2, 1905.

Joseph E. Johnston,
    Johnson, Indian Territory.

Dear Sir:

    Receipt is hereby acknowledged of the affidavits of Mary Catherine Johnston and E. Burfield to the birth of Kirkland B. Johnston son of Joseph E. and Mary Catherine Johnston, July 31, 1903, and the same have been filed with our records as an application for the enrollment of said child.

Respectfully,

Chairman.

Applications for Enrollment of Chickasaw Newborn
Act of 1905 Volume VI

Chic. N.B - 467
(Fred Cravatt
Born March 26, 1903)
(Rena Cravatt
Born January 15, 1905)

BIRTH AFFIDAVIT.

DEPARTMENT OF THE INTERIOR.
COMMISSION TO THE FIVE CIVILIZED TRIBES.

IN RE APPLICATION FOR ENROLLMENT, as a citizen of the Chickasaw Nation, of Fred Cravatt , born on the 26 day of March , 1903

Name of Father: Randers H. Cravatt a citizen of the Chick Nation.
Name of Mother: Mary Cravatt a citizen of the Chick Nation.

Postoffice Jesse I.T.

AFFIDAVIT OF MOTHER.

UNITED STATES OF AMERICA, Indian Territory, }
Southern DISTRICT. }

I, Mary Cravatt , on oath state that I am 27 years of age and a citizen by Birth , of the Chickasaw Nation; that I am the lawful wife of Randers H. Cravatt , who is a citizen, by Birth of the Chickasaw Nation; that a male child was born to me on 26th day of March , 1903; that said child has been named Fred Cravatt , and was living March 4, 1905.

Mary Cravatt

Witnesses To Mark:
{

Subscribed and sworn to before me this 25th day of April , 1905

Price Statler
Notary Public.

Applications for Enrollment of Chickasaw Newborn
Act of 1905   Volume VI

AFFIDAVIT OF ATTENDING PHYSICIAN OR MID-WIFE.

UNITED STATES OF AMERICA, Indian Territory,
Southern   DISTRICT.

I, Rena Underwood , a ———— , on oath state that I attended on Mrs. Mary Cravatt , wife of Randers H Cravatt on the 26 day of March , 1903; that there was born to her on said date a   male   child; that said child was living March 4, 1905, and is said to have been named Fred Cravatt

                                 her
Witnesses To Mark: Rena x Underwood
   { Gale Statler   mark
     William Gipson

Subscribed and sworn to before me this 25th day of   April   , 1905

                              Price Statler
                              Notary Public.

BIRTH AFFIDAVIT.
DEPARTMENT OF THE INTERIOR.
COMMISSION TO THE FIVE CIVILIZED TRIBES.

IN RE APPLICATION FOR ENROLLMENT, as a citizen of the   Chickasaw   Nation, of Rena Cravatt , born on the 16 day of Jany , 1905

Name of Father: Randers H. Cravatt   a citizen of the   Chick   Nation.
Name of Mother: Mary Cravatt   a citizen of the   Chick   Nation.

                     Postoffice   Jesse I.T.

AFFIDAVIT OF MOTHER.

UNITED STATES OF AMERICA, Indian Territory,
Southern   DISTRICT.

I, Mary Cravatt , on oath state that I am 27 years of age and a citizen by Birth , of the   Chickasaw   Nation; that I am the lawful wife of Randers H. Cravatt , who is a citizen, by Birth   of the   Chickasaw   Nation; that a Female   child was born to me on 15 day of Jany , 1905; that said child has been named Rena Cravatt , and was living March 4, 1905.

                             Mary Cravatt

Applications for Enrollment of Chickasaw Newborn
Act of 1905 Volume VI

Witnesses To Mark:

Subscribed and sworn to before me this 25th day of April , 1905

Price Statler
Notary Public.

AFFIDAVIT OF ATTENDING PHYSICIAN OR MID-WIFE.

UNITED STATES OF AMERICA, Indian Territory,
Southern DISTRICT.

I, Rena Underwood , a ———— , on oath state that I attended on Mrs. Mary Cravatt , wife of Randers H Cravatt on the 15th day of Jany , 1905; that there was born to her on said date a Female child; that said child was living March 4, 1905, and is said to have been named Rena Cravatt

her
Rena x Underwood
mark

Witnesses To Mark:
- Gale Statler
- William Gipson

Subscribed and sworn to before me this 25th day of April , 1905

Price Statler
Notary Public.

9-308

Muskogee, Indian Territory, May 1, 1905.

Randers H. Cravatt,
Jesse, Indian Territory.

Dear Sir:

Receipt is hereby acknowledged of the affidavits of Mary Cravatt and Rena Underwood to the birth of Fred Cravatt and Rena Cravatt children of Randers H. and Mary Cravatt, March 26, 1903 and January 15, 1905, respectively, and the same have been filed with our records as applications for the enrollment of said children.

Applications for Enrollment of Chickasaw Newborn
Act of 1905 Volume VI

Respectfully,

Chairman.

Chic. N.B - 468
  (Jackson McCarter
  Born June 11, 1903)

BIRTH AFFIDAVIT.

DEPARTMENT OF THE INTERIOR.
COMMISSION TO THE FIVE CIVILIZED TRIBES.

IN RE APPLICATION FOR ENROLLMENT, as a citizen of the   Chickasaw   Nation, of   Jackson McCarter   , born on the   11th day of   June   , 1903

Name of Father: Somie McCarter   a citizen of the   Chickasaw   Nation.
Name of Mother: Sarah McCarter   a citizen of the   Chickasaw   Nation.

Postoffice   Jesse I.T.

AFFIDAVIT OF MOTHER.

UNITED STATES OF AMERICA, Indian Territory,
        Southern   DISTRICT.

I,   Sarah McCarter   , on oath state that I am   26   years of age and a citizen by   Birth   , of the   Chickasaw   Nation; that I am the lawful wife of   Somie McCarter   , who is a citizen, by   Birth   of the   Chickasaw   Nation; that a male   child was born to me on   11th day of   June   , 1903; that said child has been named   Jackson McCarter   , and was living March 4, 1905.

                                Sarah McCarter
Witnesses To Mark:

Subscribed and sworn to before me this   19th day of   April   , 1905

                                Price Statler
                                Notary Public.

101

Applications for Enrollment of Chickasaw Newborn
Act of 1905   Volume VI

AFFIDAVIT OF ATTENDING PHYSICIAN OR MID-WIFE.

UNITED STATES OF AMERICA, Indian Territory, }
Southern   DISTRICT.

I, Julia McLeod, a Chickasaw, on oath state that I attended on Mrs. Sarah McCarter, wife of Somie McCarter on the 11th day of June, 1903; that there was born to her on said date a male child; that said child was living March 4, 1905, and is said to have been named Jackson McCarter

                                            her
                                Julia x McLeod
Witnesses To Mark: mark
{ Price Statler
  (Name Illegible)

Subscribed and sworn to before me this 19th day of April, 1905

                              Price Statler
                                  Notary Public.
My Commission expires Jan. 1st 1906

                      Muskogee, Indian Territory, April 24, 1905.

Somie McCarter,
    Jesse, Indian Territory.

Dear Sir:

    Receipt is hereby acknowledged of the affidavits of Sarah Mc Carter[sic] and Julia McLeod to the birth of Jackson McCarter son of Somie and Sarah McCarter, June 11, 1903.

    It is stated in the affidavit of the mother that she is a citizen by blood of the Chickasaw Nation. If this is correct you are requested to state the name under which she was enrolled, the names of her parents, and if she has selected an allotment of the lands of the Choctaw or Chickasaw Nation please give her roll number as it appears upon her allotment certificate.

                Respectfully,

                                      Chairman.

Applications for Enrollment of Chickasaw Newborn
Act of 1905   Volume VI

(COPY)

Jesse, Ind. Terr.
April 27, 1905.

The Commission to the Five Civilized Tribes,
Muskogee, I. T.

Sir:--

Yours of the 24 Inst was received and contents noted that you require me to send you no or roll of my wife, Sarah McCarter. in relation to application w put in to have enroll our baby. Sarah McCarter is daughter of Roman Monroe and Nancy Monroe. Her first name used to be Sarah Monroe in on the roll Chickasaw by blood Roll No. 475.

I think they got my name on roll by Somie McCarty instead of Somie McCarter. My proper name is McCarter.

9--147.

Muskogee, Indian Territory, May 2, 1905.

Somie McCarter,
    Jesse, Indian Territory.

Dear Sir:

Receipt is hereby acknowledged of your letter of April 27, giving information relative to the enrollment of your wife and the same has enabled us to identify her upon our records and the affidavits heretofore forwarded to the birth of your child, Jackson McCarter, have been filed with our records as an application for the enrollment of said child.

Respectfully,

Chairman.

Chic. N.B - 469
  *(Uldean Garrett
  Born March 18, 1904)*

Applications for Enrollment of Chickasaw Newborn
Act of 1905 Volume VI

BIRTH AFFIDAVIT.

DEPARTMENT OF THE INTERIOR.
COMMISSION TO THE FIVE CIVILIZED TRIBES.

IN RE APPLICATION FOR ENROLLMENT, as a citizen of the Chickasaw Nation, of Uldean Garrett, born on the 18th day of March, 1904

Name of Father: Jesse A Garrett — a non citizen ~~of the~~ ~~Nation.~~
Name of Mother: Lula Lucretia Garrett — a citizen of the Chickasaw Nation.

Postoffice Tishomingo I.T.

AFFIDAVIT OF MOTHER.

UNITED STATES OF AMERICA, Indian Territory,
Southern DISTRICT.

I, Lula Lucretia Garrett, on oath state that I am 25 years of age and a citizen by Blood, of the Chickasaw Nation; that I am the lawful wife of Jesse A Garrett, who is a non citizen, ~~by~~ of the Nation; that a female child was born to me on 18th day of March, 1904; that said child has been named Uldean Garrett, and was living March 4, 1905.

Lula Lucretia Garrett

Witnesses To Mark:

Subscribed and sworn to before me this 24th day of April, 1905

H.O. Newman
Notary Public.

AFFIDAVIT OF ATTENDING PHYSICIAN OR MID-WIFE.

UNITED STATES OF AMERICA, Indian Territory,
Southern DISTRICT.

I, W.W. Vannoy, a M.D., on oath state that I attended on Mrs. Lula L Garrett, wife of Jesse A Garrett on the 18th day of March, 1904; that there was born to her on said date a female child; that said child was living March 4, 1905, and is said to have been named Uldean Garrett

W.W. Vannoy M.D.

Witnesses To Mark:

Applications for Enrollment of Chickasaw Newborn
Act of 1905   Volume VI

Subscribed and sworn to before me this 25th day of   April   , 1905

>   H.O. Newman
>   Notary Public.

>   9-922.

>   Muskogee, Indian Territory, Maw[sic] 2, 1905.

Young & Newman,
    Attorneys at Law,
        Tishomingo, Indian Territory.

Gentlemen:

   Receipt is hereby acknowledged of your letter of April 25, enclosing the affidavits of Lula Lucretia Garrett and W. W. Vannoy to the birth of Uldean Garrett, daughter of Jesse A. and Lula L. Garrett, March 18, 1904, and the same have been filed with our records as an application for the enrollment of said child.

>   Respectfully,

>   Chairman.

Chic. N.B - 470
    (Pauline Colbert
    Born February 15, 1903)

BIRTH AFFIDAVIT.

   IN RE-APPLICATION FOR ENROLLMENT, as a citizen of the   Chickasaw   Nation, of   Pauline Colbert   , born on the   15   day of Feb   , 190 3

Name of Father: Charley Colbert   a citizen of the Chickasaw   Nation.
Name of Mother: Abbie Colbert   a citizen of the Chickasaw   Nation.

>   Postoffice   Bee I.T.

Applications for Enrollment of Chickasaw Newborn
Act of 1905   Volume VI

AFFIDAVIT OF MOTHER.

UNITED STATES OF AMERICA, INDIAN TERRITORY,}
  Central   District.

I, Abbie Colbert, on oath state that I am 28 years of age and a citizen by marriage, of the Chickasaw Nation; that I am the lawful wife of Charley Colbert, who is a citizen, by blood of the Chickasaw Nation; that a female child was born to me on 15 day of Feb, 1903, that said child has been named Pauline Colbert, and is now living.

Abbie Colbert

Witnesses To Mark:

Subscribed and sworn to before me this 12 day of Apr, 1905.

D.O. Slaughter
Notary Public.
Central Dist.

AFFIDAVIT OF ATTENDING PHYSICIAN OR MID-WIFE.

The State of Texas,}
  County of Tarrant   ~~District~~.

I, G.T. Sampson, a physician & surgeon, on oath state that I attended on Mrs. Abbie Colbert, wife of Charley Colbert on the 15th day of Feby, 1903; that there was born to her on said date a female child; that said child is now living and is said to have been named Pauline Colbert

G.T. Sampson M.D.

Witnesses To Mark:
  (Name Illegible)

Subscribed and sworn to before me this 26th day of April, 1905.

(Name Illegible)
Notary Public.

Applications for Enrollment of Chickasaw Newborn
Act of 1905   Volume VI

Chickasaw 1632.

Muskogee, Indian Territory, May 2, 1905.

Charley Colbert,
    Bee, Indian Territory.

Dear Sir:

    Receipt is hereby acknowledged of your letter of April 26, transmitting the affidavits of Abbie Colbert and G. L. Sampson to the birth of Pauline Colbert, daughter of Charley and Abbie Colbert, February 15, 1903, and the same have been filed with our records as an application for the enrollment of said child.

Respectfully,

Chairman.

Chic. N.B - 471
    (Lavada Abbott
    Born April 14, 1904)

BIRTH AFFIDAVIT.

DEPARTMENT OF THE INTERIOR.
COMMISSION TO THE FIVE CIVILIZED TRIBES.

IN RE APPLICATION FOR ENROLLMENT, as a citizen of the   Chickasaw   Nation, of   Lavada Abbott   , born on the 14   day of   April   , 1904

Name of Father: J A Abbott   a citizen of the   U S   Nation.
Name of Mother: Zona Abbott   a citizen of the   Chickasaw   Nation.

Postoffice   Ada, I.T.

AFFIDAVIT OF MOTHER.

UNITED STATES OF AMERICA, Indian Territory,
    Southern   DISTRICT.

    I,   Zona Abbott (Nee Smith)   , on oath state that I am   22   years of age and a citizen by   blood   , of the   Chickasaw   Nation; that I am the lawful wife of

Applications for Enrollment of Chickasaw Newborn
Act of 1905   Volume VI

J A Abbott   , who is a citizen, by   birth   of the   United States   Nation; that a female   child was born to me on   the 14th day of   April   , 1904; that said child has been named   Lavada Abbott   , and was living March 4, 1905.

               Zona Abbott

Witnesses To Mark:

  Subscribed and sworn to before me this   27   day of   April   , 1905

               JE Williams
                 Notary Public.

AFFIDAVIT OF ATTENDING PHYSICIAN OR MID-WIFE.

UNITED STATES OF AMERICA, Indian Territory,
 Southern   DISTRICT.

  I,   W T Nolen   , a   physician   , on oath state that I attended on Mrs.   Zona Abbott   , wife of   J A Abbott   on the   14 day of   April   , 1904; that there was born to her on said date a   female   child; that said child was living March 4, 1905, and is said to have been named   Levada[sic] Abbott

               W T Nolen

Witnesses To Mark:

  Subscribed and sworn to before me this   27   day of   April   , 1905

               JE Williams
                 Notary Public.

                  9--1212.

        Muskogee, Indian Territory, May 2, 1905.

J. A. Abbott,
  Ada, Indian Territory.

Dear Sir:

  Receipt is hereby acknowledged of the affidavits of Zona Abbott and W. T. Noley[sic] to the birth of Levada[sic] Abbott, daughter of J. A. and Zona Abbott, April 14, 1904, and the same have been filed with our records as an application for the enrollment of said child.

Applications for Enrollment of Chickasaw Newborn
Act of 1905 Volume VI

Respectfully,

Chairman.

Chic. N.B - 472
*(Thompson Pickens
Born April 5, 1904)*

BIRTH AFFIDAVIT.

DEPARTMENT OF THE INTERIOR.
COMMISSION TO THE FIVE CIVILIZED TRIBES.

IN RE APPLICATION FOR ENROLLMENT, as a citizen of the Chickasaw Nation, of Thompson Pickens , born on the 5 day of April , 1904

Name of Father: Johnie[sic] Pickens   a citizen of the Chickasaw Nation.
Name of Mother: Ollie Pickens   a citizen of the By Marage[sic] Nation.

Postoffice   Lebanon Ind Ter

AFFIDAVIT OF MOTHER.

UNITED STATES OF AMERICA, Indian Territory,
22   DISTRICT.

I, Ollie Pickens , on oath state that I am Eigteen[sic] years of age and a citizen by Marige[sic] , of the Chickasaw Nation; that I am the lawful wife of Johnie Pickens , who is a citizen, by Blood of the Chickasaw Nation; that a Male child was born to me on 5 day of April , 1904; that said child has been named Thompson Pickens , and was living March 4, 1905.

Ollie Pickens

Witnesses To Mark:

Subscribed and sworn to before me this 26 day of April , 1905

Joe Simpson
Notary Public.

Applications for Enrollment of Chickasaw Newborn
Act of 1905   Volume VI

AFFIDAVIT OF ATTENDING PHYSICIAN OR MID-WIFE.

UNITED STATES OF AMERICA, Indian Territory,　}
　　　　22　　　　DISTRICT.

　　I,　Eda Elizabeth Edington　, a　midwife　　　, on oath state that I attended on Mrs.　Ollie Pickens　, wife of　Johnie Pickens　on the　5　day of　April　, 1904; that there was born to her on said date a　male　child; that said child was living March 4, 1905, and is said to have been named　Thompson Pickens

　　　　　　　　　　　　　　　　　Eda X Elizabeth Edington
Witnesses To Mark:
　{ C H Ross
　 (Name Illegible)

　　Subscribed and sworn to before me this　27　day of　April　, 1905

　　　　　　　　　　　　　Joe Simpson
　　　　　　　　　　　　　　　Notary Public.

_____

Applications for Enrollment of Chickasaw Newborn
Act of 1905 Volume VI

Certificate of Record of Marriage

DEPARTMENT OF THE INTERIOR,
COMMISSION TO THE FIVE CIVILIZED TRIBES.

FILED

Apr 28 1905

Tams Bixby CHAIRMAN.

United States of America,
Indian Territory, } sct.
Southern District.

I, C. M. CAMPBELL, Clerk of the United States Court, in the Territory and District aforesaid DO HEREBY CERTIFY, that the License for and Certificate of Marriage of

MR   John Pickens   and

M   Ollie Kizziar

were filed in my office in said Territory and District the   17"   day of
March   A.D., 190 3
and duly recorded in Book   G
of Marriage Record, Page   191

WITNESS my hand and Seal of said Court, at Ardmore,
this   17"   day of
March   A.D. 190 3

C. M. Campbell
CLERK.

FILED
AT ARDMORE.
MAR 17 1903 2 PM
C. M. CAMPBELL, Clerk
and Exofficio Recorder.
District No 21 Ind. Ter.

 MARRIAGE LICENSE

UNITED STATES OF AMERICA,
  INDIAN TERRITORY,   } ss:
  SOUTHERN DISTRICT.

To Any Person Authorized by Law to Solemnize Marriage, Greeting:

𝔜ou are hereby commanded to solemnize the Rite and publish the Banns of Matrimony between Mr.   John Pickens
of   McMillan   in the Indian Territory, aged   22   years, and
M   Ollie Kizziar   of   Weaverton
in the Indian Territory, aged   16   years, according to law; and do you officially sign and return this License to the parties therein named.

Applications for Enrollment of Chickasaw Newborn
Act of 1905   Volume VI

Witness my hand and official Seal, this   7   day of   March   A. D. 190 3

CM Campbell
Clerk of the United States Court.

| Certificate of Marriage. |

UNITED STATES OF AMERICA,
INDIAN TERRITORY,   ss:
SOUTHERN DISTRICT.   I,   J. F. Edington
_____ do hereby certify that on the   8   day of   March 8 , A. D. 190 3 , I did duly according to law, as commanded in the foregoing License, solemnize the Rite and publish the Banns of Matrimony between the parties therein named.

Witness my hand this   8   day of   March   A. D. 190 3

My credentials are recorded in the office of the Clerk of the United States Court, Indian Territory, Southern District, at Ardmore, Book   C , Page 8

(NOTE-The person officiating should fill in the spaces for book and page and sign here.)

J F Edington
a   minister of the gospel

NOTE (a)-The License and Certificate of Marriage must be returned to the office of the Clerk of the United States Court in the Indian Territory, at Ardmore, within sixty days from the date thereof, or the party to whom the License was issued will be liable in the amount of One Hundred Dollars ($100).

NOTE (b)-No person is authorized to perform the Marriage Ceremony in the Southern District unless the proper credentials have first been recorded in the Clerk's office.

9-768.

Muskogee, Indian Territory, May 2, 1905.

Johnnie Pickens,
    Lebanon, Indian Territory.

Dear Sir:

Receipt is hereby acknowledged of the affidavits of Ollie Pickens and Eda Elizabeth Edington to the birth of Thompson Pickens, son of Johnnie and Ollie Pickens, April 5, 1904, and the same have been filed with our records as an application for the enrollment of said child.

Applications for Enrollment of Chickasaw Newborn
Act of 1905   Volume VI

Receipt is also acknowledged of the marriage license and certificate between John Pickens and Ollie Kizziar which you offer in support of the application for the enrollment of the above named child.

Respectfully,

Chairman.

Chic. N.B - 473
   (Ruby Chigley
   Born July 7, 1904)

BIRTH AFFIDAVIT.

DEPARTMENT OF THE INTERIOR.
COMMISSION TO THE FIVE CIVILIZED TRIBES.

IN RE APPLICATION FOR ENROLLMENT, as a citizen of the   Chickasaw   Nation, of   Ruby Chigley   , born on the   7   day of   July   , 1904

Name of Father: Wyatt Chigley   a citizen of the   Chickasaw   Nation.
Name of Mother: Belle Chigley   a citizen of the   Chickasaw   Nation.

Postoffice   Paoli I.T.

AFFIDAVIT OF MOTHER.

UNITED STATES OF AMERICA, Indian Territory,
   So.   **DISTRICT.**

I,   Bell Chigley   , on oath state that I am   23   years of age and a citizen by   Blood   , of the   Chickasaw   Nation; that I am the lawful wife of   Wyatt Chigley   , who is a citizen, by   Blood   of the   Chickasaw   Nation; that a   Female   child was born to me on   7   day of   July   , 1904, that said child has been named   Ruby Chigley   , and is now living.

Belle Chigley

Witnesses To Mark:

Applications for Enrollment of Chickasaw Newborn
Act of 1905   Volume VI

Subscribed and sworn to before me this   2   day of   Feb   , 1905.

          Simp Dulin
          Notary Public.

AFFIDAVIT OF ATTENDING PHYSICIAN OR MID-WIFE.

UNITED STATES OF AMERICA, Indian Territory, }
 Southern   DISTRICT.

  I,   James Whitfield   , a Physician   , on oath state that I attended on Mrs.   Lizzie Bell Chigley   , wife of   Wyatt Chigley   on the   4th   day of   July , 1904; that there was born to her on said date a   Girl Female   child; that said child is now living and is said to have been named   Ruby Chigley

         James Whitfield M.D.
Witnesses To Mark:
{

  Subscribed and sworn to before me this   10th day of   February   , 1905.

         Jno. W. Massey
         Notary Public.

BIRTH AFFIDAVIT.
     DEPARTMENT OF THE INTERIOR.
COMMISSION TO THE FIVE CIVILIZED TRIBES.

  IN RE APPLICATION FOR ENROLLMENT, as a citizen of the   Chickasaw   Nation, of   Ruby Chigley   , born on the   7th day of   July , 1904

Name of Father: Wyatt Chigley   a citizen of the   Chickasaw Nation.
Name of Mother: Lizzie Belle Chigley a citizen of the " Nation.

       Postoffice Paoli, I.T.

AFFIDAVIT OF MOTHER.

UNITED STATES OF AMERICA, Indian Territory, }
 Southern Judicial DISTRICT.

  I,   Lizzie Belle Chigley   , on oath state that I am   23   years of age and a citizen by   blood   , of the   Chickasaw   Nation; that I am the lawful wife of Wyatt Chigley   , who is a citizen, by   blood   of the   Chickasaw

Applications for Enrollment of Chickasaw Newborn
Act of 1905   Volume VI

Nation; that a female child was born to me on 7th day of July , 1904; that said child has been named Ruby , and was living March 4, 1905.

                                        Belle Chigley

Witnesses To Mark:

{

    Subscribed and sworn to before me this 10 day of April , 1905

My Commission expires April 10-1907   Simp Dulin
                                        Notary Public.

AFFIDAVIT OF ATTENDING PHYSICIAN OR MID-WIFE.

UNITED STATES OF AMERICA, Indian Territory, }
   Southern Judicial   DISTRICT. }

    I, James Whitfield , a Physician , on oath state that I attended on Mrs. Lizzie Belle Chigley , wife of Wyatt Chigley on the 7th day of July , 1904; that there was born to her on said date a female child; that said child was living March 4, 1905, and is said to have been named Ruby

                                    James Whitfield

Witnesses To Mark:

{

    Subscribed and sworn to before me this 22 day of March , 1905

                                  Jno. W. Massey
                                        Notary Public.

BIRTH AFFIDAVIT.
DEPARTMENT OF THE INTERIOR.
COMMISSION TO THE FIVE CIVILIZED TRIBES.

    IN RE APPLICATION FOR ENROLLMENT, as a citizen of the Chickasaw Nation, of Ruby Chigley , born on the 7th day of July , 1904

Name of Father: Wyatt Chigley   a citizen of the Chickasaw Nation.
Name of Mother: Lizzie Bell Chigley nee Young a citizen of the Chickasaw Nation.

                            Postoffice   Paoli Ind Ter

Applications for Enrollment of Chickasaw Newborn
Act of 1905   Volume VI

AFFIDAVIT OF MOTHER.

UNITED STATES OF AMERICA, Indian Territory,
Southern DISTRICT.

I, Lizzie Bell Chigley, on oath state that I am 23 years of age and a citizen by blood, of the Chickasaw Nation; that I am the lawful wife of Wyatt Chigley, who is a citizen, by blood of the Chickasaw Nation; that a female child was born to me on 7th day of July, 1904; that said child has been named Ruby Chigley, and was living March 4, 1905.

Lizzie Bell Chigley nee Young

Witnesses To Mark:

Subscribed and sworn to before me this 14 day of July, 1905
My commission expires
April 10-1907   Simp Dulin
Notary Public.

AFFIDAVIT OF ATTENDING PHYSICIAN OR MID-WIFE.

UNITED STATES OF AMERICA, Indian Territory, DISTRICT.

I, ..., a ...., on oath state that I attended on Mrs. ...., wife of .... on the ...... day of ...., 1......; that there was born to her on said date a .... child; that said child was living March 4, 1905, and is said to have been named ....

Witnesses To Mark:

Subscribed and sworn to before me this ...... day of ...., 1905.

Notary Public.

Applications for Enrollment of Chickasaw Newborn
Act of 1905 Volume VI

Muskogee, Indian Territory, April 20, 1905.

Wyatt Chigley,
    Paoli, Indian Territory.

Dear Sir:

    Receipt is hereby acknowledged of the affidavits of Belle Chigley and James Whitfield to the birth of Ruby Chigley, daughter of Wyatt and Lizzie Belle Chigley, July 7, 1904.

    It is stated in the affidavit of the mother that she is a citizen by blood of the Chickasaw Nation. If this is correct you are requested to state the name under which she was enrolled, the names of her parents, and if she has selected an allotment of the lands of the Choctaw or Chickasaw Nation please give her roll number as it appears upon her allotment certificate.

Respectfully,

Chairman.

(COPY)

Paoli, I. T.
April 28, 1905.

Comis to the five Tribe

    In receipt of yours of April the 20th requesting me to send you my wife Roll Number (1562). She was enrolled by the name of Lizzie Belle Young. her parents Granville W. Young and Adaline Young. She has taken her enrollment in the Chickasaw Nation.

Resp
Wyatt Chigley

9--530.

Muskogee, Indian Territory, May 6, 1905.

Wyatt Chigley,
    Paoli, Indian Territory.

Dear Sir:

    Receipt is hereby acknowledged of your letter of April 28, stating that your wife was enrolled as Lizzie Bell Young and giving her roll number.

Applications for Enrollment of Chickasaw Newborn
Act of 1905   Volume VI

This information has enabled us to identify her upon our records as an enrolled citizen by blood of the Chickasaw Nation and the affidavits heretofore forwarded to the birth of Ruby Chigley have been filed with our records as an application for the enrollment of said child.

Respectfully,

Commissioner in Charge.

9-NB-473

Muskogee, Indian Territory, July 10, 1905.

Wyatt Chigley,
    Paoli, Indian Territory.

Dear Sir:

There is inclosed you herewith affidavit to be executed by Lizzie Bell Chigley mother of your infant child, Ruby Chigley, born July 7, 1904, for whose enrollment application was made March 28, 1905.

The affidavit of the mother heretofore filed in this case is signed "Belle Chigley". It appears from the records of this office that she is enrolled under her maiden name of Lizzie Bell Young.

In having the inclosed affidavit executed please see that your wife signs her name as it appears in the body of the affidavit.

This matter should receive your immediate attention as no further action can be taken relative to the enrollment of your child until the evidence requested is supplied.

Respectfully,

LM-10-7

Commissioner.

Applications for Enrollment of Chickasaw Newborn
Act of 1905   Volume VI

9-NB-473

Muskogee, Indian Territory July 20, 1905.

Wyatt Chigley,
    Paoli, Indian Territory.

Dear Sir:

    Receipt is hereby acknowledged of the affidavit of Lizzie Bell Chigley, nee Young, to the birth of Ruby Chigley, daughter of Wyatt Chigley and Lizzie Bell Chigley, nee Young July 7, 1904, and the same has been filed with the records of this office in the matter of the enrollment of said child.

Respectfully,

Commissioner.

Chic. N.B - 474
    (Eliza Pickens
    Born July 8, 1904)

DEPARTMENT OF THE INTERIOR,
COMMISSION TO THE FIVE CIVILIZED TRIBES.
SOUTH MCALESTER, IND. Ter. APRIL 28, 1905.

    In the matter of the application for the enrollment of Eliza Pickens as a citizen by blood of the Chickasaw Nation.

Isom Pickens being first duly sworn testifies as follows:

    EXAMINATION BY THE COMMISSION:

Q What is your name? A Isom Pickens.
Q What is your age? A Thirty-three.
Q What is your post office address? A Blanco, Indian Territory.
Q You have this day made application fo[sic] your child Eliza Pickens xx ; when was Eliza Pickens born? A July 8, 1904.
Q Was she living on March 4, 1905? A Yes, sir.
Q Of what nation are you a citizen? A I am a Choctaw.
Q What is your wife's name? A Jincy.
Q Of what nation is she a citizen? A Chickasaw.

Applications for Enrollment of Chickasaw Newborn
Act of 1905   Volume VI

Q In what nation do you desire to have your child Eliza Pickens take her allotment of lands and distribution of money? A Chickasaw.

Witness excused.

Chas. T. Difendafer being first duly sworn states that the above and foregoing is a full, true and correct transcript of his stenographic notes taken in said cause on said date.

Chas. T. Difendafer

Subscribed and sworn to before me this 28th day of April 1905.

OL Johnson
Notary Public.

---

7 - 742   9 3532

BIRTH AFFIDAVIT.

DEPARTMENT OF THE INTERIOR.
COMMISSION TO THE FIVE CIVILIZED TRIBES.

IN RE APPLICATION FOR ENROLLMENT, as a citizen of the   Chickasaw   Nation, of   Eliza Pickens   , born on the   8 day of   July   , 1904

Name of Father: Isom Pickens   a citizen of the   Choc   Nation.
Name of Mother: Jincy Pickens   a citizen of the   Chickasaw   Nation.

Postoffice   Blanco I.T.

AFFIDAVIT OF MOTHER.

UNITED STATES OF AMERICA, Indian Territory, }
         Central   DISTRICT.

I, Jincy Pickens , on oath state that I am 30 years of age and a citizen by blood , of the   Chickasaw   Nation; that I am the lawful wife of   Isom Pickens , who is a citizen, by blood   of the   Choctaw   Nation; that a   female   child was born to me on   8 day of   July   , 1904; that said child has been named   Eliza Pickens , and was living March 4, 1905.   her
Jincy x Pickens
mark

Witnesses To Mark:
   { Joe Rich
   { JH Isbell

Applications for Enrollment of Chickasaw Newborn
Act of 1905 Volume VI

Subscribed and sworn to before me this 1st day of May, 1905

Martin Savage
My commission expires Feb 28-1909 Notary Public.

AFFIDAVIT OF ATTENDING PHYSICIAN OR MID-WIFE.

UNITED STATES OF AMERICA, Indian Territory,
Central DISTRICT.

I, Clemeakey Logan, a midwife, on oath state that I attended on Mrs. Jincy Pickens, wife of Isom Pickens on the 8 day of July, 1904; that there was born to her on said date a female child; that said child was living March 4, 1905, and is said to have been named Eliza Pickens

                                          her
                               Clemeakey x Logan
Witnesses To Mark: mark
 { Joe Rich
 { JH Isbell

Subscribed and sworn to before me this 1st day of May, 1905

Martin Savage
My commission expires Feb 28-1909 Notary Public.

BIRTH AFFIDAVIT.

DEPARTMENT OF THE INTERIOR.
COMMISSION TO THE FIVE CIVILIZED TRIBES.

IN RE APPLICATION FOR ENROLLMENT, as a citizen of the Chickasaw Nation, of Eliza Pickens, born on the 8th day of July, 1904

Name of Father: Isom Pickens   a citizen of the Choctaw Nation.
Name of Mother: Gincy Pickens   a citizen of the Chickasaw Nation.

Postoffice   Blanco I.T.

AFFIDAVIT OF MOTHER.

UNITED STATES OF AMERICA, Indian Territory,
Central DISTRICT.

I, Gincy Pickens, on oath state that I am 30 years of age and a citizen by Blood, of the Chickasaw Nation; that I am the lawful wife of Isom

Applications for Enrollment of Chickasaw Newborn
Act of 1905   Volume VI

Pickens, who is a citizen, by Blood of the Choctaw Nation; that a Female child was born to me on 8th day of July, 1904; that said child has been named Eliza Pickens, and was living March 4, 1905.

>   her
> Gincy x Pickens
>   mark

Witnesses To Mark:
{ T W Fry
  S L Stubblefield

Subscribed and sworn to before me this 1st day of June, 1905

Martin Savage
My commission expires Feb 28-09   Notary Public.

AFFIDAVIT OF ATTENDING PHYSICIAN OR MID-WIFE.

UNITED STATES OF AMERICA, Indian Territory, }
   Central   DISTRICT.   }

I, Clemia Key Logan, a Midwife, on oath state that I attended on Mrs. Gincy Pickens, wife of Isom Pickens on the 8th day of July, 1904; that there was born to her on said date a Female child; that said child was living March 4, 1905, and is said to have been named Eliza Pickens

>   her
> Clemia x Key Logan
>   mark

Witnesses To Mark:
{ T W Fry
  S L Stubblefield

Subscribed and sworn to before me this 1st day of June, 1905

Martin Savage
My commission expires Feb 28-09   Notary Public.

Applications for Enrollment of Chickasaw Newborn
Act of 1905 Volume VI

9-NB-474.

Muskogee, Indian Territory, May 20, 1905.

Isom Pickens,
    Blanco, Indian Territory.

Dear Sir:

    There is enclosed you herewith for execution application for the enrollment of your infant child, Eliza Pickens, born July 8, 1904.

    The application heretofore filed in this office contained neither the affidavit of the mother nor that of the attending physician or mid-wife. It will, therefore, be necessary that you execute the enclosed affidavits and return them to this office.

    In having these affidavits executed care should be exercised to see that all names are written in full, as they appear in the body of the affidavit, and in the event that either of the persons signing the affidavit are unable to write, signatures by mark must be attested by two witnesses. Each affidavit must be executed before a Notary Public and the notarial seal and signature of the officer must be attached to each separate affidavit.

    Respectfully,

    Chairman.

VR 20-8.

---

9 N.B. 474

Muskogee, Indian Territory, June 1, 1905.

Isom Pickens,
    Blanco, Indian Territory.

Dear Sir:

    Receipt is hereby acknowledged of the affidavits of Jincy Pickens and Clemeakey Logan to the birth of Eliza Pickens daughter of Isom and Jincy Pickens, July 8, 1904, and the same have been filed with our records in the matter of the enrollment of said child.

    Respectfully,

    Commissioner in Charge.

Applications for Enrollment of Chickasaw Newborn
Act of 1905 Volume VI

9 N.B. 474.

Muskogee, Indian Territory, June 5, 1905.

Isom Pickens,
    Blanco, Indian Territory.

Dear Sir:

    Receipt is hereby acknowledged of the affidavits of Gincy Pickens and Clemia Key Logan to the birth of Eliza Pickens, daughter of Isom and Gincy Pickens, July 8, 1904, and the same have been filed with our records in the matter of the enrollment of said child.

        Respectfully,

        Commissioner in Charge.

Chic. N.B - 475
    (Gouldy Sealy
    Born March 16, 1904)

BIRTH AFFIDAVIT.

IN RE-APPLICATION FOR ENROLLMENT, as a citizen of the Chickasaw Nation, of Gouldy Sealy, born on the 16 day of March, 190 4

Name of Father: Adam Sealy   a citizen of the Chickasaw Nation.
Name of Mother: Laticy[sic] Sealy   a citizen of the Chickasaw Nation.

    Postoffice   Arpelar

AFFIDAVIT OF MOTHER.

UNITED STATES OF AMERICA, INDIAN TERRITORY,
    Central   District.

    I, Laticy Sealy, on oath state that I am 32 years of age and a citizen by blood, of the Chickasaw Nation; that I am the lawful wife of Adam Sealy, who is a citizen, by blood of the Chickasaw Nation; that a female child was born to me on 16 day of March, 1904, that said child has been named Gouldy Sealy, and is now living.

        Latisy Sealy

Applications for Enrollment of Chickasaw Newborn
Act of 1905   Volume VI

Witnesses To Mark:
{ Lynch Arpelar
{ JH Bruce

Subscribed and sworn to before me this 28   day of Feb   , 1905.

Sam Wooley
Notary Public.

AFFIDAVIT OF ATTENDING PHYSICIAN OR MID-WIFE.

UNITED STATES OF AMERICA, INDIAN TERRITORY,
Central   District.

I, Henry Sealy   , a ...., on oath state that I ~~attended on~~ *know* Mrs. Liticy Sealy , wife of Adam Sealy   on the 16 day of March , 190 4; that there was born to her on said date a female child; that said child is now living and is said to have been named Gouldy Sealy

Henry Sealy

Witnesses To Mark:
{ Lynch Arpelar
{ JH Bruce

Subscribed and sworn to before me this 28   day of Feb   , 1905.

Sam Wooley
Notary Public.

BIRTH AFFIDAVIT.

DEPARTMENT OF THE INTERIOR.
COMMISSION TO THE FIVE CIVILIZED TRIBES.

IN RE APPLICATION FOR ENROLLMENT, as a citizen of the   Chickasaw   Nation, of   Gouldy Sealey   , born on the 16th day of March , 1904

Name of Father: Adam Sealey   a citizen of the Chickasaw Nation.
Name of Mother: Ledicy Sealey   a citizen of the Chickasaw Nation.

Postoffice   Arpelar I.T.

Applications for Enrollment of Chickasaw Newborn
Act of 1905 Volume VI

AFFIDAVIT OF MOTHER.

UNITED STATES OF AMERICA, Indian Territory,　}
　　Central　　　　　DISTRICT.

　　I, Ledicy Sealey, on oath state that I am 32 years of age and a citizen by Blood, of the Chickasaw Nation; that I am the lawful wife of Adam Sealey, who is a citizen, by Blood of the Chickasaw Nation; that a Female child was born to me on 16th day of March, 1904; that said child has been named Gouldy Sealey, and was living March 4, 1905.

　　　　　　　　　　　　　　　　　Ledisy[sic] Sealey
Witnesses To Mark:
{

　　Subscribed and sworn to before me this 7th day of June, 1905

　　　　　　　　　　　　　　　　　WG Weimer
Commission expires May 11 1909　　　　　Notary Public.

AFFIDAVIT OF ATTENDING PHYSICIAN OR MID-WIFE.

UNITED STATES OF AMERICA, Indian Territory,　}
　　Central　　　　　DISTRICT.

　　I, Tennessee Nelson, a Mid wife, on oath state that I attended on Mrs. Ledicy Sealey, wife of Adam Sealey on the 16th day of March, 1904; that there was born to her on said date a Female child; that said child was living March 4, 1905, and is said to have been named Gouldy Sealey
　　　　　　　　　　　　　　　　　　her
　　　　　　　　　　　　　Tennessee x Nelson
Witnesses To Mark:　　　　　　　mark
　{ Dr. A. Griffith
　　B.F. Jobe

　　Subscribed and sworn to before me this 7th day of June, 1905

　　　　　　　　　　　　　　　　　WG Weimer
Commission expires May 11 1909　　　　　Notary Public.

Applications for Enrollment of Chickasaw Newborn
Act of 1905   Volume VI

(The affidavit below typed as given.)

UNITED STATES OF AMERICA:
INDIAN TERRITORY: S.S.
CENTRAL-------------DISTRICT:

    Personally appeared before the ~~the~~ undersigned authority a Notary Public duly Commissioned and acting for the District and Territory aforesaid, Mrs. Ledicy Hawkins of Arpelar, Indian Territory first by me duly sworn, deposes says that she is a mother of Gouldy Sealy, who is a citicen by blood of the Chickasaw Nation, and daughter of of herself and that of her husband Adam Sealy, and that he was a citizen by blood of the Chickasaw Nation.

    The affiant further states that her enrolled as a citizen of the Chickasaw Nation by blood and that her roll No. is 2242, which is appears upon the record of the Commissions to the Five Civilized Tribes. And that she further states that this one Gouldy Sealy was enrolled by the name of Gouldy Sealy and who was born on the 16th day of March 1904. Affiant further states that said Adam Sealy a father of this one Gouldy Sealy is ~~a~~ her present husband, and who died on the 12th day of October 1904. Yet she was enrolled by her former marriage name and signed the same according to record of the Commission, as appears, thereto.

                                                               Ledicy Hawkins

Sworn to and subscribed before me this 26th day of April 1905.

                                                 (Illegible) Collins

My Commission Expires Jan. 25th. 1908   Notary Public.

                                      Muskogee, Indian Territory, April 19, 1905.

Adam Sealy,
    Arpealer[sic], Indian Territory.

Dear Sir:

    Receipt is hereby acknowledged of the affidavits of Litisy Sealy and Henry Sealy to the birth of Gouldy Sealy daughter of Adam and Luticy Sealy, March 16, 1904.

    It is stated in the affidavit of the mother that she is a citizen by blood of the Chickasaw Nation. If this is correct you are requested to state the name under which she was enrolled, the names of her parents, and if she or yourself have selected an allotment of the lands of the Choctaw or Chickasaw Nation please give your roll numbers as they appear upon her allotment certificates.

                                                        Respectfully,
                                                        Tams Bixby
                                                         Chairman.

Applications for Enrollment of Chickasaw Newborn
Act of 1905   Volume VI

W^mO.B.

COMMISSIONERS:
TAMS BIXBY,
THOMAS B. NEEDLES,
C.R. BRECKINBRIDGE.

WM. O. BEALL
Secretary

**DEPARTMENT OF THE INTERIOR,
COMMISSIONER TO THE FIVE CIVILIZED TRIBES.**

REFER IN REPLY TO THE FOLLOWING:

9--757.

ADDRESS ONLY THE
COMMISSION TO THE FIVE CIVILIZED TRIBES.

Muskogee, Indian Territory, May 4, 1905.

Dicey Hawkins,
    South McAlester, Indian Territory.

Dear Madam:

    Receipt is hereby acknowledged of your letter of April 25, transmitting the affidavit of Ledicy Hawkins and the information contained therein has enabled us to identify her upon our records as an enrolled citizen by blood of the Choctaw Nation, and the affidavits heretofore forwarded to the birth of your child, Gouldy Sealy, have been filed with our records as an application for the enrollment of said child.

                  Respectfully,
                  Tams Bixby
                        Chairman

9-NB-475.

Muskogee, Indian Territory, May 22, 1905.

Adam Sealey,
    Arpelar, Indian Territory.

Dear Sir:

    There is enclosed you herewith for execution application for the enrollment of your infant child, Gouldy Sealey, born March 16, 1904.

    The affidavits heretofore filed with the Commission show the child was living on February 28, 1905. It is necessary, for the child to be enrolled, that she was living on March 4, 1905.

    In having these affidavits executed care should be exercised to see that all names are written in full, as they appear in the body of the affidavit, and in the event that either of the persons signing the affidavit are unable to write, signatures by mark must be

Applications for Enrollment of Chickasaw Newborn
Act of 1905   Volume VI

attested by two witnesses. Each affidavit must be executed before a Notary Public and the notarial seal and signature of the officer must be attached to each separate affidavit.

Respectfully,
Tams Bixby
Chairman.

VR 22-4.

---

9 NB 475

Muskogee, Indian Territory, June 12, 1905.

Adam Sealy,
    Arpealer[sic], Indian Territory.

Dear Sir:

Receipt is hereby acknowledged of the affidavits of Ledicy Sealey and Tennessee Nelson to the birth of Gouldy Sealey, daughter of Adam and Ledicy Sealey, March 16, 1904, and the same have been filed in the matter of the enrollment of said child.

Respectfully,
Tams Bixby
Chairman.

Chic. N.B - 476
    (Tams L. Mullin
    Born September 14, 1904)

BIRTH AFFIDAVIT.
DEPARTMENT OF THE INTERIOR.
COMMISSION TO THE FIVE CIVILIZED TRIBES.

IN RE APPLICATION FOR ENROLLMENT, as a citizen of the Chickasaw Nation, of Tams L. Mullin, born on the 14 day of Sept , 1904.

Name of Father: Seth J. Mullin   a citizen of the U.S. ~~Nation~~.
Name of Mother: Cornealia Eldora Mullin   a citizen of the Chickasaw Nation.

Applications for Enrollment of Chickasaw Newborn
Act of 1905 Volume VI

Postoffice Antlers I.T.

AFFIDAVIT OF MOTHER.

UNITED STATES OF AMERICA, Indian Territory, }
Central DISTRICT. }

I, Cornelia Eldora Mullin, on oath state that I am 34 years of age and a citizen by blood, of the Chickasaw Nation; that I am the lawful wife of Seth J. Mullin, who is a citizen, by _____ of the United States ~~Nation~~; that a male child was born to me on 14th day of Sept, 1904; that said child has been named Tams L Mullin, and was living March 4, 1905.

Cornelia Eldora Mullin

Witnesses To Mark:
{

Subscribed and sworn to before me this 8th day of April, 1905

A.J. Arnote
Notary Public.

State of Illinois
Cook County AFFIDAVIT OF ATTENDING PHYSICIAN OR MID-WIFE.
UNITED STATES OF AMERICA, Indian Territory, }
Central DISTRICT. }

I, Isaac D. Walker, a Physician, on oath state that I attended on Mrs. Cornelia Eldora Mullin, wife of Seth J. Mullin on the 14th day of Sept, 1904; that there was born to her on said date a male child; that said child was living March 4, 1905, and is said to have been named Tams L. Mullin

Isaac D Walker MD

Witnesses To Mark:
{

Subscribed and sworn to before me this 11th day of April, 1905

Robert J Goldsmith
Notary Public.

Applications for Enrollment of Chickasaw Newborn
Act of 1905   Volume VI

Chic. N.B - 477
   (Georgian Pitchlynn
   Born February 24, 1904)

BIRTH AFFIDAVIT.

DEPARTMENT OF THE INTERIOR.
COMMISSION TO THE FIVE CIVILIZED TRIBES.

IN RE APPLICATION FOR ENROLLMENT, as a citizen of the Chickasaw Nation, of Georgian Pitchlynn, born on the 24th day of Feb, 1904

Name of Father: George Pitchlynn   a citizen of the Chickasaw Nation.
Name of Mother: Emma Pitchlynn   a citizen of the U. S. ~~Nation~~.

Postoffice   Pauls Valley I.T.

AFFIDAVIT OF MOTHER.

UNITED STATES OF AMERICA, Indian Territory, }
     Southern   DISTRICT.

     I, Emma Pitchlynn, on oath state that I am 22 years of age and a citizen by marriage, of the Chickasaw Nation; that I am the lawful wife of George Pitchlynn, who is a citizen, by blood of the Chickasaw Nation; that a Girl child was born to me on 24th day of February, 1904; that said child has been named Georgian Pitchlynn, and was living March 4, 1905.

                           Emma Pitchlynn

Witnesses To Mark:
   { W M Freeman
     Evelyn Pitchlynn

     Subscribed and sworn to before me this 25th day of April, 1905

                           J.W. Shumate
                               Notary Public.

Applications for Enrollment of Chickasaw Newborn
Act of 1905   Volume VI

AFFIDAVIT OF ATTENDING PHYSICIAN OR MID-WIFE.

UNITED STATES OF AMERICA, Indian Territory,　}
　　Southern　　　　　　　DISTRICT.

I, Icia Jacobs of Hennepin I.T. , a   Midwife   , on oath state that I attended on Mrs.   Emma Pitchlynn   , wife of   George Pitchlynn   on the 24th day of   Feb, 1904; that there was born to her on said date a   Girl   child; that said child was living March 4, 1905, and is said to have been named   George Ann Pitchlynn

　　　　　　　　　　　　　　　　　　　her
　　　　　　　　　　　　　　　　Icia x Jacobs
Witnesses To Mark:　　　　　　　　mark
　{ D.T. Strawn
　 Ardil C Meeks

　　Subscribed and sworn to before me this   20   day of   Apr   , 1905

　　　　　　　　　　　　　　(Name Illegible)
　　　　　　　　　　　　　　　　Notary Public.
My com. ex. Nov 29th 1908　　　17 District I.T.

Applications for Enrollment of Chickasaw Newborn
Act of 1905 Volume VI

CERTIFICATE OF
RECORD OF MARRIAGE

UNITED STATES OF AMERICA,
INDIAN TERRITORY,   } sct.
SOUTHERN DISTRICT.

DEPARTMENT OF THE INTERIOR,
COMMISSION TO THE FIVE CIVILIZED TRIBES.

FILED
JUL 6 1905
Tams Bixby CHAIRMAN.

I, C. M. CAMPBELL, Clerk of the United States Court, in the Territory and District aforesaid DO HEREBY CERTIFY, that the License for and Certificate of Marriage of

Mr. George Pitchlynn   and

M ISS[sic] Emma Curra

were filed in my office in said Territory and District the   15th   day of   December   A.D., 190 2   and duly recorded in Book   G   of Marriage Record, Page 48

WITNESS my hand and Seal of said Court, at Ardmore, this   15th   day of   December   A.D. 190 2

C. M. Campbell
CLERK.

No person is authorized to perform the Marriage Ceremony in the Indian Territory unless the proper credentials have first been recorded in the Clerk's office.

MARRIAGE LICENSE.

No. 1833

UNITED STATES OF AMERICA,
INDIAN TERRITORY,   } SS.
SOUTHERN DISTRICT.

To Any Person Authorized by Law to Solemnize Marriage, Greeting:

YOU ARE HEREBY COMMANDED to solemnize the Rite and publish the Banns of Matrimony between Mr.   George Pitchlynn
of   Wynnewood   in the Indian Territory, aged   38   years, and M iss Emma Curra   of   Wynnewood   in the Indian Territory, aged   19   years, according to law; and do you officially sign and return this license to the parties therein named.

Applications for Enrollment of Chickasaw Newborn
Act of 1905   Volume VI

WITNESS my hand and official Seal, this 10" day of December A. D. 190 2

C. M. Campbell
Clerk of the United States Court.

Certificate of Marriage.

UNITED STATES OF AMERICA,
INDIAN TERRITORY,   } SS.
SOUTHERN DISTRICT.   I,   B. C. Combs

_____ do hereby certify that on the 11" day of December A. D. 190 2 , I did duly and according to law, as commanded in the foregoing License, solemnize the Rite and publish the Banns of Matrimony between the parties therein named.

WITNESS my hand this 13" day of December A. D. 190 2

My credentials are recorded in the office of the Clerk of the United States Court, Indian Territory, Southern District, at Ardmore, Book C , Page 132

B. C. Combs

NOTE. (a)- This License and Certificate of Marriages must be returned to the office of the Clerk of the United States Court in the Indian Territory, at Ardmore, within sixty days from the date thereof, or the party to whom the License was issued will be liable in the amount of ONE HUNDRED DOLLARS ($100).

Indian Territory,
Southern District.

    I, C. M. Campbell, Clerk of the United States Court, Southern District, Indian Territory, do hereby certify that the above and foregoing is a true and correct copy of the Marriage License and Certificate of Marriage of George Pitchlynn and Emma Curra, filed for record in my office at Ardmore on the 15th day of December, 1902 and duly recorded in Book G., page 48 of Marriage Records.

    IN TESTIMONY WHEREOF, I have hereunto set my hand and affixed the seal of said Court, at my office in Ardmore, this 26th day of June, A.D. 1905.

C. M. Campbell, Clerk,

By   NH McCoy   Chief Deputy.

Applications for Enrollment of Chickasaw Newborn
Act of 1905   Volume VI

(The letter below typed as given.)

W. M. FREEMAN, President   CARL A. SHUMATE, Vice Pres

Office of
The Freeman-Sipes Company

Incorporated

Wholesale and Retail General Merchandise

C. B. SIPES   SEC'Y, TREAS. AND GEN'L MANAGER

PAULS VALLEY, IND. TER., June, 24th.1905. 190__

Mr. C.M. Campbell, Clerk,
Ardmore, I.T.
Dear sir:-

Please send me at once a certified copy of my mariage license. I would like to have the original license, which I think you have on file, but if you have not then I want a certified copy of the license.
I have reference to the license which was recroded there in Dec. 19o2 or in Jan. 19o3. My wifes name was Emma Curry. The license was sent to xx you by the minister Mr. Ben Combs. Please send at once.

Yours truly,

George Pitchlynn

(George Pitchlynn)

I will remit you as soon as I know the bill for the above copy. He xxxx also wants the certificate of his mariage, if it is a separate document. He has to have these papers in order to get his infant child enrolled as A Chickasaw citizen.

Yours truly,

W.M. Freeman

Ardmore, I.T., June 26, 1905.
Beg to say that the charges on the enclosed certified copy of
Marriage License and Certificate of Marriage, are $1.00, which
you will please remit at your early convenience.

C. M. Campbell, Clerk U.S. Court,

George Pitchlynn

Applications for Enrollment of Chickasaw Newborn
Act of 1905 Volume VI

9-1282.

Muskogee, Indian Territory, May 3, 1905.

George Pitchlynn,
    Pauls Valley, Indian Territory.

Dear Sir:

   Receipt is hereby acknowledged of your letter of April 25, enclosing the affidavits of Emma Pitchlynn and Icia Jacobs to the birth of George Ann Pitchlynn, daughter of George and Emma Pitchlynn, February 24, 1904, and the same have been filed with our records as an application for the enrollment of said child.

Respectfully,

Chairman.

9--N.B. 477.

Muskogee, Indian Territory, May 9, 1905.

George Pitchlynn,
    Pauls Valley, Indian Territory.

Dear Sir:

   Receipt is hereby acknowledged of your letter of May 4, stating that some days ago you forwarded application for the enrollment of your daughter, Georgian Pitchlynn, but have not received an acknowledgment of the same. You therefore ask if the application has been received at this office.

   In reply to your letter you are advised that the affidavits heretofore forwarded to the birth of your child, Georgian Pitchlynn, have been filed with our records as an application for the enrollment of said child.

Respectfully,

Commissioner in Charge.

Applications for Enrollment of Chickasaw Newborn
Act of 1905   Volume VI

9-NB-477.

Muskogee, Indian Territory, May 18, 1905.

George Pytchlyn[sic],
    Pauls Valley, Indian Territory.

Dear Sir:

    Referring to the application for the enrollment of your infant child, Georgian Pytchlyn, born February 24, 1904, it is noted that the applicant claims through you.

    It will, therefore, be necessary that you file with the Commission either the original or a certified copy of the license and certificate of your marriage to the applicant's mother, Emma Pytchlyn.

                      Respectfully,

                        Chairman.

$W^m O.B.$

COMMISSIONERS:
TAMS BIXBY,
THOMAS B. NEEDLES,
C.R. BRECKINBRIDGE.

**DEPARTMENT OF THE INTERIOR,
COMMISSIONER TO THE FIVE CIVILIZED TRIBES.**

REFER IN REPLY TO THE FOLLOWING:

9 NB 477

WM. O. BEALL
Secretary

ADDRESS ONLY THE
COMMISSION TO THE FIVE CIVILIZED TRIBES.

Muskogee, Indian Territory, June 30, 1905.

George Pytchlyn[sic],
    Pauls Valley, Indian Territory.

Dear Sir:

    Receipt is hereby acknowledged of your letter of June 24, 1905, in which you state that you will forward a certified copy of your marriage license and certificate as soon as you can secure the same from the Clerk of the United States Court at Ardmore, Indian Territory.

    In reply to your letter you are advised that this evidence of marriage should be forwarded as early as practicable in order that disposition may be made of the application for the enrollment of your daughter Georgian Pytchlyn.

                      Respectfully,

                      Tams Bixby   Commissioner.

Applications for Enrollment of Chickasaw Newborn
Act of 1905 Volume VI

9-NB-477

Muskogee, Indian Territory, July 6, 1905.

George Pitchlynn,
    Pauls Valley, Indian Territory.

Dear Sir:

    Receipt is hereby acknowledged of your letter of July 1, 1905, inclosing certified copy of the marriage license and certificate between yourself and Emma Curra, which you offer in support of the application for the enrollment of your infant child, Georgian Pitchlynn, and the same has been filed with the records in this case.

Respectfully,

Commissioner.

Chic. N.B - 478
    (Paul Fussell
    Born February 15, 1904)

BIRTH AFFIDAVIT.

    IN RE-APPLICATION FOR ENROLLMENT, as a citizen of the Chickasaw Nation, of Paul Fussell, born on the 15th day of Feby, 1904

Name of Father: James E Fussell   a citizen of the Chickasaw Nation.
Name of Mother: Alice M Fussell   a citizen of the Chickasaw Nation.

    Postoffice   Fitzhugh Ind T.

Applications for Enrollment of Chickasaw Newborn
Act of 1905 Volume VI

AFFIDAVIT OF MOTHER.

UNITED STATES OF AMERICA, INDIAN TERRITORY, }
Southern District District.

I, Alice M Fussell , on oath state that I am 28 years of age and a citizen by Blood , of the Chickasaw Nation; that I am the lawful wife of James E. Fussell , who is a citizen, by Intermarriage of the Chickasaw Nation; that a Male child was born to me on 15th day of February , 1904 , that said child has been named Paul Fussell , and is now living.

Alice M Fussell

Witnesses To Mark:
{

Subscribed and sworn to before me this 22" day of March , 1905.

JE White
Notary Public.

My Commission expires
March 26th 1907

AFFIDAVIT OF ATTENDING PHYSICIAN OR MID-WIFE.

UNITED STATES OF AMERICA, INDIAN TERRITORY, }
Southern District District.

I, Dovie Backus , a Mid wife , on oath state that I attended on Mrs. Alice M Fussell , wife of James E Fussell on the 15th day of Feby , 190 4; that there was born to her on said date a Male child; that said child is now living and is said to have been named Paul Fussell

Dovie Backus

Witnesses To Mark:
{

Subscribed and sworn to before me this 22 day of March , 1905.

JE White
Notary Public.

My Commission expires
March 26th 1907

Applications for Enrollment of Chickasaw Newborn
Act of 1905   Volume VI

9-55.

Muskogee, Indian Territory, May 3, 1905.

James E. Fussell,
Fitzhugh, Indian Territory.

Dear Sir:

Receipt is hereby acknowledged of the affidavits of Alice M. Fussell and Dovie Backus to the birth of Paul Fussell, son of James E. and Alice M. Fussell, February 15, 1904, and the same have been filed with our records as an application for the enrollment of said child.

Respectfully,

Chairman.

Chic. N.B - 479
(Claud Laten Harris
Born February 21, 1903)

BIRTH AFFIDAVIT.

IN RE-APPLICATION FOR ENROLLMENT, as a citizen of the Chickasaw Nation, of Claud Laten Harris, born on the 21st day of Feby, 190 3

Name of Father: Benjamin Franklin Harris   a citizen of the Chickasaw Nation.
Name of Mother: Ella May Harris   a citizen of the United States ~~Nation~~.

Postoffice   Tishomingo, Ind. Ter.

AFFIDAVIT OF MOTHER.

UNITED STATES OF AMERICA, INDIAN TERRITORY,
Southern   District.

I, Ella May Harris, on oath state that I am twenty Five years of age and a citizen by blood, of the United States ~~Nation~~; that I am the lawful wife of Benjamin Franklin Harris, who is a citizen, by Blood of the Chickasaw

140

Applications for Enrollment of Chickasaw Newborn
Act of 1905   Volume VI

Nation; that a   male   child was born to me on   21st day of   Feby , 1903 , that said child has been named   Claud Laten Harris   , and is now living.

her
Ella May x Harris
mark

Witnesses To Mark:
{ Charles Milligan
{ B G Grahan

    Subscribed and sworn to before me this   27th day of   April   , 1905.

H. Schneider
Notary Public.

AFFIDAVIT OF ATTENDING PHYSICIAN OR MID-WIFE.

UNITED STATES OF AMERICA, INDIAN TERRITORY, }
   Southern   District.   }

    I,   Lucinda Rushing   , a   midwife   , on oath state that I attended on Mrs.   Ella May Harris   , wife of   Benjamin Franklin Harris   on the   21st day of   Feby , 190 3; that there was born to her on said date a   male   child; that said child is now living and is said to have been named   Claud Laten Harris

her
Lucinda x Rushing
mark

Witnesses To Mark:
{ Charles Milligan
{ B G Grahan

    Subscribed and sworn to before me this   27th day of   April   , 1905.

H. Schneider
Notary Public.

My commission expires
March 17th 1909

Chickasaw 894.

Muskogee, Indian Territory, May 3, 1905.

Benjamin Franklin Harris,
    Tishomingo, Indian Territory.

Dear Sir:

    Receipt is hereby acknowledged of your letter of April 27, enclosing the affidavits of Ella May Harris and Lucinda Rushing to the birth of Claud Laten Harris, February 21,

Applications for Enrollment of Chickasaw Newborn
Act of 1905   Volume VI

1903, son of Benjamin Franklin and Ella May Harris, and the same have been filed with our records as an application for the enrollment of said child.

Respectfully,

Chairman.

Chic. N.B - 480
  (Rubey Massey
  Born September 20, 1903)

BIRTH AFFIDAVIT.

DEPARTMENT OF THE INTERIOR.
COMMISSION TO THE FIVE CIVILIZED TRIBES.

IN RE APPLICATION FOR ENROLLMENT, as a citizen of the   Chickasaw   Nation, of   Rubey Massey   , born on the 20   day of Sept   , 1903

Name of Father: John W. Massey   a citizen of the   Chickasaw   Nation.
Name of Mother: Juel Massey   a citizen of the   Chickasaw   Nation.

Postoffice   Berwyn, I.T.

AFFIDAVIT OF MOTHER.

UNITED STATES OF AMERICA, Indian Territory, }
  Southern   DISTRICT.

I, Juel Massey , on oath state that I am 25 years of age and a citizen by blood , of the Chickasaw Nation; that I am the lawful wife of John W Massey, who is a citizen, by Intermarriage   of the   Chickasaw   Nation; that a   female child was born to me on 20th   day of   September   , 1903; that said child has been named   Rubey Massey   , and was living March 4, 1905.

Juel Massey

Witnesses To Mark:

Applications for Enrollment of Chickasaw Newborn
Act of 1905 Volume VI

Subscribed and sworn to before me this 26th day of   April   , 1905

                                                        H.C. MIller
                                                       Notary Public.

AFFIDAVIT OF ATTENDING PHYSICIAN OR MID-WIFE.

UNITED STATES OF AMERICA, Indian Territory, ⎫
.... DISTRICT. ⎭

      I, ..., a ...., on oath state that I attended on Mrs. ...., wife of .... on the .... day of ...., 1......; that there was born to her on said date a .... child; that said child was living March 4, 1905, and is said to have been named ....

Witnesses To Mark:
{ ....
  ....

                        ....

Subscribed and sworn to before me this .... day of ...., 1905.

                                                  Notary Public.

BIRTH AFFIDAVIT.

DEPARTMENT OF THE INTERIOR.
COMMISSION TO THE FIVE CIVILIZED TRIBES.

      IN RE APPLICATION FOR ENROLLMENT, as a citizen of the .... Nation, of ...., born on the .... day of ...., 1........

Name of Father: .... a citizen of the .... Nation.
Name of Mother .... a citizen of the .... Nation.

                                    Postoffice ....

AFFIDAVIT OF MOTHER.

UNITED STATES OF AMERICA, Indian Territory, ⎫
.... DISTRICT. ⎭

      I, ..., on oath state that I am .... years of age and a citizen by ...., of the .... Nation; that I am the lawful wife of ...., who is a citizen, by .... of the .... Nation; that a

Applications for Enrollment of Chickasaw Newborn
Act of 1905 Volume VI

.... child was born to me on ..... day of ...., 1......., that said child has been named ...., and was living March 4, 1905.

Witnesses To Mark:
{ ....
....

Subscribed and sworn to before me this .... day of ...., 1905.

Notary Public.

AFFIDAVIT OF ATTENDING PHYSICIAN OR MID-WIFE.

UNITED STATES OF AMERICA, Indian Territory, }
  Southern   DISTRICT.

I, Rachel A Massey , a Mid-wife , on oath state that I attended on Mrs. Juel Massey , wife of John W. Massey on the 20 day of September, 1903; that there was born to her on said date a female child; that said child was living March 4, 1905, and is said to have been named Rubey Massey

Rachel A Massey

Witnesses To Mark:
{
  Subscribed and sworn to before me this 27 day of April , 1905

T.J. Carson
Notary Public.

9-846.

Muskogee, Indian Territory, May 3, 1905.

John W. Massey
  Berwyn, Indian Territory.

Dear Sir:

Receipt is hereby acknowledged of the affidavits of Juel Massey and Rachel A. Massey to the birth of Rubey Massey, daughter of John W. and Juel Massey, September 20, 1903, and the same have been filed with our records as an application for the enrollment of said child.

Applications for Enrollment of Chickasaw Newborn
Act of 1905   Volume VI

Respectfully,

Chairman.

(The letter above given again.)

Chic. N.B - 481
  (Wisie Shields
  Born March 3, 1905)

BIRTH AFFIDAVIT.

DEPARTMENT OF THE INTERIOR.
COMMISSION TO THE FIVE CIVILIZED TRIBES.

IN RE APPLICATION FOR ENROLLMENT, as a citizen of the Chickasaw Nation, of Wisie Shields , born on the 3 day of March , 1905

Name of Father: Simian Shields   a citizen of the Chickasaw Nation.
Name of Mother: Manda Shields   a citizen of the Chickasaw Nation.

Postoffice   Allen

AFFIDAVIT OF MOTHER.

UNITED STATES OF AMERICA, Indian Territory,
  Central   DISTRICT.

I, Manda Shields , on oath state that I am 27 years of age and a citizen by blood , of the Chickasaw Nation; that I am the lawful wife of Simian Shields , who is a citizen, by blood of the Chickasaw Nation; that a female child was born to me on 3 day of March , 1905; that said child has been named Wisie Shields , and was living March 4, 1905.

Manda Shields

Witnesses To Mark:

Applications for Enrollment of Chickasaw Newborn
Act of 1905 Volume VI

Subscribed and sworn to before me this 27 day of April, 1905

My commission expires J. L. Cart
June 27 -1908 Notary Public.

AFFIDAVIT OF ATTENDING PHYSICIAN OR MID-WIFE.

UNITED STATES OF AMERICA, Indian Territory, }
  Central DISTRICT. }

I, Leffy Jackson, a midwife, on oath state that I attended on Mrs. Manda Shields, wife of Simian Shields on the 3 day of March, 1905; that there was born to her on said date a female child; that said child was living March 4, 1905, and is said to have been named Wisie Shields

                      her
             Leffy x Jackson
Witnesses To Mark: mark
{ J W Jones
{ *(Name Illegible)*

Subscribed and sworn to before me this 27 day of April, 1905

My commission expires J. L. Cart
June 27 -1908 Notary Public.

9-85.

Muskogee, Indian Territory, May 3, 1905.

Simion[sic] Shields,
    Allen, Indian Territory.

Dear Sir:

Receipt is hereby acknowledged of the affidavits of Manda Shields and Leffy Jackson to the birth of Esau Shields and Wisie Shields, children of Simion and Manda Shields, September 25, 1902, and March 3, 1905, respectively, and the same have been filed with our records as an application for the enrollment of said child.

                Respectfully,

                           Chairman.

Applications for Enrollment of Chickasaw Newborn
Act of 1905 Volume VI

Chic. N.B - 482
    (Evert Allen Turner
    Born May 19, 1904)

BIRTH AFFIDAVIT.   #85

DEPARTMENT OF THE INTERIOR.
COMMISSION TO THE FIVE CIVILIZED TRIBES.

IN RE APPLICATION FOR ENROLLMENT, as a citizen of the   Chickasaw   Nation, of   Evert Allen Turner   , born on the   19   day of   May   , 1904

Name of Father: Andrew Jackson Turner   a citizen of the   Chickasaw   Nation.
Name of Mother: Maud Miller Turner   a citizen of the   Chickasaw   Nation.

                Postoffice   Kemp

AFFIDAVIT OF MOTHER.

UNITED STATES OF AMERICA, Indian Territory, }
    Central   DISTRICT. }

    I,   Maud Miller Turner   , on oath state that I am   21   years of age and a citizen by   blood   , of the   Chickasaw   Nation; that I am the lawful wife of   Andrew Jackson Turner   , who is a citizen, by   intermarriage   of the   Chickasaw   Nation; that a   male   child was born to me on   19   day of   May   , 1904, that said child has been named   Evert Allen   , and is now living.

Witnesses To Mark:
  { J.W. Connelly
    Hannah Connelly

    Subscribed and sworn to before me this   13   day of   February   , 1905.

                        S M Mead
                        Notary Public.

AFFIDAVIT OF ATTENDING PHYSICIAN OR MID-WIFE.

UNITED STATES OF AMERICA, Indian Territory, }
    .... DISTRICT. }

    I, ..., a ...., on oath state that I attended on Mrs. ...., wife of .... on the .... day of

Applications for Enrollment of Chickasaw Newborn
Act of 1905   Volume VI

..................................., 1..........; that there was born to her on said date a ....
child; that said child is now living and is said to have been named ....

Witnesses To Mark:
{ J.W. Connelly
{ Hannah Connelly

Subscribed and sworn to before me this..........day of.........................., 190....

Notary Public.

BIRTH AFFIDAVIT.

DEPARTMENT OF THE INTERIOR.
COMMISSION TO THE FIVE CIVILIZED TRIBES.

IN RE APPLICATION FOR ENROLLMENT, as a citizen of the   Chickasaw   Nation, of   Evert Allen Turner   , born on the 19   day of   May   , 1904

Name of Father: Andrew Jackson Turner   a citizen of the   Chickasaw   Nation.
Name of Mother: Maude Turner   a citizen of the   Chickasaw   Nation.

Postoffice   Kemp Ind Ter

AFFIDAVIT OF MOTHER.

UNITED STATES OF AMERICA, Indian Territory, }
Central   DISTRICT. }

I,   Maude Turner   , on oath state that I am   21   years of age and a citizen by   birth   , of the   Chickasaw   Nation; that I am the lawful wife of   Andrew Jackson Turner   , who is a citizen, by marriage   of the   Chickasaw Nation; that a   Male   child was born to me on   19   day of   May   , 1904; that said child has been named   Evert Allen Turner   , and was living March 4, 1905.

Maude Turner

Witnesses To Mark:
{

Subscribed and sworn to before me this   29   day of   March   , 1905

S. T. Johns
Notary Public.

Applications for Enrollment of Chickasaw Newborn
Act of 1905   Volume VI

AFFIDAVIT OF ATTENDING PHYSICIAN OR MID-WIFE.

UNITED STATES OF AMERICA, Indian Territory, }
   Central   DISTRICT.

I,   G. H. Ellis   , a   Physician   , on oath state that I attended on Mrs.   Maude Turner   , wife of   A J Turner   on the   19 day of   May   , 1904; that there was born to her on said date a   male   child; that said child was living March 4, 1905, and is said to have been named   Evert Allen Turner

G H Ellis MD

Witnesses To Mark:
{

Subscribed and sworn to before me this 29   day of   March   , 1905

S. T. Johns
Notary Public.

Feb 11th 1905
#85

I G H Ellis a Physician do swear that I attended Maud Turner a citizen by birth on the 19th day of May 1904 and that she gave birth to a male child and said child is now living and is named Everett[sic] Allen.
Given under my hand the 11th day of Feby 1905

GH Ellis MD

Subscribed and sworn to before me this 11th day of Feb 1905

EL Mead
Mayor

(The letter below typed as given.)

Kemp, I. T.
   April 25, 1905.

Maud Turner enrollment No. 3566 fild March 7, 1904 Maud Duckworth her father name Berry Duckworth and mother Lou Duckworth.

Yours Andrew J. Turner

P S Please let me know if this is correct or all that is needed in the above case.

Applications for Enrollment of Chickasaw Newborn
Act of 1905 Volume VI

Muskogee, Indian Territory, April 22, 1905.

Andrew Jackson Turner,
 Kemp, Indian Territory.

Dear Sir:

Receipt is hereby acknowledged of the affidavits of Maude Turner and G. H. Ellis to the birth of Evert Allen Turner, son of A. J. and Maude Turner, May 19, 1904.

It appears from the affidavit of the mother that she is a citizen by blood of the Chickasaw Nation, and if this is correct you are requested to state her full name, the names of her parents, and if she has made a selection of the lands of the Choctaw and Chickasaw Nations, please give her roll number as the same appears upon her allotment certificate.

This matter should receive immediate attention in order that proper disposition may be made of the application for the enrollment of your child.

Respectfully,

Chairman.

Chic. N.B - 483
 (Henretta Pickens
 Born April 22, 1903)
 (Hylam Pickens
 Born August 9, 1904)

BIRTH AFFIDAVIT.

DEPARTMENT OF THE INTERIOR.
COMMISSION TO THE FIVE CIVILIZED TRIBES.

IN RE APPLICATION FOR ENROLLMENT, as a citizen of the Chickasaw Nation, of Henretta Pickens , born on the 22nd day of April , 1903

Name of Father: Thomas Pickens a citizen of the Chickasaw Nation.
Name of Mother: Lucy Pickens a citizen of the Chickasaw Nation.

Postoffice McMillan I.T.

Applications for Enrollment of Chickasaw Newborn
Act of 1905   Volume VI

AFFIDAVIT OF MOTHER.

UNITED STATES OF AMERICA, Indian Territory, }
Southern   DISTRICT.

I,   Lucy Pickens   , on oath state that I am   18   years of age and a citizen by Blood   , of the   Chickasaw   Nation; that I am the lawful wife of   Thomas Pickens   , who is a citizen, by Blood   of the   Chickasaw   Nation; that a Female   child was born to me on 22nd day of   Aprial[sic]   , 1903; that said child has been named   Henretta Pickens   , and was living March 4, 1905.

Lucy Pickens

Witnesses To Mark:

{ Subscribed and sworn to before me this 27   day of   march   , 1905

Joe Simpson
Notary Public.

AFFIDAVIT OF ATTENDING PHYSICIAN OR MID-WIFE.

UNITED STATES OF AMERICA, Indian Territory, }
Southern   DISTRICT.

I,   Elsie Norton   , a   Midwife   , on oath state that I attended on Mrs.   Lucy Pickens   , wife of   Thomas Pickens   on the 22nd day of   April , 1903; that there was born to her on said date a   female   child; that said child was living March 4, 1905, and is said to have been named   Henretta Pickens

                                                  her
                                          Elsie x Norton
Witnesses To Mark: mark
{ B J Dabney
  B.H. Key

Subscribed and sworn to before me this 6th day of   April   , 1905

W.H. Pittman
Notary Public.

Applications for Enrollment of Chickasaw Newborn
Act of 1905   Volume VI

BIRTH AFFIDAVIT.

DEPARTMENT OF THE INTERIOR.
COMMISSION TO THE FIVE CIVILIZED TRIBES.

IN RE APPLICATION FOR ENROLLMENT, as a citizen of the   Chickasaw   Nation, of   Hylam Pickens   , born on the   9th day of   August   , 1904

Name of Father: Thomas Pickens   a citizen of the   Chickasaw   Nation.
Name of Mother: Lucy Pickens   a citizen of the   Chickasaw   Nation.

Postoffice   McMillan I.T.

AFFIDAVIT OF MOTHER.

UNITED STATES OF AMERICA, Indian Territory,}
Southern   DISTRICT.

I,   Lucy Pickens   , on oath state that I am   18   years of age and a citizen by Blood   , of the   Chickasaw   Nation; that I am the lawful wife of   Thomas Pickens   , who is a citizen, by Blood   of the   Chickasaw   Nation; that a Male   child was born to me on   9th day of   August   , 1904; that said child has been named   Hylam Pickens   , and was living March 4, 1905.

                                        Lucy Pickens
Witnesses To Mark:
{ Subscribed and sworn to before me this   27   day of   march   , 1905

                                        Joe Simpson
                                        Notary Public.

AFFIDAVIT OF ATTENDING PHYSICIAN OR MID-WIFE.

UNITED STATES OF AMERICA, Indian Territory,}
Southern   DISTRICT.

I,   Elsie Norton   , a   Midwife   , on oath state that I attended on Mrs.   Lucy Pickens   , wife of   Thomas Pickens   on the   9th day of   August   , 1904; that there was born to her on said date a   male   child; that said child was living March 4, 1905, and is said to have been named   Hylam Pickens

                                        her
                                    Elsie x Norton
Witnesses To Mark: mark
{ B.H. Key
  J B Pittman

Applications for Enrollment of Chickasaw Newborn
Act of 1905 Volume VI

Subscribed and sworn to before me this 6th day of April , 1905

W.H. Pittman
Notary Public.

Muskogee, Indian Territory, April 13, 1905.

Thomas Pickens,
    McMillan, Indian Territory.

Dear Sir:

    Receipt is hereby acknowledged of the affidavits of Lucy Pickens and Elsie Norton to the birth of Henretta Pickens and Hylam Pickens, children of Thomas and Lucy Pickens, April 22, 1903 and August 9, 1904, respectively.

    It appears from the affidavits that the mother of these children is a citizen by blood of the Chickasaw Nation. If this is correct, you are requested to state the name under which she was enrolled, the names of her parents and if she has selected her allotment, please give her roll number as it appears upon her allotment certificate.

    This matter should receipt immediate attention in order that proper disposition may be made of the application for the enrollment of the above named children.

Respectfully,

Commissioner in Charge.

(C O P Y)

Madill, I. T.

April 29th, 1905.

Commission to the Five Civilized Tribes,
    Muskogee, I. T.

Gentlemen;-

    I am in receipt of your letter of the 13th., inst., wherein you state that it appears from the affidavits of Henretta Pickens and Hylam Pickens birth that the mother of these children is a citizen by blood, and you desire to know the name under which she was enrolled, the names of her parents, and her roll number. You are advised that the mother, Lucy Pickens, was enrolled as Lucy Brown. Her father has been dead for sometime. Her mother's name is Elsie Brown. The mothers roll number is 2158. The numbers of her

Applications for Enrollment of Chickasaw Newborn
Act of 1905   Volume VI

certificates of allotment are Nos. 3496 and 3146.   Advise me if you need further information. Is the application sufficient?

Very respectfully,
Tom Pickens.

9--731.

Muskogee, Indian Territory, May 5, 1905.

Tom. Pickens,
    Madill, Indian Territory.

Dear Sir:

    Receipt is hereby acknowledged of your letter of April 29, stating that Lucy Pickens was enrolled as Lucy Brown and giving her roll number, and this information has enabled us to identify her upon our records as an enrolled citizen by blood of the Chickasaw Nation, and the affidavits heretofore forwarded to the birth of Henretta and Hylam Pickens have been filed with our records as applications for the enrollment of said children.

Respectfully,

Commissioner in Charge.

Chic. N.B - 484
    (Lillie May Keener
    Born August 25, 1903)

BIRTH AFFIDAVIT.   No 38

DEPARTMENT OF THE INTERIOR.
COMMISSION TO THE FIVE CIVILIZED TRIBES.

    IN RE APPLICATION FOR ENROLLMENT, as a citizen of the   Chickasaw   Nation, of   Lillie May Keener   , born on the   25th day of   August   , 1903

Name of Father: _____   a citizen of the _____ Nation.
Name of Mother: Maulsey Keener   a citizen of the   Chickasaw Nation.

Postoffice   Ada, Ind. Ty.

Applications for Enrollment of Chickasaw Newborn
Act of 1905   Volume VI

AFFIDAVIT OF MOTHER.

UNITED STATES OF AMERICA, Indian Territory, }
Southern   DISTRICT.

I,   Mauley[sic] Keener   , on oath state that I am   24   years of age and a citizen by   blood   , of the   Chickasaw   Nation; that I am the lawful wife of Jackson Reed   , who is a citizen, by .... of the   United States   Nation; that a   female   child was born to me on   25th day of   August   , 1903, that said child has been named   Lillie May Keener   , and is now living.

              Molsey[sic] Keener

Witnesses To Mark:
{

  Subscribed and sworn to before me this 7th   day of   December   , 1904

My commission expires   Tom D. McKeown
 Nov. 12 - 1907   Notary Public.

AFFIDAVIT OF ATTENDING PHYSICIAN OR MID-WIFE.

UNITED STATES OF AMERICA, Indian Territory, }
Southern   DISTRICT.

I,   Artie Cupps   , a   Mid-wife   , on oath state that I attended on Mrs.   Maulsey Keener   , wife of   Jackson Reed   on the   25   day of   August   , 1903; that there was born to her on said date a   female   child; that said child is now living and is said to have been named   Lillie May Keener

              Artie Cupps

Witnesses To Mark:
{ Newton Oliver
 John I McCoole

  Subscribed and sworn to before me this   30   day of   December   , 1904

             John I McCoole
My com ex Feb 11th 1907   Notary Public.

Applications for Enrollment of Chickasaw Newborn
Act of 1905 Volume VI

BIRTH AFFIDAVIT.

DEPARTMENT OF THE INTERIOR.
COMMISSION TO THE FIVE CIVILIZED TRIBES.

IN RE APPLICATION FOR ENROLLMENT, as a citizen of the Chickasaw Nation, of Lillie May Keener , born on the 25 day of August , 1904[sic]

Name of Father: Stokes Keener a citizen of the Chickasaw Nation.
Name of Mother: Molsey Keener a citizen of the Chickasaw Nation.

Postoffice Ada, I.T.

AFFIDAVIT OF MOTHER.

UNITED STATES OF AMERICA, Indian Territory, }
Southern DISTRICT. }

I, Molsey Keener , on oath state that I am 24 years of age and a citizen by blood , of the Chickasaw Nation; that I am the lawful wife of Stokes Keener , who is a citizen, by blood of the Chickasaw Nation; that a female child was born to me on the 25th day of August , 1904; that said child has been named Lillie May Keener , and was living March 4, 1905.

Molsey Keener

Witnesses To Mark:
{

Subscribed and sworn to before me this 29 day of April , 1905

JE Williams
Notary Public.

AFFIDAVIT OF ATTENDING PHYSICIAN OR MID-WIFE.

UNITED STATES OF AMERICA, Indian Territory, }
DISTRICT. }

I, ..., a ...., on oath state that I attended on Mrs. ...., wife of .... on the .... day of ...., 1......; that there was born to her on said date a .... child; that said child was living March 4, 1905, and is said to have been named ....

Witnesses To Mark:
{

Applications for Enrollment of Chickasaw Newborn
Act of 1905   Volume VI

Subscribed and sworn to before me this .... day of ...., 1905.

....

Notary Public.

BIRTH AFFIDAVIT.

DEPARTMENT OF THE INTERIOR.
COMMISSION TO THE FIVE CIVILIZED TRIBES.

IN RE APPLICATION FOR ENROLLMENT, as a citizen of the   Chickasaw   Nation, of   Lillie May ~~Keener~~ Reed   , born on the 25th day of   August   , 1903

Name of Father: ─────────────────a citizen of the─────────Nation.
Name of Mother: Molsey Keener   a citizen of the   Chickasaw   Nation.

Postoffice   Ada I. T.

AFFIDAVIT OF MOTHER.

UNITED STATES OF AMERICA, Indian Territory, }
    Southern   DISTRICT.
                Reed
    I,   Molsey ~~Keener~~   , on oath state that I am   24   years of age and a citizen by   Blood   , of the   Chickasaw   Nation; that I am the lawful wife of   Jackson Reed   , who is a citizen, by─────── of the ─────── Nation; that a   Female child was born to me on 25th day of   August   , 1903; that said child has been named   Lillie May ~~Keener~~ Reed   , and was living March 4, 1905.

                        Molsey Reed
Witnesses To Mark:
{

    Subscribed and sworn to before me this   4   day of   Sept   , 1905

                        John I McCoole
MY COMMISSION EXPIRES FEBY. 11TH. 1907.   Notary Public.

Applications for Enrollment of Chickasaw Newborn
Act of 1905   Volume VI

AFFIDAVIT OF ATTENDING PHYSICIAN OR MID-WIFE.

UNITED STATES OF AMERICA, Indian Territory, }
Southern   DISTRICT.

I, Artie Cupps, a midwife, on oath state that I attended on Mrs. Molsey ~~Keener~~ Reed, wife of ———— on the 25th day of August, 1903; that there was born to her on said date a Female child; that said child was living March 4, 1905, and is said to have been named Lillie May ~~Keener~~ Reed

Witnesses To Mark:
{

                                    Artie Cupps

    Subscribed and sworn to before me this 31 day of August, 1905

                              W Hugh *(Illegible)*
                                  Notary Public.

United States of America
Southern District, Indian Territory

    Artie Cupps being on oath deposes and says that she is a midwife an attended on Moley Keener during the birth of a female child on the 25 day of Aug. 1904, that said child has been named Lillie May Keener and is now living

                              Artie Cupps

Subscribed and sworn to before me, a Notary Public, in and for the Southern District, Indian Territory, on this the 28 day of April 1905

MY COMMISSION EXPIRES FEBY. 11TH. 1907.   John I McCoole
                                        Notary Public.

Applications for Enrollment of Chickasaw Newborn
Act of 1905   Volume VI

9--1387.

Muskogee, Indian Territory, May 4, 1905.

Stokes Keener,
    Ada, Indian Territory.

Dear Sir:

    Receipt is hereby acknowledged of the affidavits of Molsey Keener and Artie Cuffs[sic] to the birth of Lillie May Keener, daughter of Stokes and Molsey Keener, August 25, 1904, and the same have been filed with our records as an application for the enrollment of said child.

    Respectfully,

Chairman.

9-NB-484.

Muskogee, Indian Territory, May 20, 1905.

Molsey Keener,
    Ada, Indian Territory.

Dear Madam:

    There is enclosed you herewith for execution application for the enrollment of your infant child, Lillie May Keener.

    Referring to your affidavit, executed December 7, 1904, and that of Artie Cupps, executed December 30, 1904, to the birth of the above mentioned applicant, it appears that Jackson Reed was your husband and that the applicant was born on August 25, 1903, while in your affidavit of the 29th ultimo, you state that you are the lawful wife of Stokes Keener and also mention him as the father of this applicant. Artie Cupps, the attending mid-wife, in her affidavit of the 29th ultimo fails to mention your husband or the father of the child. In the two affidavits last mentioned the birth of the applicant is given as August 25, 1904.

    In the enclosed application both the name of the father and the date of birth of the applicant have been left blank, which you will please insert before execution these affidavits.

    In having these affidavits executed care should be exercised to see that all names are written in full, as they appear in the body of the affidavit, and in the event that either of the persons signing the affidavit are unable to write, signatures by mark must be

Applications for Enrollment of Chickasaw Newborn
Act of 1905 Volume VI

attested by two witnesses. Each affidavit must be executed before a Notary Public and the notarial seal and signature of the officer must be attached to each separate affidavit.

                Respectfully,

                                      Chairman.

VR 20-7.

                                7[sic]-N.B.-484.

                Muskogee, Indian Territory, June 10, 1905.

Tom D. McKeown,
    Attorney at Law,
        Ada, Indian Territory.

Dear Sir:

    Receipt is hereby acknowledged of your letter of June 5, relative to the enrollment of Lillie May Keener, child of Maulsey Keener, in which you state that she is enrolled opposite No. 3874, upon the approved roll of citizens by blood of the Chickasaw Nation; that she refuses to disclose the name of the father of her child, and you ask if she can execute affidavits with the name of the father left blank.

    In reply to your letter you are advised that the name of Maulsey Keener appears opposite No. 3894, upon the approved roll of citizens by blood of the Chickasaw Nation, and it is believed that your letter was in error in stating that she was enrolled opposite No. 3874.

    You are advised that Maulsey Keener may, if she insists, execute the affidavit to the birth of her child, Lillie May Keener, with the name of the father left blank.

                Respectfully,

                                      Chairman.

Applications for Enrollment of Chickasaw Newborn
Act of 1905   Volume VI

9-NB-484.

Muskogee, Indian Territory, August 17, 1905.

Maulsey Keener,
    Ada, Indian Territory.

Dear Madam:

    On May 20, 1905, the Commission to the Five Civilized Tribes addressed a letter to you requesting you to furnish this office with proper proof of the birth of your infant child Lillie May Keener and inclosed with said letter a blank for proof of birth. To such letter no response has been received.

    Referring to your affidavit executed December 7, 1904, and the affidavit of Artie Cupps, executed December 30, 1904, as to the birth of said child it appears that said child was born August 25, 1903, while in your affidavits of April 29, 1905, and the affidavit of the said Artie Cupps of April 28, 1905, the date of the birth of said child is given as August 25, 1904.

    In one set of affidavits you state that you are [sic] lawful wife of Jackson Reed, while in the other set [sic] davits it is alleged that you are the lawful wif [sic] Keener and that Stokes Kenner is the father [sic] child.

    In order that these discrepancies may be explained and corrected there is inclosed herewith another blank for proof of birth which you are requested to have filled out, executed and returned to this office in the inclosed envelope. In having the same executed be careful to see that all blank spaces are properly filled; that the correct date of the birth of said child is given, and that the notary public before whom the affidavits are sworn to attached his name and seal to each affidavit. In case any signature is by mark the same must be attested by two witnesses.

    Please give this matter your immediate attention.

    Respectfully,

    Acting Commissioner.

B C
Env.

Applications for Enrollment of Chickasaw Newborn
Act of 1905   Volume VI

REFER IN REPLY TO THE FOLLOWING:
7-NB-484

DEPARTMENT OF THE INTERIOR,
COMMISSIONER TO THE FIVE CIVILIZED TRIBES.

Muskogee, Indian Territory, September 7, 1905.

Maulsey Reed,
    Ada, Indian Territory.

Dear Madam:

    Receipt is hereby acknowledged of your affidavit and also that of Artie Cupps, the midwife, to the birth of your infant child, Lillie May Reed, born August 25, 1903, offered in support of the application for the enrollment of said child as a citizen by blood of the Chickasaw Nation. Said affidavits have been filed with the records in this case.

                        Respectfully,
                        Wm O. Beall
                        Acting Commissioner.

9-NB-484

Muskogee, Indian Territory, January 30, 1906.

James B. Vandiver,
    Roff, Indian Territory.

Dear Sir:

    Receipt is hereby acknowledged of your letter of January 26, 1906, in which you give information relative to Lillie Kinner[sic] and state that her mother Mulsey[sic] Kinner may have been enrolled as Mulsey King as her parents were Anderson and Susan King; that she has a brother Hayes King who is enrolled and the application for the enrollment of Lillie Kinner was made in the fall of 1904 as nearly as you can obtain information.

    In reply to your letter you are advised that the information contained therein has enabled this office to identify the mother of the child referred to in your letter as Maulsey Keener and her child to whom you refer has been enrolled as a new born citizen of the Chickasaw Nation under the name of Lillie May Reed and her enrollment as such was approved by the Secretary of the Interior, November 24, 1905.

                        Respectfully,

                        Acting Commissioner.

Applications for Enrollment of Chickasaw Newborn
Act of 1905 Volume VI

Chic. N.B - 485
(Jesse Keel
Born September 2, 1903)

BIRTH AFFIDAVIT.

DEPARTMENT OF THE INTERIOR.
COMMISSION TO THE FIVE CIVILIZED TRIBES.

IN RE APPLICATION FOR ENROLLMENT, as a citizen of the   Chickasaw   Nation, of   Jesse Keel   , born on the 2nd day of Sept , 1903

Name of Father: Sanders Keel   a citizen of the   Chickasaw   Nation.
Name of Mother: Belle Keel   a citizen of the .... Nation.

Postoffice   Lebanon I.T.

AFFIDAVIT OF MOTHER.

UNITED STATES OF AMERICA, Indian Territory, }
     Southern   DISTRICT.

I,   Belle Keel   , on oath state that I am 18   years of age and a citizen by ...., of the .... Nation; that I am the lawful wife of   Sanders Keel   , who is a citizen, by Blood   of the   Chickasaw   Nation; that a .... child was born to me on 2nd day of   September   , 1903; that said child has been named   Jesse Keel   , and was living March 4, 1905.

Belle Keel

Witnesses To Mark:
{

Subscribed and sworn to before me this 28 day of   Mar   , 1905

F J Hamilton
Notary Public.

AFFIDAVIT OF ATTENDING PHYSICIAN OR MID-WIFE.

UNITED STATES OF AMERICA, Indian Territory, }
     Southern   DISTRICT.

I,   JM Hanna   , a physician   , on oath state that I attended on Mrs.   Belle Keel   , wife of   Sanders Keel   on the 2nd day of   September   ,

Applications for Enrollment of Chickasaw Newborn
Act of 1905   Volume VI

1903; that there was born to her on said date a .... child; that said child was living March 4, 1905, and is said to have been named Jessie[sic] Keel

Dr. JM Hanna

Witnesses To Mark:
{

Subscribed and sworn to before me this 28 day of   Mar   , 1905

F J Hamilton
Notary Public.

ACKNOWLEDGMENT

INDIAN TERRITORY,   }
   SOUTHERN DISTRICT.   On this the 3^d day of   July   190 0 before me, the undersigned, a Notary Public in and for the Southern District, Indian Territory, appeared in person   Sanders Keel   to me personally well known to be the person whose name appears upon the within and foregoing instrument as the party grantor, and stated to me that he had executed the same for the consideration and purposes therein mentioned and set forth, and I do so certify.

   In testimony whereof, I have hereunto set my hand and seal of office as such Notary Public, the day and year above written.

F J Hamilton
SEAL   Notary Public. Southern District, Indian Territory.

Certificate of Marriage:

United States of America }
Indian Territory   } ss.
Southern District   }

I, J. F. Edington   A Minister of the Gospel. Do hereby certify that on the 13th day of September AD 1901 I did duly and according to law, as commanded in the foregoing License, Solemnize the Rite and publish the Banns of Matrimony between the parties therein named.

   Witness my hand this 13th day of September AD 1901.

My credentials are recorded in the office of the Clerk of the United States Court Indian Territory, Southern District at Ardmore Book C, Page 8.

J. F. Edington
A Minister of the Gospel

Applications for Enrollment of Chickasaw Newborn
Act of 1905   Volume VI

United States of America
Indian Territory } ss.
Southern District

   I Sanders Keel of Lebanon Ind Ter Do Solemnly swear that the above is a true and correct coppy[sic] of my marriage license & certificate with Belle Clarborn

       Signed. Sanders Keel

      Marriage License.

United States of America   (No 1226)
Indian Territory } ss.
Southern District

To any person authorized by law to Solemnize Marriage = Greeting:

 You are hereby commanded to Solemnize the Rite and publish the Banns of Matrimony between Mr. Sanders Keel of Lebanon in the Indian Territory aged 20 years, and Miss Belle Clarborn of Lebanon in the Indian Territory aged 18 years. According to law and do you officially sign and return this License to the parties there in named.

 Witness my hand and official seal this 12th day of September AD 1901

       C.M. Campbell
       Clerk of the United States Court.

          9--979.

    Muskogee, Indian Territory, May 4, 1905.

Sanders Keel,
 Lebanon, Indian Territory.

Dear Sir:

 Receipt is hereby acknowledged of the affidavits of Belle Keel and Dr. J. M. Hanna to the birth of Jessie Keel, daughter of Sanders and Belle Keel, September 2, 1903, and the same have been filed with our records as an application for the enrollment of said child.

      Respectfully,

        Chairman.

Applications for Enrollment of Chickasaw Newborn
Act of 1905   Volume VI

9-NB-485.

Muskogee, Indian Territory, May 19, 1905.

Sandus[sic] Keel,
    Lebanon, Indian Territory.

Dear Sir:

    Referring to the application for the enrollment of your infant child, Jesse Keel, born September 2, 1903, it is noted that the applicant claims through you.

    If this is correct it will be necessary for you to file with the Commission either the original or a certified copy of the license and certificate of your marriage to the applicant's mother, Belle Keel.

                          Respectfully,

                                    Chairman.

9-NB-485

Muskogee, Indian Territory, July 6, 1905.

Sanders Keel,
    Lebanon, Indian Territory.

Dear Sir:

    On May 19, 1905, the Commission to the Five Civilized Tribes addressed you a communication in which you were requested to furnish either the original or a certified copy of the license and certificate of marriage of yourself and Belle Keel to be filed in support of the application for the enrollment of your infant child, Jesse Keel, born September 2, 1903, to which you have not replied.

    You are advised that no further action can be taken relative to the enrollment of said child until the can be be[sic] taken in the matter of the application for the enrollment of said child, until the evidence requested is supplied, and you should give this matter your immediate attention.

                          Respectfully,

                                   Commissioner.

Applications for Enrollment of Chickasaw Newborn
Act of 1905   Volume VI

9-NB-485

Muskogee, Indian Territory, July 10, 1905.

Sanders Keel,
    Lebabon[sic], Indian Territory.

Dear Sir:

    Receipt is hereby acknowledged of a certified copy of the marriage license and certificate between yourself and Belle Clarborn which you offer in support of the application for the enrollment of your child Jesse Keel as a citizen by blood of the Chickasaw Nation and the same has been filed with the record in this case.

                  Respectfully,

                              Commissioner.

Chic. N.B - 486
    (Jewell Benton
    Born December 27, 1904)

DEPARTMENT OF THE INTERIOR,
COMMISSIONER TO THE FIVE CIVILIZED TRIBES,
CHOCTAW LAND OFFICE.
---:---
Atoka, Indian Territory, September 14, 1905.
---:---

    In the matter of the enrollment of Jewell Benton, Chickasaw By Blood New Born, Card No. 486, Approved Roll No. 395.

    Earnest Benton, being first duly sworn, testified as follows:

EXAMINATION BY THE COMMISSIONER,

Q. What is your name ?
A. Earnest Benton.
Q. What is your postoffice address ?
A. Owl.
Q. How old are you ?
A. 29.

Applications for Enrollment of Chickasaw Newborn
Act of 1905   Volume VI

Q. What is the name of your father?
A. Davis Benton.
Q. What is the name of your mother?
A. Louisa Benton.
Q. Are you a recognized and enrolled citizen by blood of the Chickasaw Nation?
A. Yes, sir.

Witness is identified on Chickasaw Field Care No. 320, Approved Roll No. 1020.

Q. Are [sic] the father of Jewell Benton?
A. Yes, sir.
Q. When was Jewell Benton born?
A. Last December, the 27th.
Q. What year?
A. 1904.
Q. What is the name of the mother of Jewell Benton?
A. Miggey Benton - was Miggey Miller.
Q. Is Miggey Miller a citizen of either the Choctaw or Chickasaw Nation?
A. She was a court claimant in the Choctaw Nation.
Q. Was she ever enrolled as a citizen of the Choctaw Nation?
A. They never been approved, but they were court claimants.
Q. What was he name of Miggey Benton's father?
A. Henry Miller.
Q. What was the name of her mother?
A. Sallie Miller.
Q. When were you married to Miggey Miller?
A. The 12th day of October, 1904.
Q. You present here a certified copy of marriage license and certificate issued to earnest Benton and Miss Miggey Miller, are younthe[sic] identical person named in this marriage certificate as Earnest Benton?
A. Yes, sir.
Q. And is your wife the same person whose name appears in here as Miggey Miller?
A. Yes, sir.
Q. And she is the mother of your infant child, Jewell Benton?
A. Yes, sir.
Q. Is Miggey Miller your second wife?
Q. Yes, sir.
Q. What was the name of your first wife?
A. Maggie Benton.
Q. What was the name of her father?
A. James Lee.
Q. What was the name of her mother?
A. I don't know. She was an orphan girl when I married her.
Q. Is your former wife, Maggie Benton, dead?
A. Yes, sir.
Q. Was she dead before you married Miggey Miller?
A. Yes, sir.

Applications for Enrollment of Chickasaw Newborn
Act of 1905   Volume VI

Q Your former wife, Maggie Benton, is not the mother of Jewell Benton?
A. No, sir.
Q. Did you fill out affidavits relative to the birth of Jewell Benton and forward them to the Commission?
A. Yes, sir.
Q. Did your wife, Miggey Benton, sign one of these affidavits?
A. Yes, sir.
Q. Do you know how she spelled her name when she signed the affidavit?
A. She put it down Miggey Benton.
Q. Do you know how she spelled the name, Miggey?
A. No, sir.
Q. You state that Maggie Benton, who was the daughter of James Lee, was not the mother of Jewell Benton?
A. No, sir.
Q. But the mother of Jewell Benton is Miggey Benton, formerly Miggey Miller, and she is not an enrolled citizen of the Choctaw or Chickasaw Nations?
A. No, sir.
Q. You have not heretofore furnished the Commission nor the Commissioner to the Five Civilized Tribes with a certified copy of your marriage license and certificate to your present wife, Miggey Benton?
A. No.

Miggey Benton, being first duly sworn, testified as follows:

Q. What is your name?
A. Miggey Benton.
Q. How old are you?
A. 18.
Q. What is your postoffice address?
A. Owl.
Q. Are you the wife of Earnest Benton?
A. Yes, sir.
Q. Is he a recognized and enrolled citizen by blood of the Chickasaw Nation?
A. Yes, sir.
Q. When were you married to Earnest Benton?
A. October 12th, 1904.
Q. Are you the mother of Jewell Benton?
A. Yes, sir.
Q. And is Earnest Benton the father of this child?
A. Yes, sir.
Q. Did you know Earnest Benton's former wife?
A. No, sir.
Q. Do you know what his for wife's name was?
A. Maggie Benton.
Q. Do you know whether she's dead?
A. Yes, sir; she's dead.

Applications for Enrollment of Chickasaw Newborn
Act of 1905   Volume VI

Q. Was she dead before you married Earnest Benton?
A. Yes, sir.
Q. Maggie Benton, the former wife of Earnest Benton, is not the mother of Jewell Benton?
A. No, sir.
Q. You are the mother of this child?
A. Yes, sir.
Q. Are you a citizen of either the Choctaw or Chickasaw Nations[sic]?
A. Choctaw.
Q. Have you been finally enrolled as a citizen of the Chickasaw Nation the Choctaw Nation?
A. No.
Q. Have you an application now pending before the Commission to the Five Civilized Tribes for enrollment as a citizen of the Choctaw Nation?
A. I don't know whether I have or not.
Q. You never have received notice that you have been approved by the Secretary of the Interior?
A. No, sir.
Q. Are you the same person referred to in this certified copy of marriage license and certificate presented by your husband as Miggey Miller?
A. Yes, sir.
Q. Your maiden name was Miggey Miller?
A. Yes, sir.
Q. When was Jewell Benton born?
A. 27th day of December, 1904.
Q. Do you know when Maggie Benton, the former wife of your husband, died?
A. She died in October.
Q. What year?
A. I don't know.
Q. She died though before you married Earnest Benton?
A. Yes, sir.
Q. And before the birth of Jewell Benton?
A. Yes, sir.
Q. If the records of the Commissioner show that Maggie Benton is the mother of Jewell Benton is that a mistake?
A. Yes, sir.
Q. Did you sign an affidavit relative to the birth of Jewell Benton and send to the Commission to the Five Civilized Tribes at Muskogee?
A. Yes, sir.
Q. How did you sign that affidavit?
A. Miggey Benton.

Wm. L. Martin, stenographer to the Commissioner to the Five Civilized Tribes, upon oath states that the above and foregoing is a full, true and correct transcript of his stenographic notes taken in said cause on said date.

Applications for Enrollment of Chickasaw Newborn
Act of 1905   Volume VI

W^mL. Martin

Subscribed and sworn to before me this the 25th day of September, 1905.

W.H. Angell
Notary Public.

BIRTH AFFIDAVIT.

DEPARTMENT OF THE INTERIOR.
COMMISSION TO THE FIVE CIVILIZED TRIBES.

IN RE APPLICATION FOR ENROLLMENT, as a citizen of the Chickasaw Nation, of Jewell Benton , born on the 27 day of Dec , 1904

Name of Father: Earnest Benton   a citizen of the Chickasaw Nation.
Name of Mother: Miggie[sic] M. Benton   a citizen of the U.S. ~~Nation~~.

Postoffice Owl I.T.

AFFIDAVIT OF MOTHER.

UNITED STATES OF AMERICA, Indian Territory, }
Central   DISTRICT. }

I, Miggie M. Benton , on oath state that I am 17 years of age and a citizen by ——— of the U. S. ~~Nation~~; that I am the lawful wife of Ernest[sic] Benton , who is a citizen, by Blood of the Chickasaw Nation; that a Female child was born to me on 27 day of Dec , 1904; that said child has been named Jewell Benton , and was living March 4, 1905.

Miggie M Benton

Witnesses To Mark:
{

Subscribed and sworn to before me this 29 day of April , 1905

R.T. Breedlove
Notary Public.

Applications for Enrollment of Chickasaw Newborn
Act of 1905 Volume VI

AFFIDAVIT OF ATTENDING PHYSICIAN OR MID-WIFE.

UNITED STATES OF AMERICA, Indian Territory,
Central   DISTRICT.

I, J.H. Arnold, a Physician, on oath state that I attended on Mrs. Miggie M. Benton, wife of Ernest Benton on the 27 day of Dec, 1904; that there was born to her on said date a Female child; that said child was living March 4, 1905, and is said to have been named Jewell Benton

J.H. Arnold, M.D.

Witnesses To Mark:

Subscribed and sworn to before me this 29 day of April, 1905

R.T. Breedlove
Notary Public.

No. 2299

Certificate of Record of Marriages.

United States of America,
The Indian Territory, sct.
Central *District.*

I, E. J. Fannin   Clerk of the United States Court, in the Indian Territory and District aforesaid, do hereby CERTIFY, that the License for and Certificate of the Marriage of

Mr. Earnest Benton   and
M   Miggey Miller   was

filed in my office in said Territory and District the 1 day of Nov A.D., 190 4, and duly recorded in Book 2 of Marriage Record, Page 532

WITNESS my hand and Seal of said Court, at Atoka this 14" day of Sept A.D. 190 5

E.J. Fannin   Clerk.
By J.H. Catlin   Deputy.

P. O.   Owl

**Applications for Enrollment of Chickasaw Newborn
Act of 1905   Volume VI**

No. 2299

MARRIAGE LICENSE

United States of America,   The Indian Territory,
                                                     Central   DISTRICT, SS.

To any Person Authorized by Law to Solemnize Marriage, Greeting:

You are hereby commanded to Solemnize the Rite and publish the Banns of Matrimony between Mr. Earnest Benton
of Owl *in the Indian Territory, aged* 28 *years,
and M* iss Miggey Miller *of* Owl
in the Indian Territory., aged 17 *years, according to law, and do you officially sign and return this License to the parties therein named.*

WITNESS *my hand and official seal, this* 12 *day
of* Oct   *A. D. 190* 4

(Seal)

E.J. Fannin
Clerk of the United States Court.

J.H. Catlin   Deputy

Certificate of Marriage.

United States of America,
  The Indian Territory, } ss.
  Central   District.   I,   J.H. Buzbee

a ...., *do hereby certify, that on the* 19 *day
of* October *A. D. 190* 4 *, I did, duly and according to law, as commanded in the foregoing License, solemnize the Rite and publish the Banns of Matrimony between the parties therein named.*

Witness my hand, this 19 *day of* October *A. D. 190* 4

*My credentials are recorded in the office of the Clerk of
the United States Court in the Indian Territory,
Central District, Book* A *, Page* 78   *a* ....
                          Ardmore

Note—This License and Certificate of Marriage must be returned to the Office of the Clerk of the United States Court of the Indian Territory, from whence it was issued, within sixty days from the date thereof, or the party to whom the License was issued will be liable in the amount of the One Hundred Dollars ($100.00).

Applications for Enrollment of Chickasaw Newborn
Act of 1905   Volume VI

9-320.

Muskogee, Indian Territory, May 4, 1905.

Ernest Benton,
    Owl, Indian Territory.

Dear Sir:

    Receipt is hereby acknowledged of the affidavits of Miggie M. Benton and J. H. Arnold to the birth of Jewell Benton, daughter of Ernest and Miggie M. Benton, December 27, 1904, and the same have been filed with our records as an application for the enrollment of said child.

    Respectfully,

    Chairman.

9-NB-486.

COPY.

Muskogee, Indian Territory, September 30, 1905

Chief Clerk,
    Chickasaw Land Office,
        Ardmore, Indian Territory.

Dear Sir:

    Chickasaw new born card No. 486 has been corrected so that it appears therefrom that the mother of Jewell Benton, roll number 395, is Miggie M. Benton, a noncitizen, instead of Maggie Benton, roll number IW 544.

    You are requested to correct the duplicate card in your possession in like manner.

    Respectfully,

    SIGNED   *Tams Bixby*
    Commissioner.

Applications for Enrollment of Chickasaw Newborn
Act of 1905 Volume VI

Chic. N.B - 487
(Ruby Isabelle Watkins
Born October 5, 1902)
(Henry Furman Watkins
Born August 11, 1904)

BIRTH AFFIDAVIT.

DEPARTMENT OF THE INTERIOR.
COMMISSION TO THE FIVE CIVILIZED TRIBES.

IN RE APPLICATION FOR ENROLLMENT, as a citizen of the Chickasaw Nation, of Ruby Isabelle Watkins , born on the 5th day of Oct , 1902

Name of Father: W. R. Watkins   a citizen of the Chickasaw Nation.
Name of Mother: Lou Catherine Watkins   a citizen of the Chickasaw Nation.

Postoffice   Petersburg

AFFIDAVIT OF MOTHER.

UNITED STATES OF AMERICA, Indian Territory,
Southern   DISTRICT.

I, Mrs Lou Catherine Watkins , on oath state that I am Twenty three years of age and a citizen by blood , of the Chickasaw Nation; that I am the lawful wife of W. R. Watkins , who is a citizen, by .... of the Chickasaw Nation; that a .... child was born to me on 5th day of Oct , 1902; that said child has been named Ruby Isabelle , and was living March 4, 1905.

                         Lou Catherine Watkins

Witnesses To Mark:
   { Robt E. Lee
     Ola Halloway

Subscribed and sworn to before me this 1st day of April , 1905

                         Ola Halloway
                         Notary Public.

Applications for Enrollment of Chickasaw Newborn
Act of 1905   Volume VI

AFFIDAVIT OF ATTENDING PHYSICIAN OR MID-WIFE.

UNITED STATES OF AMERICA, Indian Territory,
Southern DISTRICT.

I, Dr. Walter Hardy, a Physician, on oath state that I attended on Mrs. Lou Catherine Watkins, wife of W.R. Watkins on the 5th day of Oct, 1902; that there was born to her on said date a female child; that said child was living March 4, 1905, and is said to have been named Ruby Isabelle

W. Hardy M.D.

Witnesses To Mark:
{ Robt E Lee

Subscribed and sworn to before me this 1st day of April, 1905

Ola Halloway
Notary Public.

BIRTH AFFIDAVIT.

DEPARTMENT OF THE INTERIOR.
COMMISSION TO THE FIVE CIVILIZED TRIBES.

IN RE APPLICATION FOR ENROLLMENT, as a citizen of the Chickasaw Nation, of Henry Furman Watkins, born on the 11th day of August, 1904

Name of Father: W. R. Watkins   a citizen of the Chickasaw Nation.
Name of Mother: Lou Catherine Watkins   a citizen of the Chickasaw Nation.

Postoffice   Petersburg Ind Ter

AFFIDAVIT OF MOTHER.

UNITED STATES OF AMERICA, Indian Territory,
Southern DISTRICT.

I, Mrs Lou Catherine Watkins, on oath state that I am Twenty Three years of age and a citizen by blood, of the Chickasaw Nation; that I am the lawful wife of W. R. Watkins, who is a citizen, by blood of the Chickasaw Nation; that a male child was born to me on 11th day of August, 1904; that said child has been named Henry Furman Watkins, and was living March 4, 1905.

Lou Catherine Watkins

Applications for Enrollment of Chickasaw Newborn
Act of 1905   Volume VI

Witnesses To Mark:
{ Robt E. Lee
{ Ola Halloway

    Subscribed and sworn to before me this 1st   day of   April   , 1905

                        Ola Halloway
                        Notary Public.

AFFIDAVIT OF ATTENDING PHYSICIAN OR MID-WIFE.

UNITED STATES OF AMERICA, Indian Territory, }
Southern   DISTRICT.   }

    I,   Mrs Lizzie Wells   , a Wet Nurse   , on oath state that I attended on Mrs.   Lou Catherine Watkins   , wife of   W.R. Watkins   on the 11th day of August   , 1904; that there was born to her on said date a   male   child; that said child was living March 4, 1905, and is said to have been named   Henry Furman Watkins

                        Mrs Lizzie Wels

Witnesses To Mark:
{ *(Name Illegible)*

    Subscribed and sworn to before me this   14th   day of   April   , 1905

                        L. L. Lee
                        Notary Public.

                Muskogee, Indian Territory, April 21, 1905.

W. R. Watkins,
    Petersburg, Indian Territory.

Dear Sir:

    Receipt is hereby acknowledged of the affidavits of Lou Catherine Watkins and W. Hardy to the birth of Ruby Isabelle Watkins, daughter of W. R. and Lou Catherine Watkins, October 5, 1902; also affidavits of Lou Catherine Watkins and Mrs Lizzie Wells to the birth of Henry Furman Watkins, son of W R. and Lou Catherine Watkins, August 11, 1904.

    It is stated in the affidavit of the mother that she is a citizen by blood of the Chickasaw Nation. If this is correct you are requested to state the name under which she was enrolled, the names of her parents, and if she has selected an allotment of the lands

Applications for Enrollment of Chickasaw Newborn
Act of 1905   Volume VI

of the Choctaw or Chickasaw Nation please give her roll number as it appears upon her allotment certificate.

>Respectfully,
>
>Chairman.

>Petersburg, I. T. April 30, 1905.

Commission to the Five Civilized Tribes,
   Muskogee, I. T.

This is to certify that I Lula Catherine Watkins am a Chickasaw by blood and on the roll as Lulu Catherine Bourland which was my maiden name. The daughter of William Howard Bourland. I was married to W. R. Watkins Jr., July 23, 1901. My certificate numvers[sic] are Homestead No. 2044.

   Exclusive of a homestead No. 2182.

Roll number 4381.
Filed July 23, 1903.

>Respectfully,
>Mrs. Lulu Catherine Watkins.

Chic. N.B - 488
   (Susan Johnson
   Born October 16, 1904)

BIRTH AFFIDAVIT.   *No. 9*

DEPARTMENT OF THE INTERIOR.
COMMISSION TO THE FIVE CIVILIZED TRIBES.

IN RE APPLICATION FOR ENROLLMENT, as a citizen of the   Chickasaw   Nation, of   Susan Johnson   , born on the 16th day of   Oct   , 1904

Name of Father: Thomas Johnson   a citizen of the   Chickasaw   Nation.
Name of Mother: Louisa Johnson   a citizen of the   Chickasaw   Nation.

>Postoffice   Conway IT

Applications for Enrollment of Chickasaw Newborn
Act of 1905   Volume VI

AFFIDAVIT OF MOTHER.

UNITED STATES OF AMERICA, Indian Territory, }
16th   DISTRICT.

I,   Louisa Johnson   , on oath state that I am   20   years of age and a citizen by   Blood   , of the   Chickasaw   Nation; that I am the lawful wife of Thomas Johnson   , who is a citizen, by   Blood   of the   Chickasaw   Nation; that a   female   child was born to me on   16th   day of   Oct   , 1904, that said child has been named   Susan   , and is now living.

                                          her
                                  Louisa x Johnson
Witnesses To Mark: mark
{ W N Allison
{ G.F. Byrd

Subscribed and sworn to before me this   19th   day of   Jan   , 1905.

                                  W N Allison
                                  Notary Public.

AFFIDAVIT OF ATTENDING PHYSICIAN OR MID-WIFE.

UNITED STATES OF AMERICA, Indian Territory, }
16th   DISTRICT.

I,   Nancy Johnson   , a   Midwife   , on oath state that I attended on Mrs.   Louisa Johnson   , wife of   Thomas Johnson   on the   16th   day of Oct , 1904; that there was born to her on said date a   female   child; that said child is now living and is said to have been named   Susan

                                  her
                                Nancy x Johnson
Witnesses To Mark: mark
{ W N Allison
{ G.F. Byrd

Subscribed and sworn to before me this   19th   day of   Jan   , 1905.

                                  W N Allison
                                  Notary Public.

Applications for Enrollment of Chickasaw Newborn
Act of 1905 Volume VI

BIRTH AFFIDAVIT.

DEPARTMENT OF THE INTERIOR.
COMMISSION TO THE FIVE CIVILIZED TRIBES.

IN RE APPLICATION FOR ENROLLMENT, as a citizen of the Chickasaw Nation, of Susan Johnson, born on the 16 day of October, 1904

Name of Father: Thompson Johnson   a citizen of the Chickasaw Nation.
Name of Mother: Louise Johnson Sealey   a citizen of the Chickasaw Nation.

Postoffice   Conway, I. T.

AFFIDAVIT OF MOTHER.

UNITED STATES OF AMERICA, Indian Territory,
Southern District   DISTRICT.

I, Louise Johnson, on oath state that I am 26 years of age and a citizen by Blood, of the Chickasaw Nation; that I am the lawful wife of Thompson Johnson, who is a citizen, by Blood of the Chickasaw Nation; that a girl child was born to me on 16 day of October, 1904; that said child has been named Susan Johnson, and was living March 4, 1905.

                 her
         Louise x Johnson
Witnesses To Mark: mark
   B.P. Ford
   Henry Shields

Subscribed and sworn to before me this 27 day of April, 1905

       B.P. Ford
       Notary Public.

AFFIDAVIT OF ATTENDING PHYSICIAN OR MID-WIFE.

UNITED STATES OF AMERICA, Indian Territory,
Southern   DISTRICT.

I, Thompson Johnson, a father, on oath state that I attended on Mrs. Louise Johnson, wife of Thompson Johnson on the 16 day of October, 1904; that there was born to her on said date a girl child; that said child was living March 4, 1905, and is said to have been named Susan Johnson

       Thompson Johnson

Applications for Enrollment of Chickasaw Newborn
Act of 1905 Volume VI

Witnesses To Mark:
{ B.P. Ford
 Henry Shields

Subscribed and sworn to before me this 27 day of   April   , 1905

B.P. Ford
Notary Public.

BIRTH AFFIDAVIT.

DEPARTMENT OF THE INTERIOR.
COMMISSION TO THE FIVE CIVILIZED TRIBES.

IN RE APPLICATION FOR ENROLLMENT, as a citizen of the   Chickasaw   Nation, of   Susan Johnson   , born on the 16th day of October   , 1904

Name of Father: Thompson Johnson   a citizen of the Chickasaw Nation.
Name of Mother: Louisa Johnson   a citizen of the Chickasaw Nation.

Postoffice   Conway Ind Ter

AFFIDAVIT OF MOTHER.

UNITED STATES OF AMERICA, Indian Territory, }
Central   DISTRICT.

I, Louisa Johnson   , on oath state that I am 26 years of age and a citizen by   Blood   , of the   Chickasaw   Nation; that I am the lawful wife of Thompson Johnson   , who is a citizen, by Blood   of the   Chickasaw Nation; that a   Female   child was born to me on 16th   day of October   , 1904; that said child has been named   Susan Johnson   , and was living March 4, 1905.

Louisa x Johnson
Witnesses To Mark: mark
{ Albert Campbell
 Francis Johnson

Subscribed and sworn to before me this 22 day of February   , 1906

W.W. Jones
My Com Exp Jan 8 1907   Notary Public.

Applications for Enrollment of Chickasaw Newborn
Act of 1905   Volume VI

AFFIDAVIT OF ATTENDING PHYSICIAN OR MID-WIFE.

UNITED STATES OF AMERICA, Indian Territory, }
Central   DISTRICT.

I, Nancy Johnson, a Indian Doctor, on oath state that I attended on Mrs. Louisa Johnson, wife of Thompson Johnson on the 16th day of October, 1904; that there was born to her on said date a Female child; that said child was living March 4, 1905, and is said to have been named Susan Johnson

                                   her
                        Nancy x Johnson
Witnesses To Mark: mark
 { Albert Campbell
   Francis Johnson

Subscribed and sworn to before me this 22 day of February, 1906

                        W.W. Jones
My Com Exp Jan 8 1907   Notary Public.

9--1477.

Muskogee, Indian Territory, May 4, 1905.

Thompson Johnson,
     Conway, Indian Territory.

Dear Sir:

     Receipt is hereby acknowledged of the affidavits of Leuise[sic] Johnson and Thompson Johnson to the birth of Susan Johnson, daughter of Thompson and Leuise Johnson, October 16, 1904, and the same have been filed with our records as an application for the enrollment of said child.

                    Respectfully,

                                 Chairman.

Applications for Enrollment of Chickasaw Newborn
Act of 1905 Volume VI

9-NB-488.

Muskogee, Indian Territory, May 20, 1905.

Thompson Johnson,
    Conway, Indian Territory.

Dear Sir:

    There is enclosed you herewith for execution application for the enrollment of your infant child, Susan Johnson, born October 16, 1904.

    It is noted from the affidavits heretofore filed with the Commission that you, the father of the above mentioned applicant, executed the affidavit intended for the attending physician or mid-wife. Before this matter can be finally determined it will be necessary for you to file in this office the affidavits of two disinterested persons, who have actual knowledge of the facts that the child was born, the date of her birth; that she was living on March 4, 1905, and that Louisa Johnson is her mother.

    In having these affidavits executed care should be exercised to see that all names are written in full, as they appear in the body of the affidavit, and in the event that either of the persons signing the affidavit are unable to write, signatures by mark must be attested by two witnesses. Each affidavit must be executed before a Notary Public and the notarial seal and signature of the officer must be attached to each separate affidavit.

    Respectfully,

    Chairman.

VR 20-5.

Muskogee, Indian Territory, June 9, 1905.

Thomas Johnson,
    Conway, Indian Territory.

Dear Sir:

    Receipt is hereby acknowledged of the affidavits of Louisa Johnson and Nancy Johnson to the birth of Susan Johnson daughter of Thomas and Louisa Johnson, October 16, 1904.

    It is stated in the affidavit of the mother that she is a citizen by blood of the Chickasaw Nation. If this is correct you are requested to state the name under which she was enrolled, the names of her parents and if she has selected an allotment of the lands of the Choctaw or Chickasaw Nation please give her number as it appears upon her allotment certificate.

Applications for Enrollment of Chickasaw Newborn
Act of 1905   Volume VI

                                        Respectfully,

                                                               Chairman.

9-NB-488.

                                Muskogee, Indian Territory, August 17, 1905.

Thompson Johnson,
    Conway, Indian Territory.

Dear Sir:

    On May 20, 1905 the Commission to the Five Civilized Tribes addressed a letter to you requesting you to furnish this office with proper proof of the birth of your child Susan Johnson and inclosed herewith a blank for proof of birth of said child.

    It appears from the affidavits heretofore filed with the Commission to the Five Civilized Tribes that you, the father of the above named child, executed the affidavit intended for the attending physician or midwife.

    Before the matter of the enrollment of said child can be finally determined it will be necessary for you to file with this office the affidavit of the attending physician or midwife who attended upon your wife at the birth of said child, but in the event that there was no one in attendance when said child was born it will be necessary for you to furnish this office the affidavits of two disinterested persons as to the birth of said child. Said affidavits of two disinterested persons must set forth said child's name, the date of her birth, the names of her parents and whether or not she was living on March 4, 1905.

                                  Respectfully,

                                                 Acting Commissioner.

B C
Env.

Applications for Enrollment of Chickasaw Newborn
Act of 1905   Volume VI

9-NB-488

Muskogee, Indian Territory, November 28, 1905.

Thompson Johnson,
    Conway, Indian Territory.

Dear Sir:

    You are again advised that it will be necessary for you to forward the affidavit of the attending physician or midwife to the birth of your child Susan Johnson, or in the event there was no one in attendance at the birth of said child, the affidavits of two disinterested persons as to her birth, the date of her birth, the names of her parents, and whether or not she was living March 4, 1905.

    This matter should receive your immediate attention as until evidence requested has been furnished no action can be taken in the matter of the enrollment of your child.

    Respectfully,

    Acting Commissioner.

9-NB-488

Muskogee, Indian Territory, February 13, 1906.

Thompson Johnson,
    Conway, Indian Territory.

Dear Sir:

    In the matter of the application for the enrollment of your child, Susan Johnson, you are advised that you should forward at once the affidavit of the physician or mid wife in attendance at her birth, or in the event no one was in attendance, the affidavits of two disinterested persons, giving the date of her birth, the names of her parents and whether or not she was living on March 4, 1905.

    This matter should receive your immediate attention.

    Respectfully,

    Acting Commissioner.

Applications for Enrollment of Chickasaw Newborn
Act of 1905   Volume VI

9-NB-488

Muskogee, Indian Territory, February 27, 1906.

Thompson Johnson,
    Conway, Indian Territory.

Dear Sir:

    Receipt is hereby acknowledged of the affidavits of Louisa Johnson and Nancy Johnson to the birth of Susan Johnson, October 16, 1904, and the same have been filed with the record in the matter of the enrollment of said child.

                        Respectfully,

                        Acting Commissioner.

Chic. N.B - 489
    (Ceral Reynolds
    Born August 14, 1903)

DEPARTMENT OF THE INTERIOR,
COMMISSION TO THE FIVE CIVILIZED TRIBES.

    Record in the matter of the application for enrollment as a citizen by blood of the Chickasaw Nation of:

        CERAL REYNOLDS   9-NB-489

Applications for Enrollment of Chickasaw Newborn
Act of 1905   Volume VI

DEPARTMENT OF THE INTERIOR.
COMMISSION TO THE FIVE CIVILIZED TRIBES.

In the matter of the death of   Carial[sic] Reynolds a citizen of the   Chickasaw   Nation, who formerly resided at or near   Kemp   , Ind. Ter., and died on the   16   day of   May   , 1904

AFFIDAVIT OF RELATIVE.

UNITED STATES OF AMERICA, Indian Territory, }
Central   DISTRICT.

I,   Vina Lee Reynolds   , on oath state that I am   24   years of age and a citizen by ...., of the   United States   Nation; that my postoffice address is   Kemp   , Ind. Ter.; that I am   Mother   of   Carial Reynolds   who was a citizen, by blood   , of the   Chickasaw   Nation and that said   Carial Reynolds   died on the   16   day of   May   , 1904

Witnesses To Mark:
{

Vina Lee Reynolds

Subscribed and sworn to before me this   2   day of   June   , 1906

O.R. Fowler
Notary Public.

AFFIDAVIT OF ACQUAINTANCE.

UNITED STATES OF AMERICA, Indian Territory, }
Central   DISTRICT.

I,   Permelia Skinner   , on oath state that I am   25   years of age, and a citizen by blood   of the   Chickasaw   Nation; that my postoffice address is   Kemp   , Ind. Ter.; that I was personally acquainted with   Carial Reynolds   who was a citizen, by blood   , of the   Chickasaw   Nation; and that said   Carial Reynolds   died on the   16   day of   May   , 1904

Permelia Skinner
Witnesses To Mark:
{

Subscribed and sworn to before me this   2   day of   June   , 1906

O.R. Fowler
Notary Public.

Applications for Enrollment of Chickasaw Newborn
Act of 1905   Volume VI

BIRTH AFFIDAVIT.

DEPARTMENT OF THE INTERIOR.
COMMISSION TO THE FIVE CIVILIZED TRIBES.

IN RE APPLICATION FOR ENROLLMENT, as a citizen of the Chickasaw Nation, of Ceral Reyonlds[sic], born on the 14 day of August, 1903

Name of Father: Frank Reynolds   a citizen of the Chickasaw Nation.
Name of Mother: Vina Lee Reynolds   a citizen of the Chickasaw Nation.

Postoffice   Kemp

AFFIDAVIT OF MOTHER.

UNITED STATES OF AMERICA, Indian Territory, }
Central   DISTRICT. }

I, Vina Lee Reynolds, on oath state that I am 24 years of age and a citizen by intermarrage[sic], of the Chickasaw Nation; that I am the lawful wife of Frank Reynolds, who is a citizen, by Blood of the Chickasaw Nation; that a male child was born to me on 14 day of August, 1904, that said child has been named Ceral, [sic] and is now living.

Vina Lee Reynolds

Witnesses To Mark:
{ Permelia Skinner
{ W. L. Skinner

Subscribed and sworn to before me this 19 day of January, 1905.

S.M. Mead
Notary Public.

AFFIDAVIT OF ATTENDING PHYSICIAN OR MID-WIFE.

UNITED STATES OF AMERICA, Indian Territory, }
                           DISTRICT. }

I, ..., a ...., on oath state that I attended on Mrs. ...., wife of .... on the .... day of ...., 1......... ; that there was born to her on said date a .... child; that said child is now living and is said to have been named ....

Applications for Enrollment of Chickasaw Newborn
Act of 1905   Volume VI

Witnesses To Mark:
{ Permelia Skinner
{ W.L. Skinner

Subscribed and sworn to before me this............day of................................., 190.....

....
Notary Public.

W.J.
9-NB-489.

DEPARTMENT OF THE INTERIOR,
COMMISSION TO THE FIVE CIVILIZED TRIBES.

In the matter of the application for the enrollment of Ceral Reynolds as a citizen by blood of the Chickasaw Nation.

---oOo---

It appears from the record herein that on April 26, 1905, there was received by the Commission application for the enrollment of Ceral Reynolds as a citizen by blood of the Chickasaw Nation.

It further appears from the record herein and the records of the Commission that the applicant was born August 14, 1903; that he is a son of Frank Reynolds, a recognized and enrolled citizen by blood of the Chickasaw Nation whose name appears as number 3426 upon the final roll of citizens by blood of the Chickasaw Nation, approved by the Secretary of the Interior December 12, 1902, and Vina Lee Reynolds, a citizen of the United States; and that said applicant died on May 16, 1904.

The Act of Congress approved March 3, 1905 (Public No. 212) among other things provides:

"That the Commission to the Five Civilized Tribes is authorized for sixty days after the date of the approval of this act to receive and consider applications for enrollment of children born subsequent to September twenty-fifth, nineteen hundred and two, and prior to March fourth, nineteen hundred and five, and who were living on said latter date, to citizens by blood of the Choctaw and Chickasaw tribes of Indians whose enrollment has been approved by the Secretary of the Interior prior to the date of the approval of this act; and to enroll and make allotments to such children."

It is, therefore, hereby ordered that the application for the enrollment of Ceral Reynolds as a citizen by blood of the Chickasaw Nation be dismissed in accordance with the order of the Commission of March 31, 1905.

COMMISSION TO THE FIVE CIVILIZED TRIBES,

Applications for Enrollment of Chickasaw Newborn
Act of 1905   Volume VI

Tams Bixby
Commissioner.

Muskogee, Indian Territory.
JUN 28 1905

9-NB-489.

Muskogee, Indian Territory, May 20, 1905.

Frank Reynolds,
    Kemp, Indian Territory.

Dear Sir:

    Referring to the application for the enrollment of your infant child, Ceral Reynolds, born August 14, 1903, it appears from the affidavit of the mother, heretofore filed in this office, that the applicant is dead.

    If this is correct you will kindly execute the enclosed proof of death and return to this office.

    In having these affidavits executed care should be exercised to see that all names are written in full, as they appear in the body of the affidavit, and in the event that either of the persons signing the affidavit are unable to write, signatures by mark must be attested by two witnesses. Each affidavit must be executed before a Notary Public and the notarial seal and signature of the officer must be attached to each separate affidavit.

Respectfully,

SIGNED *Tams Bixby*
Chairman.

Encl. D-C.

9-NB-489

Muskogee, Indian Territory, June 7, 1905.

Vina Lee Reynolds,
    Kemp, Indian Territory.

Dear Madam:

    Receipt is hereby acknowledged of your affidavit and the affidavit of Permelia Skinner to the death of your child Cerial[sic] Reynolds as citizen by blood of the

Applications for Enrollment of Chickasaw Newborn
Act of 1905   Volume VI

Chickasaw Nation which occurred May 16, 1904, and the same have been filed as evidence of death of the above named child.

                        Respectfully,

                                  Commissioner in Charge.

9-NB-489

Muskogee, Indian Territory, June 22, 1905.

Frank Reynolds,   **COPY.**
    Kemp, Indian Territory.

Dear Sir:

    Inclosed herewith you will find a copy of the order of this Commission, dated June 22, 1905, dismissing the application for the enrollment of your infant child, Ceral Reynolds as a citizen by blood of the Chickasaw Nation.

                      Respectfully,
                          SIGNED
                             Tams Bixby

Registered.   Chairman.
Incl. 9-NB-489.

9-NB-489

Muskogee, Indian Territory, June 22, 1905.

Mansfield, McMurray & Cornish,   **COPY.**
    Attorneys for Choctaw and Chickasaw Nations,
        South McAlester, Indian Territory.

Gentlemen:

    Inclosed herewith you will find a copy of the order of this Commission, dated June 22, 1905, dismissing the application for the enrollment of your infant child, Ceral Reynolds as a citizen by blood of the Chickasaw Nation.

                      Respectfully,
                          SIGNED

                             Tams Bixby
Incl. 9-NB-489.   Chairman.

Applications for Enrollment of Chickasaw Newborn
Act of 1905   Volume VI

Chic. N.B - 490
  (Marguerite N. Warren
  Born July 29, 1904)

BIRTH AFFIDAVIT.

DEPARTMENT OF THE INTERIOR.
COMMISSION TO THE FIVE CIVILIZED TRIBES.

IN RE APPLICATION FOR ENROLLMENT, as a citizen of the Chickasaw Nation, of Marguerite N. Warren, born on the 29th day of July, 1904

Name of Father: William F. Warren   a citizen of the Chickasaw Nation.
Name of Mother: Nannie B. Warren   a citizen of the Chickasaw Nation.

Postoffice   Ardmore, Indian Territory.

AFFIDAVIT OF MOTHER.

UNITED STATES OF AMERICA, Indian Territory, }
  Southern   DISTRICT.

I, Nannie B. Warren, on oath state that I am 32 years of age and a citizen by blood, of the Chickasaw Nation; that I am the lawful wife of William F. Warren, who is a citizen, by intermarriage of the Chickasaw Nation; that a female child was born to me on 29th day of July, 1904; that said child has been named Marguerite N. Warren, and was living March 4, 1905.

Nannie B. Warren

Witnesses To Mark:
{

Subscribed and sworn to before me this 26th day of April, 1905

L. L. Tye
Notary Public.

AFFIDAVIT OF ATTENDING PHYSICIAN OR MID-WIFE.

UNITED STATES OF AMERICA, Indian Territory, }
  Southern   DISTRICT.

I, James Whitfield, a Physician, on oath state that I attended on Mrs. Nannie B. Warren, wife of W^m F Warren on the 29 day of July,

Applications for Enrollment of Chickasaw Newborn
Act of 1905   Volume VI

1904; that there was born to her on said date a   Female   child; that said child was living March 4, 1905, and is said to have been named Marguerite Nancy Warren

James Whitfield

Witnesses To Mark:
{

Subscribed and sworn to before me this 15th day of April , 1905

Jno. W. Massey
Notary Public.

Chic. N.B - 491
    (Vinnie May Seely
    Born May 15, 1903)

BIRTH AFFIDAVIT.   No 79

DEPARTMENT OF THE INTERIOR.
COMMISSION TO THE FIVE CIVILIZED TRIBES.

IN RE APPLICATION FOR ENROLLMENT, as a citizen of the   Chickasaw   Nation, of Vinnie May Seely , born on the 15th day of May , 1903

Name of Father: Esau Seely   a citizen of the Chickasaw Nation.
Name of Mother: Etta Columbus   a citizen of the Chickasaw Nation.

Postoffice Coatsworth

AFFIDAVIT OF MOTHER.

UNITED STATES OF AMERICA, Indian Territory, }
    Central   DISTRICT.

I, Etta Columbus , on oath state that I am 21 years of age and a citizen by Blood , of the Chickasaw Nation; that I am^ the lawful wife of Esau Seely Born out of wedlock , who is a citizen, by Blood of the Chickasaw Nation; that a Female child was born to me on 15th day of May , 1903, that said child has been named Vinnie May Seely , and is now living.

Etta Columbus

193

Applications for Enrollment of Chickasaw Newborn
Act of 1905   Volume VI

Witnesses To Mark:
{

    Subscribed and sworn to before me this 26th day of Jan , 1905.

                                  E.J. Ball
                                    Notary Public.

AFFIDAVIT OF ATTENDING PHYSICIAN OR MID-WIFE.

UNITED STATES OF AMERICA, Indian Territory, }
   Central   DISTRICT. }

    I, Lerna Underwood , a midwife , on oath state that I attended on ~~Mrs.~~ Etta Columbus , wife of .... on the 15th day of May , 1903; that there was born to her on said date a Female child; that said child is now living and is said to have been named Vinnie May Seely

                              Lerna Underwood

Witnesses To Mark:
{

    Subscribed and sworn to before me this 26 day of Jan , 1905.

                                    E.J. Ball
                                    Notary Public.

BIRTH AFFIDAVIT.
               DEPARTMENT OF THE INTERIOR.
COMMISSION TO THE FIVE CIVILIZED TRIBES.

    IN RE APPLICATION FOR ENROLLMENT, as a citizen of the Chickasaw Nation, of Vinnie May Seely , born on the 15th day of May , 1903

Name of Father: Esau Seely   a citizen of the Chickasaw Nation.
Name of Mother: Etta Columbus   a citizen of the Chickasaw Nation.

                        Postoffice   Coatsworth I.T.

Applications for Enrollment of Chickasaw Newborn
Act of 1905   Volume VI

AFFIDAVIT OF MOTHER.

UNITED STATES OF AMERICA, Indian Territory, }
22 Southern   DISTRICT.

I,   Etta Columbus   , on oath state that I am   21   years of age and a citizen by   Blood   , of the   Chickasaw   Nation; that I am the lawful wife of   Esau Seely   , who is a citizen, by Blood   of the   Chickasaw   Nation; that a Female   child was born to me on   15th   day of   May   , 1903; that said child has been named   Vinnie May Seely   , and was living March 4, 1905.

Etta Columbus

Witnesses To Mark:
{

Subscribed and sworn to before me this   23   day of   August   , 1905

T.C. Keller
Notary Public.

AFFIDAVIT OF ATTENDING PHYSICIAN OR MID-WIFE.

UNITED STATES OF AMERICA, Indian Territory, }
22 Southern   DISTRICT.

I,   Lernah[sic] Underwood   , a ...., on oath state that I attended on Mrs.   Etta Columbus   not the, wife of   Esau Seely   on the   15th day of   May   , 1903; that there was born to her on said date a   Female   child; that said child was living March 4, 1905, and is said to have been named   Vinnie May Seely

Lerna Underwood

Witnesses To Mark:
{

Subscribed and sworn to before me this   23   day of   August   , 1905

T.C. Keller
Notary Public.

Applications for Enrollment of Chickasaw Newborn
Act of 1905   Volume VI

9-NB-491.

Muskogee, Indian Territory, May 22, 1905.

Esau Seely,
    Coatsworth, Indian Territory,

Dear Sir:

    There is enclosed you herewith for execution application for the enrollment of your infant child, Vinnie May Seely, born May 15, 1903.

    The affidavits heretofore filed with the Commission show the child was living on January 26, 1905. It is necessary, for the child to be enrolled, that she was living on March 4, 1905.

    In having these affidavits executed care should be exercised to see that all names are written in full, as they appear in the body of the affidavit, and in the event that either of the persons signing the affidavit are unable to write, signatures by mark must be attested by two witnesses. Each affidavit must be executed before a Notary Public and the notarial seal and signature of the officer must be attached to each separate affidavit.

    Respectfully,

    Chairman.

VR 22-5.

(Copy)

Walker, I. T.

June 11, 1905.

Department of the Interior.

Commission to the Five Civilized Tribes.

    Sir & Friend:

    I do no endorse for any child to be enrolled as I have no children.

    You are asked by me not to enroll said Vinnie May Seely in my name for I am not the father of any children.

    Yours respectfully

    E. D. Seely.

Applications for Enrollment of Chickasaw Newborn
Act of 1905   Volume VI

9 NB 491

Muskogee, Indian Territory, June 16, 1905.

E. B. Sealy[sic],
    Walker, Indian Territory.

Dear Sir:

    Receipt is hereby acknowledged of your letter of June 11, 1905, in which you state that Vinnie May Sealy is not your child.

    This information has been made a matter of record.

Respectfully,

Chairman.

9-NB-491.

Muskogee, Indian Territory, June 17, 1905.

Etta Columbus,
    Coatsworth, Indian Territory.

Dear Madam:

    There is enclosed herewith for execution application for the enrollment of your infant child, Vinnie May Seely, born May 15, 1903.

    The affidavits heretofore filed with the Commission show that the child was living on January 26, 1904. For the child to be enrolled it is necessary that she was living on March 4, 1905.

    In having these affidavits executed care should be exercised to see that all names are written in full, as they appear in the body of the affidavit, and in the event that either of the persons signing the affidavit are unable to write, signatures by mark must be attested by two witnesses. Each affidavit must be executed before a Notary Public and the notarial seal and signature of the officer must be attached to each separate affidavit.

    This matter should receive your immediate attention.

Respectfully,

DeB--1/17   Chairman.

Applications for Enrollment of Chickasaw Newborn
Act of 1905   Volume VI

9-NB-491

Muskogee, Indian Territory, August 26, 1905.

Etta Columbus,
    Coatsworth, Indian Territory.

Dear Madam:

    Receipt is hereby acknowledged of your affidavit and the affidavit of Lema[sic] Underwood, to the birth of Vinnie May Seely, May 15, 1905, and the same have been filed with the records in this case.

        Respectfully,

            Commissioner.

Chic. N.B - 492
    (Liza Richardson
    Born May 29, 1903)

BIRTH AFFIDAVIT.   *No 58*

DEPARTMENT OF THE INTERIOR.
COMMISSION TO THE FIVE CIVILIZED TRIBES.

    IN RE APPLICATION FOR ENROLLMENT, as a citizen of the   Chickasaw   Nation, of   Liza Richardson   , born on the   29th day of   May   , 1903

Name of Father: Walton Richardson   a citizen of the   Chickasaw   Nation.
Name of Mother: Nevina Richardson   a citizen of the   Chickasaw   Nation.

        Postoffice   Conway

AFFIDAVIT OF MOTHER.

UNITED STATES OF AMERICA, Indian Territory, }
    16th   DISTRICT. }

    I,   Nevina Richardson   , on oath state that I am   20   years of age and a citizen by   Blood   , of the   Chickasaw   Nation; that I am the lawful wife of Walton Richardson   , who is a citizen, by   Blood   of the   Chickasaw

Applications for Enrollment of Chickasaw Newborn
Act of 1905   Volume VI

Nation; that a female child was born to me on 29th day of May, 1903, that said child has been named Liza, and is now living.

                                      her
                              Nevina x Richardson

Witnesses To Mark: mark
  { WN Allison
    Dore Richardson

Subscribed and sworn to before me this 31st day of Dec, 1904

                              WN Allison
                                  Notary Public.

AFFIDAVIT OF ATTENDING PHYSICIAN OR MID-WIFE.

UNITED STATES OF AMERICA, Indian Territory, }
   16th   DISTRICT.

    I, Dore Richardson, a Mid wife, on oath state that I attended on Mrs. Nevina Richardson, wife of Walton Richardson on the 29th day of May, 1903; that there was born to her on said date a female child; that said child is now living and is said to have been named Liza

                              Dore Richardson

Witnesses To Mark:
  { WN Allison

Subscribed and sworn to before me this 31st day of Dec, 1904

                              W.H. Allison
                              Notary Public.

BIRTH AFFIDAVIT.
DEPARTMENT OF THE INTERIOR.
COMMISSION TO THE FIVE CIVILIZED TRIBES.

    IN RE APPLICATION FOR ENROLLMENT, as a citizen of the ....Nation, of Liza Richardson, born on the 29 day of May, 1903

Name of Father: Walton Richardson   a citizen of the Chickasaw Nation.
Name of Mother: Lovinie Richardson   a citizen of the Chickasaw Nation.

                        Postoffice   Conway I.T.

Applications for Enrollment of Chickasaw Newborn
Act of 1905 Volume VI

AFFIDAVIT OF MOTHER.

UNITED STATES OF AMERICA, Indian Territory,　
Southern　　　　　　DISTRICT.

I, Louvinia Richardson, on oath state that I am 27 years of age and a citizen by blood, of the Chickasaw Nation; that I am the lawful wife of Walton Richardson (deceased, who was a citizen, by his mother Chick., his father of the Chickasaw Nation; that a female child was born to me on 29 day of May, 1903; that said child has been named Liza, and was living March 4, 1905.

　　　　　　　　　　　　her x mark
　　　　　　　　　　　　Louvinia Richardson

Witnesses To Mark:
{ Dore Richardson
{ *(Name Illegible)*

Subscribed and sworn to before me this 17 day of July, 1905

　　　　　　　　　　　　H.T. Lyles
　　　　　　　　　　　　Notary Public.

AFFIDAVIT OF ATTENDING ~~PHYSICIAN OR MID-WIFE~~.
　　　　　　　　　　　　young woman

UNITED STATES OF AMERICA, Indian Territory,　
Southern　　　　　　DISTRICT.

　　　　　　　　　　　　　　　　was present
I, Dore Richardson, a _____, on oath state that I attended on Mrs. when Mrs Louvinia Richardson, wife of Walton Richardson on the 29 gave birth to child now named Liza - no doctor or midwife day of May 1903, I........; that there was born to her on said date a female child; that said child was living March 4, 1905, and is said to have been named Liza

　　　　　　　　　　　　Dore Richardson

Witnesses To Mark:
{　**said to be no physician or midwife**

Subscribed and sworn to before me this 17 day of July, 1905

　　　　　　　　　　　　H.T. Lyles
　　　　　　　　　　　　Notary Public.

Applications for Enrollment of Chickasaw Newborn
Act of 1905   Volume VI

9-NB-492.

Muskogee, Indian Territory, May 22, 1905.

Walton Richardson,
    Conway, Indian Territory.

Dear Sir:

    There is enclosed you herewith for execution application for the enrollment of your infant child, Liza Richardson, born May 29, 1903.

    The affidavits heretofore filed with the Commission show the child living on December 31, 1904. It is necessary, for the child to be enrolled, that she was living on March 4, 1905.

    In having these affidavits executed care should be exercised to see that all names are written in full, as they appear in the body of the affidavit, and in the event that either of the persons signing the affidavit are unable to write, signatures by mark must be attested by two witnesses. Each affidavit must be executed before a Notary Public and the notarial seal and signature of the officer must be attached to each separate affidavit.

Respectfully,

Chairman.

VR 22-3.

---

9 N.B. 492.

Muskogee, Indian Territory, June 1, 1905.

Walton Richardson,
    Conway, Indian Territory.

Dear Sir:

    Receipt is hereby acknowledged of the affidavits of Louvena Pettigrew (Richardson) and Dora[sic] Richardson to the birth of Liza Richardson, daughter of Walton and Louvena Richardson, May 29, 1903, and the same have been filed with our records in the matter of the enrollment of said child.

Respectfully,

Commissioner in Charge.

Applications for Enrollment of Chickasaw Newborn
Act of 1905   Volume VI

9-NB-492

Muskogee, Indian Territory, July 11, 1905.

Walton Richardson,
    Conway, Indian Territory.

Dear Sir:

    There is returned to you herewith application for the enrollment of your infant child, Liza Richardson, born May 29, 1903.

    You will note that the affidavit of your wife is signed "Louvina Pettigrew" her maiden name, when she should have signed "Louvena Richardson." You will please have the affidavit of your wife re-executed and return to this office.

    Please give this matter your immediate attention as no further action can be taken relative to the enrollment of said child until the can be taken relative to the enrollment of your child until this evidence is supplied.

                                Respectfully,

LM 11-2   Commissioner.

9-171
9-NB-492

Muskogee, Indian Territory, July 24, 1905.

Louvenia Richardson,
    Conway, Indian Territory.

Dear Madam:

    Receipt is hereby acknowledged of your affidavit and the affidavit of Dore Richardson to the birth of Liza Richardson, daughter of Walton and Lovenie Richardson, May 29, 1903; also the affidavits of yourself and Sarah Richardson to the birth of Benin Pettigrew, son of Mose Pettigrew and Lavenie Richardson, October 15, 1900, and the same have been filed with the records of this office in the matter of the enrollment of these children.

                                Respectfully,

                                              Commissioner.

Applications for Enrollment of Chickasaw Newborn
Act of 1905   Volume VI

9-NB-493[sic]

Muskogee, Indian Territory, May 9, 1906.

A. L. Allen,
 Stonewall, Indian Territory.

Dear Sir:

Receipt is hereby acknowledged of your letter of May 3, 1906, asking if Liza Richardson has been enrolled as a citizen of the Chickasaw Nation.

In reply to your letter you are advised that the enrollment of Liza Richardson as a new born citizen of the Chickasaw Nation was approved by the Secretary of the Interior, September 23, 1905.

Respectfully,

Acting Commissioner.

Chic. N.B - 493
 (Hazel Victor
 Born August 28, 1903)

BIRTH AFFIDAVIT.   #147

DEPARTMENT OF THE INTERIOR.
COMMISSION TO THE FIVE CIVILIZED TRIBES.

IN RE APPLICATION FOR ENROLLMENT, as a citizen of the   Chickasaw   Nation, of   Hazel Victor , born on the   28   day of   Aug , 1903

Name of Father: Emmet L Victor   a citizen of the   Chickasaw Nation.
Name of Mother: Lee Victor   a citizen of the   Intermarried Nation.

Postoffice   Dibble Ind Ter

Applications for Enrollment of Chickasaw Newborn
Act of 1905   Volume VI

AFFIDAVIT OF MOTHER.

UNITED STATES OF AMERICA, Indian Territory, }
Southern   DISTRICT.

I,   Lee Victor   , on oath state that I am   twenty five   years of age and a citizen by   intermarriage   , of the   Chickasaw   Nation; that I am the lawful wife of   Emmet L Victor   , who is a citizen, by   Blood   of the   Chickasaw   Nation; that a   Female   child was born to me on 28th day of   August   , 1903, that said child has been named   Hazel Victor   , and is now living.

                                                Lee Victor

Witnesses To Mark:
{ Taylor Black
{ Tom *(Illegible)*

Subscribed and sworn to before me this 21st day of   February   , 1905.

                                                Jas M Gordon
                                                   Notary Public.
My term of office expires Mch 1907

AFFIDAVIT OF ATTENDING PHYSICIAN OR MID-WIFE.

UNITED STATES OF AMERICA, Indian Territory, }
Southern   DISTRICT.

I,   Lora Roggers[sic]   , a   Mid wife   , on oath state that I attended on Mrs.   Lee Victor   , wife of   Emmet L Victor   on the   28   day of August   , 1903; that there was born to her on said date a   Female   child; that said child is now living and is said to have been named   Hazel Victor

                                                Lora Rogers

Witnesses To Mark:
{ Taylor Black
{ Tom *(Illegible)*

Subscribed and sworn to before me this   21   day of   February   , 1905.

                                              Jas M Gordon
                                                Notary Public.
My term of office expires Mch 1907

Applications for Enrollment of Chickasaw Newborn
Act of 1905   Volume VI

BIRTH AFFIDAVIT.

DEPARTMENT OF THE INTERIOR.
COMMISSION TO THE FIVE CIVILIZED TRIBES.

IN RE APPLICATION FOR ENROLLMENT, as a citizen of the Chickasaw Nation, of Hazel Victor, born on the 28 day of August, 1903

Name of Father: Emmet L Victor   a citizen of the Chickasaw Nation.
Name of Mother: Lee Victor   a citizen of the Chickasaw Intermarried Nation.

Postoffice Dibble Ind Ter

AFFIDAVIT OF MOTHER.

UNITED STATES OF AMERICA, Indian Territory,
Southern DISTRICT.

I, Lee Victor, on oath state that I am twenty five years of age and a citizen by Intermarried, of the Chickasaw Nation; that I am the lawful wife of Emmet L Victor, who is a citizen, by Blood of the Chickasaw Nation; that a female child was born to me on 28 day of August, 1903; that said child has been named Hazel Victor, and was living March 4, 1905.

Lee Victor

Witnesses To Mark:
{

Subscribed and sworn to before me this 22 day of April, 1905

JM Gordon
Notary Public.

AFFIDAVIT OF ATTENDING PHYSICIAN OR MID-WIFE.

UNITED STATES OF AMERICA, Indian Territory,
Southern DISTRICT.

I, Lora Rogers, a Midwife, on oath state that I attended on Mrs. Lee Victor, wife of Emmet L Victor on the 28 day of August, 1903; that there was born to her on said date a female child; that said child was living March 4, 1905, and is said to have been named Hazel Victor

Lora Rogers

Applications for Enrollment of Chickasaw Newborn
Act of 1905   Volume VI

Witnesses To Mark:

{

Subscribed and sworn to before me this 22 day of   April   , 1905

JM Gordon
Notary Public.

My term of office expires Mch 1907

Chickasaw NB 493

Muskogee, Indian Territory, June 28, 1905.

Emmett[sic] L. Victor,
   Dibble, Indian Territory.

Dear Sir:

   Receipt is hereby acknowledged of your letter of June 20, asking if an application for the enrollment of your baby has been received and in reply you are advised that the name of your child, Hazel Victor, has been placed upon a schedule of citizens by blood of the Chickasaw Nation prepared for forwarding to the Secretary of the Interior. You will be notified when her enrollment is approved by the Department.

Respectfully,

Chairman.

Chic. N.B - 494
   (William Jasper McMillan
   Born November 14, 1903)

Applications for Enrollment of Chickasaw Newborn
Act of 1905   Volume VI

BIRTH AFFIDAVIT.

DEPARTMENT OF THE INTERIOR.
COMMISSION TO THE FIVE CIVILIZED TRIBES.

IN RE APPLICATION FOR ENROLLMENT, as a citizen of the   Chickasaw   Nation, of   William Jasper McMillan   , born on the 14th day of   November   , 1903

Name of Father: W.A. McMillan   a citizen of the   Chickasaw   Nation.
Name of Mother: Mary McMillan   a citizen of the   Chickasaw   Nation.

Postoffice   Orr Ind. Ter.

AFFIDAVIT OF MOTHER.

UNITED STATES OF AMERICA, Indian Territory, }
  Southern   DISTRICT.

I,   Mary McMillan   , on oath state that I am   24   years of age and a citizen by   Blood   , of the   Chickasaw   Nation; that I am the lawful wife of W. A. McMillan   , who is a citizen, by Intermarriage   of the   Chickasaw Nation; that a   Male   child was born to me on   Fourteenth   day of   November , 1903; that said child has been named   William Jasper McMillan   , and was living March 4, 1905.

                                    Mary McMillan
Witnesses To Mark:
{

Subscribed and sworn to before me this   24th day of   April   , 1905

(Name Illegible)
                                    Notary Public.

AFFIDAVIT OF ATTENDING PHYSICIAN OR MID-WIFE.

UNITED STATES OF AMERICA, ~~Indian Territory~~, }
   The State f Texas   DISTRICT.
   County of Grayson

I, R.A. Gardner   , a   physician   , on oath state that I attended on Mrs.   Mary McMillan   , wife of   W^m McMillan   on the 14th day of   Nov , 1903; that there was born to her on said date a   male   child; that said child was living March 4, 1905, and is said to have been named   William Jasper McMillan

                                    R.A. Gardner M.D.

Applications for Enrollment of Chickasaw Newborn
Act of 1905   Volume VI

Witnesses To Mark:
{

Subscribed and sworn to before me this 16ᵗʰ day of   April   , 1905

(Name Illegible)
Notary Public.

Chic. N.B - 495
(Peachie Viola Duroderigo
Born January 14, 1905)

BIRTH AFFIDAVIT.
DEPARTMENT OF THE INTERIOR.
COMMISSION TO THE FIVE CIVILIZED TRIBES.

IN RE APPLICATION FOR ENROLLMENT, as a citizen of the   Chickasaw   Nation, of   Peachie Viola Durigo   , born on the 14 day of   January   , 1905

Name of Father: Albert Franklin Durigo   a citizen of the   Chickasaw   Nation.
Name of Mother: Martha Jane Durigo   a citizen of the .... Nation.

Postoffice   McMillan, I.T.

AFFIDAVIT OF MOTHER.

UNITED STATES OF AMERICA, Indian Territory, }
Southern   DISTRICT.

I,   Martha Jane Durigo   , on oath state that I am   eighteen   years of age ~~and a citizen by~~ ...., ~~of the~~ .... ~~Nation~~; that I am the lawful wife of Albert Franklin Durigo   , who is a citizen, by   blood   of the   Chickasaw   Nation; that a   female   child was born to me on 14 day of   January   , 1905; that said child has been named   Peachie Viola Durigo   , and was living March 4, 1905.

Martha Jane Durigo

Witnesses To Mark:
{

Applications for Enrollment of Chickasaw Newborn
Act of 1905   Volume VI

Subscribed and sworn to before me this 15 day of   April   , 1905

Sula E. Taylor
Notary Public.

AFFIDAVIT OF ATTENDING PHYSICIAN OR MID-WIFE.

UNITED STATES OF AMERICA, Indian Territory, }
Southern   DISTRICT.

I,   T. S. Booth   , a   Physician   , on oath state that I attended on Mrs.   Martha Jane Durigo   , wife of   Albert Franklin Durigo   on the 14 day of Jan   , 1905; that there was born to her on said date a   Female   child; that said child was living March 4, 1905, and is said to have been named   Peachie Viola Durigo

T S Booth MD

Witnesses To Mark:
{

Subscribed and sworn to before me this 15 day of   April   , 1905

Sula E. Taylor
Notary Public.

BIRTH AFFIDAVIT.
DEPARTMENT OF THE INTERIOR.
COMMISSION TO THE FIVE CIVILIZED TRIBES.

IN RE APPLICATION FOR ENROLLMENT, as a citizen of the   Chickasaw   Nation, of   Peachie Viola Duroderigo   , born on the   14th   day of   January   , 1905

Name of Father: Albert Franklin Duroderigo   a citizen of the   Chickasaw   Nation.
Name of Mother: Martha Jane Duroderigo   a citizen of the .... Nation.

Postoffice   McMillan, I.T.

AFFIDAVIT OF MOTHER.

UNITED STATES OF AMERICA, Indian Territory, }
....   DISTRICT.

I,   Martha Jane Duroderigo   , on oath state that I am   18   years of age and a citizen ~~by~~ ...., of the   United States   Nation; that I am the lawful wife of Albert Franklin Duroderigo   , who is a citizen, by   Blood   of the   Chickasaw

Applications for Enrollment of Chickasaw Newborn
Act of 1905   Volume VI

Nation; that a   Female   child was born to me on   14th   day of   January   , 1905; that said child has been named   Peachie Viola Duroderigo   , and was living March 4, 1905.

Martha Jane Duroderigo

Witnesses To Mark:
{

   Subscribed and sworn to before me this 2 day of   June   , 1905

Sula E. Taylor
Notary Public.

AFFIDAVIT OF ATTENDING PHYSICIAN OR MID-WIFE.

UNITED STATES OF AMERICA, Indian Territory,
.... DISTRICT.

   I, ... , a ...., on oath state that I attended on Mrs.   Martha Jane Duroderigo   , wife of   Albert Franklin Duroderigo   on the 14th   day of   January   , 1905; that there was born to her on said date a   Female   child; that said child was living March 4, 1905, and is said to have been named   Peachie Viola Duroderigo

T S Booth MD

Witnesses To Mark:
{

   Subscribed and sworn to before me this 5 day of   June   , 1905

Sula E. Taylor
Notary Public.

Applications for Enrollment of Chickasaw Newborn
Act of 1905   Volume VI

437

Certificate of Record of Marriage

UNITED STATES OF AMERICA,
INDIAN TERRITORY, } sct.
Southern District.

DEPARTMENT OF THE INTERIOR,
COMMISSION TO THE FIVE CIVILIZED TRIBES.

FILED

MAY 8 1905

Tams Bixby CHAIRMAN.

I, C. M. CAMPBELL, Clerk of the United States Court, in the Territory and District aforesaid, DO HEREBY CERTIFY, that the License for and Certificate of Marriage of

Mr   Albert Draughess[sic]   and

M   Mattie Simpson

were filed in my office in said Territory and District the   14   day of   Oct A.D., 190 3   and duly recorded in Book G of Marriage Record, Page 437

WITNESS my hand and Seal of said Court, at Ardmore, this   14"   day of   Oct   A.D. 190 3

C. M. Campbell
CLERK.

McMillan

MARRIAGE LICENSE.

№ 1360

United States of America,
Indian Territory, } ss
Southern District.

To Any Person Authorized by Law to
Solemnize Marriage, Greeting:

You are hereby Commanded to solemnize the Rite and publish the Banns of Matrimony between Mr.   Albert Draughess of   McMillan   in the Indian Territory, aged   21   years, and M iss   Mattie Simpson   of   McMillan   in the Indian Territory, aged   17   years, according to law; and do you officially sign and return this license to the parties therein named.

Applications for Enrollment of Chickasaw Newborn
Act of 1905 Volume VI

Witness my hand and official Seal, this 6" day of October A. D. 190 3

C.M. Campbell
Clerk of the United States Court.

Certificate of Marriage.

United States of America
Indian Territory, ss
Southern District.

I, J. F. Edington do hereby certify that on the 7 day of Oct A. D. 1903, I did duly and according to law, as commanded in the foregoing License, solemnize the Rite and publish the Banns of Matrimony between the parties therein named.

Witness my hand this 7 day of Oct A. D. 190 3

My credentials are recorded in the office of the Clerk of the United States Court, Indian Territory, Southern District, at Ardmore, Book C , Page 8

J F Edington
a minister of gospel

NOTE. (a)- This License and Certificate of Marriages must be returned to the office of the Clerk of the United States Court in the Indian Territory, at Ardmore, within sixty days from the date thereof, or the party to whom the License was issued will be liable in the amount of ONE HUNDRED DOLLARS ($100).

Indian Territory,
Southern District.

I, Albert Franklin Duroderigo, being duly sworn, on oath state that I am the person whose name appears in the affidavits heretofore filed with the Commission as Albert Franklin Durigo.

On May 8th, 1905, there was filed with the Commission license and certificate of he marriage between Albert Draughess and Mattie Simpson, and this license and certificate has been filed as evidence of my marriage to Martha Jane Duroderigo. I certify that I am the same person as Albert Draughess, mentioned in this license and certificate, and that my wife is the same as Mattie Simpson.

Dr Albert Franklin Duroderigo

Subscribed and sworn to before me this the 2nd day of June, 1905.

Sula E Taylor
Notary Public.

Applications for Enrollment of Chickasaw Newborn
Act of 1905 Volume VI

9-NB-495.

Muskogee, Indian Territory, May 19, 1905.

Albert Franklin Duroderigo,
    McMillan, Indian Territory.

Dear Sir:

    There is enclosed you herewith for execution application for the enrollment of your infant child, Peachie Viola Duroderigo, born January 14, 1905.

    In the affidavits heretofore filed with the Commission you give your name as Albert Franklin Durigo, while your name appears on the records of the Commission as Albert Franklin Duroderigo. In the enclosed affidavits your name is inserted as it appears from the records of the Commission.

    On May 8, 1905, there was filed with the Commission license and certificate of the marriage between Albert Draughess and Mattie Simpson. This license and certificate has been filed as evidence of your marriage to Martha Jane Duroderigo. If you are the same person as Albert Draughess, mentioned in this license and certificate and your wife is the same as Mattie Simpson you will please file in this office an affidavit to that effect.

    In having these affidavits executed care should be exercised to see that all names are written in full, as they appear in the body of the affidavit, and in the event that either of the persons signing the affidavit are unable to write, signatures by mark must be attested by two witnesses. Each affidavit must be executed before a Notary Public and the notarial seal and signature of the officer must be attached to each separate affidavit.

Respectfully,

Chairman.

VR 19-3.

Applications for Enrollment of Chickasaw Newborn
Act of 1905 Volume VI

9 NB 495

Muskogee, Indian Territory, June 9, 1905.

Albert F. Duroderigo,
McMillan, Indian Territory.

Dear Sir:

Receipt is hereby acknowledged of the affidavits of Martha Jane Duroderigo and T. S. Booth to the birth of Peachie Viola Duroderigo, daughter of Albert Franklin and Martha Jane Duroderigo, January 14, 1905; receipt is also acknowledged of your affidavit stating that you are the same person named in the marriage certificate recently filed by you as Albert Draughess and the same have been filed with the record in this case.

Respectfully,

Chairman.

Chic. N.B - 496
(James Bruno Mayer
Born April 12, 1904)

BIRTH AFFIDAVIT. No 77

DEPARTMENT OF THE INTERIOR.
COMMISSION TO THE FIVE CIVILIZED TRIBES.

IN RE APPLICATION FOR ENROLLMENT, as a citizen of the Chickasaw Nation, of James Bruno , born on the 12th day of April , 1904

Name of Father: Bruno Mayer   a citizen of the Chickasaw Nation.
Name of Mother: Cornelia Mayer   a citizen of the Chickasaw Nation.

Postoffice   Conway I.T.

Applications for Enrollment of Chickasaw Newborn
Act of 1905 Volume VI

AFFIDAVIT OF MOTHER.

UNITED STATES OF AMERICA, Indian Territory, }
16th   DISTRICT.

I, Cornelia Mayer, on oath state that I am 24 years of age and a citizen by Blood, of the Chickasaw Nation; that I am the lawful wife of Bruno Mayer, who is a citizen, by Marriage of the Chickasaw Nation; that a Male child was born to me on 12th day of April, 1904, that said child has been named James Bruno, and is now living.

Cornelia Mayer

Witnesses To Mark:
{

Subscribed and sworn to before me this 20th day of January, 1905.

W.H. Allison
Notary Public.

AFFIDAVIT OF ATTENDING PHYSICIAN OR MID-WIFE.

UNITED STATES OF AMERICA, Indian Territory, }
....DISTRICT.

I, Oscar F Coffey, a practicing physician, on oath state that I attended on Mrs. Cornelia Mayer, wife of James[sic] Bruno Mayer on the 12th day of April, 1904; that there was born to her on said date a male child; that said child is now living and is said to have been named James Bruno

O.F. Coffey

Witnesses To Mark:
{ Joseph S Coffman
{ (Name Illegible)

Subscribed and sworn to before me this 25 day of January, 1905.

J.C. Marshall
Notary Public.

my commission
expires Nov 2/08

Applications for Enrollment of Chickasaw Newborn
Act of 1905 Volume VI

BIRTH AFFIDAVIT.

DEPARTMENT OF THE INTERIOR.
COMMISSION TO THE FIVE CIVILIZED TRIBES.

IN RE APPLICATION FOR ENROLLMENT, as a citizen of the Chickasaw Nation, of James Bruno Mayer, born on the 12th day of April, 1904

Name of Father: Bruno Mayer   a citizen of the Chickasaw Nation.
Name of Mother: Cornelia Mayer   a citizen of the Chickasaw Nation.

Postoffice   Conway IT

AFFIDAVIT OF MOTHER.

UNITED STATES OF AMERICA, Indian Territory, }
16th   DISTRICT. }

I, Cornelia Mayer, on oath state that I am 24 years of age and a citizen by Blood, of the Chickasaw Nation; that I am the lawful wife of Bruno Mayer, who is a citizen, by Marriage of the Chickasaw Nation; that a Male child was born to me on 12th day of April, 1904; that said child has been named James Bruno Mayer, and was living March 4, 1905.

Cornelia Mayer

Witnesses To Mark:

Subscribed and sworn to before me this 1st day of May, 1905

Wade H. Allison
Notary Public.

AFFIDAVIT OF ATTENDING PHYSICIAN OR MID-WIFE.

UNITED STATES OF AMERICA, Indian Territory, }
DISTRICT. }

I, O. F. Coffey, a Physician, on oath state that I attended on Mrs. Cornelia Mayer, wife of Bruno Mayer on the 12 day of April, 1904; that there was born to her on said date a Male child; that said child was living March 4, 1905, and is said to have been named James Bruno Mayer

Dr. O.F. Coffey

Witnesses To Mark:

Applications for Enrollment of Chickasaw Newborn
Act of 1905   Volume VI

Subscribed and sworn to before me this   29th   day of   April   , 1905

                        W.H. Allison
                        Notary Public.

Chic. N.B - 497
    (Nancy Roberts
    Born October 13, 1904)

BIRTH AFFIDAVIT.   #131

IN RE-APPLICATION FOR ENROLLMENT, as a citizen of the   Chickasaw   Nation, of   Nancy Roberts   , born on the   13   day of   Oct , 190 4

Name of Father: Wilson Roberts   a citizen of the   Chickasaw   Nation.
Name of Mother: Elsa[sic] Roberts   a citizen of the   "   Nation.

        Postoffice   Owl I.T.

AFFIDAVIT OF MOTHER.

UNITED STATES OF AMERICA, INDIAN TERRITORY,
S[sic] Central   District.

I,   Elsie Roberts   , on oath state that I am   33   years of age and a citizen by Blood   , of the   Chickasaw   Nation; that I am the lawful wife of   Wilson Roberts   , who is a citizen, by   Blood   of the   Chickasaw   Nation; that a   Female   child was born to me on   13th   day of   Oct.   , 190 4, that said child has been named   Nancy Roberts   , and is now living.

                        Elsie Roberts

Witnesses To Mark:
    ME Cross
    Charlie Colbert

Subscribed and sworn to before me this   14   day of   Feb   , 1905.

                      John H Cross
                      Notary Public.

Applications for Enrollment of Chickasaw Newborn
Act of 1905 Volume VI

AFFIDAVIT OF ATTENDING PHYSICIAN OR MID-WIFE.

UNITED STATES OF AMERICA, INDIAN TERRITORY, }
Central   District.

I, Amelia Clark, a midwife, on oath state that I attended on Mrs. Elsie Roberts, wife of Wilson Roberts on the 13 day of Oct, 190 4; that there was born to her on said date a Female child; that said child is now living and is said to have been named Nancy Roberts

her
Amelia x Clark
mark

Witnesses To Mark:
{ S.S. Forrest
  M E Cross

Subscribed and sworn to before me this 22 day of Feb, 1905.

John H Cross
Notary Public.

my com expires Sept 24 1908

BIRTH AFFIDAVIT.

DEPARTMENT OF THE INTERIOR.
COMMISSION TO THE FIVE CIVILIZED TRIBES.

IN RE APPLICATION FOR ENROLLMENT, as a citizen of the Chickasaw Nation, of Nancy Roberts, born on the 14[sic] day of Oct, 1904

Name of Father: Wilson Roberts   a citizen of the Chickasaw Nation.
Name of Mother: Elsie Roberts   a citizen of the Chickasaw Nation.

Postoffice   Owl I.T.

AFFIDAVIT OF MOTHER.

UNITED STATES OF AMERICA, Indian Territory, }
Central   DISTRICT.

I, Elsie Roberts, on oath state that I am 33 years of age and a citizen by Blood, of the Chickasaw Nation; that I am the lawful wife of Wilson Roberts, who is a citizen, by Blood of the Chickasaw Nation; that a Female child was born to me on 14 day of Oct, 1904; that said child has been named Nancy Roberts, and was living March 4, 1905.

Elsie Roberts

Applications for Enrollment of Chickasaw Newborn
Act of 1905 Volume VI

Witnesses To Mark:
{

Subscribed and sworn to before me this 28 day of April , 1905

John H. Cross
Notary Public.

AFFIDAVIT OF ATTENDING PHYSICIAN OR MID-WIFE.

UNITED STATES OF AMERICA, Indian Territory, }
Central   DISTRICT.

I, Amelia Clark , a Midwife , on oath state that I attended on Mrs. Elsie Roberts , wife of Wilson Roberts on the 14 day of Oct , 1904; that there was born to her on said date a Female child; that said child was living March 4, 1905, and is said to have been named Nancy Roberts

                                             her
                                 Amelia x Clark

Witnesses To Mark: mark
{ M E Cross
  S.S. Forrest

Subscribed and sworn to before me this 28 day of April , 1905

John H. Cross
Notary Public.

BIRTH AFFIDAVIT.

DEPARTMENT OF THE INTERIOR.
COMMISSION TO THE FIVE CIVILIZED TRIBES.

IN RE APPLICATION FOR ENROLLMENT, as a citizen of the Chickasaw Nation, of Nancy Roberts , born on the 13 day of Oct , 1904

Name of Father: Wilson Roberts   a citizen of the Chickasaw Nation.
Name of Mother: Elsie Roberts   a citizen of the Chickasaw Nation.

                     Postoffice   Owl Indian Territory

Applications for Enrollment of Chickasaw Newborn
Act of 1905   Volume VI

AFFIDAVIT OF MOTHER.

UNITED STATES OF AMERICA, Indian Territory, }
Central   DISTRICT.

I,   Elsie Roberts   , on oath state that I am   33   years of age and a citizen by Blood , of the   Chickasaw   Nation; that I am the lawful wife of   Wilson Roberts , who is a citizen, by Blood   of the   Chickasaw   Nation; that a   Female   child was born to me on   13   day of   Oct   , 1904; that said child has been named   Nancy Roberts   , and was living March 4, 1905.

                        Elsie Roberts

Witnesses To Mark:
{

Subscribed and sworn to before me this   7   day of   June   , 1905

                        John H. Cross
                        Notary Public.

AFFIDAVIT OF ATTENDING PHYSICIAN OR MID-WIFE.

UNITED STATES OF AMERICA, Indian Territory, }
Central   DISTRICT.

I,   Amelia Clark   , a   Midwife   , on oath state that I attended on Mrs.   Elsie Roberts   , wife of   Wilson Roberts   on the   13   day of   Oct   , 1904; that there was born to her on said date a   Female   child; that said child was living March 4, 1905, and is said to have been named   Nancy Roberts

                        her
                    Amelia x Clark

Witnesses To Mark: mark
{ S. F. Self
  M E Cross

Subscribed and sworn to before me this   7   day of   June   , 1905

                        John H. Cross
                        Notary Public.

Applications for Enrollment of Chickasaw Newborn
Act of 1905   Volume VI

9-192.

Muskogee, Indian Territory, May 3, 1905.

Wilson Roberts.
    Owl, Indian Territory.

Dear Sir:

    Receipt is hereby acknowledged of the affidavits of Elsie Roberts and Amelia Clark to the birth of Nancy Roberts, daughter of Wilson and Elsie Roberts, October 1, 1904, and the same have been filed with our records in the matter of the enrollment of said child.

                Respectfully,

                              Chairman.

9-NB-497.

Muskogee, Indian Territory, May 20, 1905.

Wilson Roberts,
    Owl, Indian Territory.

Dear Sir:

    There is enclosed you herewith for execution application for the enrollment of your infant child, Nancy Roberts.

    In the affidavit of your wife, executed February 14, 1905, and the affidavit of Amelia Clark, executed February 22, 1905, heretofore filed with the Commission, the date of birth of the applicant is given as October 13, 1904, while their affidavits of April 28, 1905, give the date of birth as October 14, 1904. In the enclosed application the date of birth is left blank, which you will please supply before having the affidavits executed.

    In having these affidavits executed care should be exercised to see that all names are written in full, as they appear in the body of the affidavit, and in the event that either of the persons signing the affidavit are unable to write, signatures by mark must be attested by two witnesses. Each affidavit must be executed before a Notary Public and the notarial seal and signature of the officer must be attached to each separate affidavit.

                Respectfully,

                              Chairman.

VR 20-9.

Applications for Enrollment of Chickasaw Newborn
Act of 1905 Volume VI

9 NB 497

Muskogee, Indian Territory, June 16, 1905.

Wilson Roberts,
    Owl, Indian Territory.

Dear Sir:

    Receipt is hereby acknowledged of the affidavits of Elsie Roberts and Amelia Clark to the birth of Nancy Roberts, daughter of Wilson and Elsie Roberts, October 13, 1904, and the same have been filed with our records in the matter of the enrollment of said child.

        Respectfully,

                Chairman.

9-NB-497

Muskogee, Indian Territory, July 10, 1905.

Wilson Roberts,
    Owl, Indian Territory.

Dear Sir:

    Receipt is hereby acknowledged of your letter of June 29, 1905, asking the sttus of the application for the enrollment of your child.

    In reply to your letter you are advised that the name of your daughter Nancy Roberts is being placed upon a schedule of citizens by blood of the Chickasaw Nation prepared for forwarding to the Secretary of the Interior, and you will be notified when her enrollment is approved by him.

    The other matters referred to in your letter have been made the subject of a separate communication.

        Respectfully,

                Commissioner.

Applications for Enrollment of Chickasaw Newborn
Act of 1905   Volume VI

Chic. N.B - 498
(Cora Cass
Born April 13, 1903)

BIRTH AFFIDAVIT.   No 82

DEPARTMENT OF THE INTERIOR.
COMMISSION TO THE FIVE CIVILIZED TRIBES.

IN RE APPLICATION FOR ENROLLMENT, as a citizen of the Chickasaw Nation, of Cora Cass, born on the 13th day of April, 1903

Name of Father: Lewis Cass   a citizen of the Chickasaw Nation.
Name of Mother: Rhoda Cass   a citizen of the Chickasaw Nation.

Postoffice   Cope

AFFIDAVIT OF MOTHER.

UNITED STATES OF AMERICA, Indian Territory,
Central   DISTRICT.

I, Rhoda Cass, on oath state that I am 22 years of age and a citizen by Blood, of the Chickasaw Nation; that I am the lawful wife of Lewis Cass, who is a citizen, by Blood of the Chickasaw Nation; that a Female child was born to me on 13 day of April, 1903, that said child has been named Cora Cass, and is now living.

Rhoda Cass

Witnesses To Mark:

Subscribed and sworn to before me this 24 day of Jan, 1905.

E J Ball
Notary Public.

AFFIDAVIT OF ATTENDING PHYSICIAN OR MID-WIFE.

UNITED STATES OF AMERICA, Indian Territory,
Central   DISTRICT.

I, Adline Carney, a midwife, on oath state that I attended on Mrs. Rhoda Cass, wife of Lewis Cass on the 13 day of April, 1903; that

Applications for Enrollment of Chickasaw Newborn
Act of 1905   Volume VI

there was born to her on said date a   Female   child; that said child is now living and is said to have been named   Cora Cass

Adline Carney

Witnesses To Mark:
{

Subscribed and sworn to before me this   24   day of   Jan , 1905.

E J Ball
Notary Public.

BIRTH AFFIDAVIT.

DEPARTMENT OF THE INTERIOR.
COMMISSION TO THE FIVE CIVILIZED TRIBES.

IN RE APPLICATION FOR ENROLLMENT, as a citizen of the   Chickasaw   Nation, of   Cora Cass , born on the   13   day of   Aprile[sic] , 1903

Name of Father: Lewis Cass   a citizen of the   Chickasaw   Nation.
Name of Mother: Roda[sic] Cass   a citizen of the   Chickasaw   Nation.

Postoffice   Cope Ind. Ty.

AFFIDAVIT OF MOTHER.

UNITED STATES OF AMERICA, Indian Territory, }
   22nd Southern   DISTRICT.

I,   Roda Cass , on oath state that I am   22   years of age and a citizen by blood , of the   Chickasaw   Nation; that I am the lawful wife of   Lewis Cass , who is a citizen, by blood   of the   Chickasaw   Nation; that a   Female   child was born to me on   13   day of   Aprile , 1903; that said child has been named   Cora Cass , and was living March 4, 1905.

                                    her
                              Roda x Cass
Witnesses To Mark: mark
{ JH Luna
  Mollie Durant

Subscribed and sworn to before me this   13th day of   Aprile , 1905

T.C. Keller
Notary Public.

Applications for Enrollment of Chickasaw Newborn
Act of 1905   Volume VI

AFFIDAVIT OF ATTENDING PHYSICIAN OR MID-WIFE.

UNITED STATES OF AMERICA, Indian Territory,
22nd Southern   DISTRICT.

    I, Adaline[sic] Carney   , a midwife   , on oath state that I attended on Mrs. Roda Bass   , wife of Lewis Cass   on the 13 day of Aprile   , 1903; that there was born to her on said date a   Female   child; that said child was living March 4, 1905, and is said to have been named Cora Cass

Adeline Carney

Witnesses To Mark:
{

    Subscribed and sworn to before me this 28 day of   Aprile   , 1905

T. C. Keller
Notary Public.

Choctaw 54.

Muskogee, Indian Territory, April 21, 1905.

Lewis Cass,
    Cope, Indian Territory.

Dear Sir:

    Receipt is hereby acknowledged of your letter of April 17, asking if application for the enrollment of your child, Cora Cass, has been received, and if not that you be furnished a blank for that purpose.

    In reply to your letter you are advised that it does not appear from our records that affidavits to the birth of your child, Cora Cass, has been received, and in compliance with your request there is herewith enclosed blank for the enrollment of an infant child which you should have executed and returned to this office within sixty days from March 3, 1905.

Respectfully,

Chairman.

Applications for Enrollment of Chickasaw Newborn
Act of 1905   Volume VI

9-54.

Muskogee, Indian Territory, May 3, 1905.

Lewis Cass,
    Cope, Indian Territory.

Dear Sir:

    Receipt is hereby acknowledged of the affidavits of Roda Cass and Adeline Carney to the birth of Cora Cass, daughter of Lewis and Roda Cass, April 13, 1903, and the same have been filed with our records as an application for the enrollment of said child.

    Respectfully,

    Chairman.

9-NB-498.

Muskogee, Indian Territory, May 20, 1905.

Lewis Cass,
    Cope, Indian Territory.

Dear Sir:

    There is enclosed herewith application for the enrollment of your infant child, Cora Cass, born April 13, 1903, in which the Notary Public failed to insert the date of execution in the jurat attached to the affidavit of the mother.

    Please have the proper date inserted and then return the application to this office.

    Respectfully,

    Chairman.

VR 2R-16.

Applications for Enrollment of Chickasaw Newborn
Act of 1905   Volume VI

1- N.B. 498.

Muskogee, Indian Territory, May 20, 1905.

L. W. Cass,
    Cope, Indian Territory.

Dear Sir:

    Receipt is hereby acknowledged of the application for the enrollment of Cora Cass, child of Lewis and Roda Cass, which has been corrected by having the date of the execution by Roda Cass of her affidavit inserted by the notary public, and the affidavits have now been filed as an application for the enrollment of said child.

                    Respectfully,

                                  Chairman.

Chic. N.B - 499
    (Gwendoline Mintahoyo Perry
    Born August 3, 1904)

DEPARTMENT OF THE INTERIOR
COMMISSIONER TO THE FIVE CIVILIZED TRIBES
CHICKASAW LAND OFFICE
ARDMORE, I. T.
Nov. 22, 1905.

In the matter of the enrollment of Gwendoline Mintahoyo Perry, Chickasaw by blood new born card No. 499, roll No. 215.

JAMES M. PERRY, being duly sworn by H. C. Miller, Notary Public, testified as follows:

EXAMINATION BY THE COMMISSIONER:

Q What is your name? A James M. Perry.
Q How old are you Mr. Perry? A Forty-seven.
Q What is your post office address? A Ada.
Q What is your father's name? A Johnson Perry.
Q What is your mother's name? A Name was Liley Perry.

Applications for Enrollment of Chickasaw Newborn
Act of 1905 Volume VI

Q Are you married? A Yes.
Q What is your wife's name? A Minna Lee Perry.
Q She is a white woman? A Yes.
Q A non-citizen? A Yes.
Q Have you any children? A Gwendoline Mintahoyo Perry.

    The name of this witness appears upon Chickasaw Roll card No. 361, Chickasaw final roll No. 1096 as J. M. Perry.

I, Helen C. Miller, Stenographer for the Commissioner to the Five Civilized Tribes hereby swear that I took the testimony in the above matter and that same is a true and correct transcript of my stenographic notest[sic]

                                      Helen C Miller

Subscribed and sworn to before me this 22 day of November, 1905.

                                      J.H. Carlock
                                      Notary Public.

BIRTH AFFIDAVIT.   #104

    IN RE-APPLICATION FOR ENROLLMENT, as a citizen of the   Chickasaw   Nation, of Gwendolene[sic] Mintahoyo Perry   , born on the 3rd day of August , 190 4

Name of Father: James M. Perry   a citizen of the Chickasaw Nation.
Name of Mother: Minna Lee Perry   a citizen of the United States Nation.

                                Postoffice   Ada, Ind. Territory

---

                              AFFIDAVIT OF MOTHER.

UNITED STATES OF AMERICA, INDIAN TERRITORY, ⎫
     Southern   District. ⎭

    I, Minna Lee Perry   , on oath state that I am 33   years of age and a citizen ~~by~~ ...., of the United States   Nation; that I am the lawful wife of   James M. Perry , who is a citizen, by   blood   of the   Chickasaw   Nation; that a   Female child was born to me on 3rd day of   August   , 1904 , that said child has been named Gwendolene Mintahoyo Perry , and is now living.

                                      Minna Lee Perry

Witnesses To Mark:
    Isaac Impson
    Mrs Maggie Crawford

Applications for Enrollment of Chickasaw Newborn
Act of 1905 Volume VI

Subscribed and sworn to before me this 27th day of February, 1905.

C.O. Barton
Notary Public.

AFFIDAVIT OF ATTENDING PHYSICIAN OR MID-WIFE.

UNITED STATES OF AMERICA, INDIAN TERRITORY, }
Southern District.

I, W. T. Noley, a Physician, on oath state that I attended on Mrs. Minna Lee Perry, wife of James M Perry on the 3rd day of August, 190 4; that there was born to her on said date a Female child; that said child is now living and is said to have been named Gwendolene Mintahoyo Perry

W T Noley

Witnesses To Mark:
{ L. G. Barlow
{ *(Name Illegible)*

Subscribed and sworn to before me this 28th day of February, 1905.

C.O. Barton
Notary Public.

BIRTH AFFIDAVIT.

DEPARTMENT OF THE INTERIOR.
COMMISSION TO THE FIVE CIVILIZED TRIBES.

IN RE APPLICATION FOR ENROLLMENT, as a citizen of the Chickasaw Nation, of Gwendolene Mintahoyo Perry, born on the 3rd day of August, 1904

Name of Father: James M Perry a citizen of the Chickasaw Nation.
Name of Mother: Minna Lee Perry a citizen of the United States Nation.

Postoffice Ada, Indian Territory

AFFIDAVIT OF MOTHER.

UNITED STATES OF AMERICA, Indian Territory, }
Southern DISTRICT.

I, Minna Lee Perry, on oath state that I am 33 years of age and a citizen ~~by~~ ...., of the United States ~~Nation~~; that I am the lawful wife of James

Applications for Enrollment of Chickasaw Newborn
Act of 1905   Volume VI

M. Perry   , who is a citizen, by blood   of the   Chickasaw   Nation; that a Female   child was born to me on   third   day of August   , 1904; that said child has been named   Gwendolene Mintahoyo Perry   , and was living March 4, 1905.

Minna Lee Perry

Witnesses To Mark:
{

Subscribed and sworn to before me this 21 day of   April   , 1905

Jno. P. Crawford
Notary Public.

AFFIDAVIT OF ATTENDING PHYSICIAN OR MID-WIFE.

UNITED STATES OF AMERICA, Indian Territory, }
.... DISTRICT. }

I,   N.B. Shands   , a   M.D.   , on oath state that I attended on Mrs.   Minna Lee Perry   , wife of   James M. Perry   on the 3rd day of August, 1904; that there was born to her on said date a   Female   child; that said child was living March 4, 1905, and is said to have been named   Gwendolene Mintahoyo Perry

N B Shands

Witnesses To Mark:
{

Subscribed and sworn to before me this 21 day of   April   , 1905

Jno. P. Crawford
Notary Public.

Applications for Enrollment of Chickasaw Newborn
Act of 1905   Volume VI

CERTIFICATE OF RECORD OF MARRIAGE

United States Of America, ⎫
   Indian Territory, ⎬ Sct.
   Southern District. ⎭

I, C. M. CAMPBELL, Clerk of the United States Court, in the Territory and District aforesaid DO HEREBY CERTIFY, that the License for and Certificate of Marriage of

MR   J M Perry   and

Mrs. Minnie Wade

were filed in my office in said Territory and District the 19 day of Nov. A.D., 190 2 and duly recorded in Book G of Marriage Record, Page 5

DEPARTMENT OF THE INTERIOR,
COMMISSION TO THE FIVE CIVILIZED TRIBES.
FILED
MAY 3 1905
Tams Bixby CHAIRMAN.

WITNESS my hand and Seal of said Court, at Ardmore, this 19 day of Nov. A.D. 190 2

C. M. Campbell
_____
CLERK.

Return this License to the United States Clerk at Ardmore, that it may be recorded, when it will be mailed to the proper address.

Ardmoreite Steam Print.

 MARRIAGE LICENSE

UNITED STATES OF AMERICA, ⎫
   INDIAN TERRITORY, ⎬ ss:
   SOUTHERN DISTRICT. ⎭
To Any Person Authorized by Law to Solemnize Marriage, Greeting:

𝔜ou are hereby commanded to solemnize the Rite and publish the Banns of Matrimony between Mr.   J.M. Perry

Applications for Enrollment of Chickasaw Newborn
Act of 1905 Volume VI

of   Ada   in the Indian Territory, aged   42   years, and M rs Minnie Wade   of   Ada   in the Indian Territory, aged   21   years, according to law; and do you officially sign and return this License to the parties therein named.

Witness my hand and official Seal, this   15   day of   November   A. D. 190 2

C.M. Campbell
Clerk of the United States Court.
By John S. Hanna

| Certificate of Marriage. |

UNITED STATES OF AMERICA,
INDIAN TERRITORY, } ss:
SOUTHERN DISTRICT.   I,   E.A. Wesson

_____ do hereby certify that on the   17   day of   Nov.   , A. D. 190 2 , I did duly according to law, as commanded in the foregoing License, solemnize the Rite and publish the Banns of Matrimony between the parties therein named.

Witness my hand this   17   day of   Nov.   A. D. 190 2

My credentials are recorded in the office of the Clerk of the United States Court, Indian Territory, Southern District, at Ardmore, Book A , Page 232

(NOTE-The person officiating should fill in the spaces for book and page and sign here.)☞

E.A. Wesson
a   A Minister Gospel

NOTE (a)-The License and Certificate of Marriage must be returned to the office of the Clerk of the United States Court in the Indian Territory, at Ardmore, within sixty days from the date thereof, or the party to whom the License was issued will be liable in the amount of One Hundred Dollars ($100).

NOTE (b)-No person is authorized to perform the Marriage Ceremony in the Southern District unless the proper credentials have first been recorded in the Clerk's office.

Applications for Enrollment of Chickasaw Newborn
Act of 1905   Volume VI

9-NB-499

Muskogee, Indian Territory, April 22, 1906.

James M. Perry,
    Ada, Indian Territory.

Dear Sir:

    Receipt is hereby acknowledged of your letter of April 17, 1906, in which you advise that your marriage license and certificate was forwarded in the matter of the enrollment of your child Gwendoline Mintahoya[sic] Perry and replying to your previous letter in which you request the return thereof you are informed that under Departmental instructions this office is retaining all papers filed in enrollment cases, but if your desire a certified copy of your marriage license and certificate the same will be made upon request.

    The communication from this office of May 4, 1905, enclosed with your letter is herewith returned.

                                                  Respectfully,

KB 1-21   Acting Commissioner.

Chickasaw 23.

Muskogee, Indian Territory, May 4, 1905.

James M. Perry,
    Ada, Indian Territory.

Dear Sir:

    Receipt is hereby acknowledged of the affidavits of Minna Lee Perry and N. B. Shands to the birth of Gwendolene Mintahoyo Perry, daughter of James M. and Minna Lee Perry, August 3rd, 1904; also the marriage license and certificate between J. M. Perry and Mrs. Minnie Wade. These papers have been filed with our records as an application for the enrollment of said child.

                                        Respectfully,

                                                     Chairman.

Applications for Enrollment of Chickasaw Newborn
Act of 1905 Volume VI

9-NB-499

Muskogee, Indian Territory, November 28, 1905.

Chief Clerk,
    Chickasaw Land Office,
        Ardmore, Indian Territory.

Dear Sir:

    Referring to Chickasaw new born roll card No. 499, Gwendoline Mintahoyo Perry, you are advised that "father's roll number" has been changed so as to appear thereon "1096", and "for father's enrollment see Chickasaw roll card number" has been changed to read "361".

    You are therefore directed to make like changes upon the duplicate Chickasaw new born roll card No. 499 in the possession of your office.

                Respectfully,

                Acting Commissioner.

Chic. N.B - 500
    (Amanda Underwood
    Born September 14, 1904)

BIRTH AFFIDAVIT. *No 45*

DEPARTMENT OF THE INTERIOR.
COMMISSION TO THE FIVE CIVILIZED TRIBES.

    IN RE APPLICATION FOR ENROLLMENT, as a citizen of the Chickasaw Nation, of Amanda Underwood, born on the 14 day of Sept, 1904

Name of Father: _____ a citizen of the _____ Nation.
Name of Mother: Alice Underwood   a citizen of the Chickasaw Nation.

                Postoffice _____

Applications for Enrollment of Chickasaw Newborn
Act of 1905   Volume VI

AFFIDAVIT OF MOTHER.

UNITED STATES OF AMERICA, Indian Territory, }
   Southern   DISTRICT.

    I, Alice Underwood   , on oath state that I am   19"   years of age and a citizen by   blood   , of the   Chickasaw   Nation; that I am the lawful wife of   not married   , who is a citizen, by .... of the .... Nation; that a female   child was born to me on   14"   day of   Sept   , 1904, that said child has been named   Amanda   , and is now living.

                                      Alice Underwood

Witnesses To Mark:
{

    Subscribed and sworn to before me this   15   day of   Dec   , 1904

                                      Jno. P. Crawford
                                      Notary Public.

AFFIDAVIT OF ATTENDING PHYSICIAN OR MID-WIFE.

UNITED STATES OF AMERICA, Indian Territory, }
   Southern   DISTRICT.

    I,   Nancy Underwood   , a   midwife   , on oath state that I attended on Mrs.   Alice Underwood   , ~~wife of~~   not married   on the   14   day of Sept, 1904; that there was born to her on said date a .... child; that said child is now living and is said to have been named Amanda Underwood

                                      her
                              Nancy x Underwood

Witnesses To Mark: mark
{ Jas. B. Vandiver
  Jno. P. Crawford

    Subscribed and sworn to before me this   14   day of   ~~Sept~~   Dec   , 1904

                                      Jno. P. Crawford
                                      Notary Public.

Applications for Enrollment of Chickasaw Newborn
Act of 1905 Volume VI

BIRTH AFFIDAVIT.

DEPARTMENT OF THE INTERIOR.
COMMISSION TO THE FIVE CIVILIZED TRIBES.

IN RE APPLICATION FOR ENROLLMENT, as a citizen of the Chickasaw Nation, of Mandy Underwood, born on the 14 day of September, 1904

Name of Father: Won't tell father's name   a citizen of the .... Nation.
Name of Mother: Alice King   a citizen of the Chickasaw Nation.

Postoffice   Roff I.T.

AFFIDAVIT OF MOTHER.

UNITED STATES OF AMERICA, Indian Territory, }
Southern DISTRICT. }

I, Alice King, on oath state that I am 20 years of age and a citizen by blood, of the Chickasaw Nation; ~~that I am the lawful wife of~~ ...., ~~who is a citizen, by~~ .... ~~of the Nation~~; that a Female child was born to me on 14 day of September, 1904; that said child has been named Mandy Underwood, and was living March 4, 1905.

Alice King

Witnesses To Mark:
{

Subscribed and sworn to before me this 1 day of May, 1905

JE Williams
Notary Public.

AFFIDAVIT OF ATTENDING PHYSICIAN OR MID-WIFE.

UNITED STATES OF AMERICA, Indian Territory, }
Southern DISTRICT. }

I, Nancy Underwood, a Midwife, on oath state that I attended on Mrs. Alice King, ~~wife of~~ .... on the 14 day of September, 1904; that there was born to her on said date a Female child; that said child was living March 4, 1905, and is said to have been named Mandy Underwood

her
Nancy x Underwood
mark

Applications for Enrollment of Chickasaw Newborn
Act of 1905   Volume VI

Witnesses To Mark:
{ Albert Perry
{ JE Williams

    Subscribed and sworn to before me this 1 day of   May   , 1905

                        JE Williams
                        Notary Public.

BIRTH AFFIDAVIT.

DEPARTMENT OF THE INTERIOR.
COMMISSION TO THE FIVE CIVILIZED TRIBES.

    IN RE APPLICATION FOR ENROLLMENT, as a citizen of the   Chickasaw   Nation, of   Amanda Underwood   , born on the 14th   day of   September   , 1904

Name of Father: .... a citizen of the .... Nation.
Name of Mother: Alice Underwood   a citizen of the   Chickasaw   Nation.

                Postoffice   Ada I.T.

              AFFIDAVIT OF MOTHER.

UNITED STATES OF AMERICA, Indian Territory,
    Southern   **DISTRICT.**

    I,   Alice Underwood (now Alice King)   , on oath state that I am   19   years of age and a citizen by   Blood   , of the   Chickasaw   Nation; that I am the lawful wife of   Mack King   , who is a citizen, by   Blood   of the   Choctaw   Nation; that a   Female   child was born to me on   14th   day of   September   , 1904; that said child has been named   Amanda Underwood   , and was living March 4, 1905.

                        Alice Underwood
Witnesses To Mark: now Alice King
{

    Subscribed and sworn to before me this 5 day of   June   , 1905

                        John Casteel
                        Notary Public.

Applications for Enrollment of Chickasaw Newborn
Act of 1905   Volume VI

AFFIDAVIT OF ATTENDING PHYSICIAN OR MID-WIFE.

UNITED STATES OF AMERICA, Indian Territory, }
    Southern   DISTRICT. }

    I, Nancy Underwood , a Midwife , on oath state that I attended on Mrs. Alice Underwood , wife of (now) Mack King on the 14th day of September , 1904; that there was born to her on said date a Female child; that said child was living March 4, 1905, and is said to have been named Amanda Underwood

                                          her
                                Nancy x Underwood
                                    mark

Witnesses To Mark:
  { *(Name Illegible)*
    A.M. Havermale

    Subscribed and sworn to before me this 5 day of June , 1905

                              John Casteel
                                    Notary Public.

                    Muskogee, Indian Territory, May 18, 1905.

Alice King,
    Roff, Indian Territory.

Dear Madam:

    Receipt is hereby acknowledged of your affidavit and the affidavit of Nancy Underwood to the birth of Mandy Underwood daughter of Alice King, September 14, 1904.

    It is stated in your affidavit that you are a citizen by blood of the Chickasaw Nation. If this is correct you are requested to state the name under which you were enrolled, the names of your parents and if you have selected an allotment of the lands of the Choctaw or Chickasaw Nations[sic] please give your roll number as it appears upon your allotment certificate.

                              Respectfully,

                                                Chairman.

Applications for Enrollment of Chickasaw Newborn
Act of 1905   Volume VI

9-NB-500.

Muskogee, Indian Territory, May 22, 1905.

Alice Underwood,
    Ada, Indian Territory.

Dear Madam:

    There is enclosed you herewith for execution application for the enrollment of your infant child, Amanda Underwood, born September 14, 1904.

    The affidavits heretofore filed with the Commission show the child living on December 14, 1904. It is necessary, for the child to be enrolled, that she was living on March 4, 1905.

    In having these affidavits executed care should be exercised to see that all names are written in full, as they appear in the body of the affidavit, and in the event either of the persons signing the affidavit are unable to write, signatures by mark must be attested by two witnesses. Each affidavit must be executed before a Notary Public and the notarial seal and signature of the officer must be attached to each separate affidavit.

                      Respectfully,

                                  Chairman.

VR 22-7.

(COPY)

Roff, I. T. May 24, 1905.

The Commission to the Five Civilized Tribes,
    Muskogee, I. T.
Gentlemen: Yours of May 18th to hand. Replying to same beg to say.

    I am a citizen by blood of the Chickasaw Nation. and that I was enrolled as Alice Underwood, and am the daughter of Gabrel[sic] Underwood   Suckie Underwood.
My roll number is 120 as appears on my allotment certificate
My allotment was taken in the Chickasaw Nation.

                      Yours truly,

                            Alice King.

Applications for Enrollment of Chickasaw Newborn
Act of 1905   Volume VI

9 N.B. 500.

Muskogee, Indian Territory, June 1, 1905.

Alice King,
    Roff, Indian Territory.

Dear Madam:

  Receipt is hereby acknowledged of your letter of May 24, stating that you were enrolled as Alice Underwood and giving your roll number. This information has enabled us to identify you upon our records as an enrolled citizen by blood of the Chickasaw Nation, and the affidavits heretofore forwarded to the birth of your daughter, Mandy Underwood, have been filed with our records as an application for the enrollment of said child.

           Respectfully,

                [sic]

---

9 NB 500

Muskogee, Indian Territory, June 16, 1905.

Alice Underwood,
    Ada, Indian Territory.

Dear Madam:

  Receipt is hereby acknowledged of the affidavits of yourself and Nancy Underwood to the birth of Amanda Underwood, daughter of Alice Underwood, September 14, 1904, and the same have been filed with our records in the matter of the enrollment of said child.

           Respectfully,

                Chairman.

Applications for Enrollment of Chickasaw Newborn
Act of 1905   Volume VI

9-NB-500

Muskogee, Indian Territory, August 4, 1905.

Crawford & Bolen,
> Attorneys at Law,
>> Ada, Indian Territory.

Gentlemen:

Receipt is hereby acknowledged of your letter of July 25, 1905, asking if the enrollment of Jessie Underwood and Amanda Underwood has been approved.

In reply to your letter you are advised that on June 21, 1905, the Secretary of the Interior approved the enrollment of Jessie Underwood, son of Wesley and Sallie Sealy Underwood as a citizen by blood of the Chickasaw Nation.

You are further advised that the name of Amanda Underwood has not yet been placed upon a schedule of citizens by blood of the Chickasaw Nation prepared for forwarding to the Secretary of the Interior.

Respectfully,

Commissioner.

9-NB-500.

Muskogee, Indian Territory, September 22, 1905

John Casteel,
> Attorney at Law,
>> Roff, Indian Territory.

Dear Sir:

Receipt is hereby acknowledged of your letter of September 16, 1905, in which you request to be advised as to whether the name of Amanda Underwood can be changed upon the final roll of new born citizens by blood of the Chickasaw Nation to Amanda King and if so that steps are necessary on the part of the father and mother of said child to have said name so changed.

You are informed that application was made for the enrollment of this child under the name of Amanda Underwood; that on three different occasions proof of birth was filed for this child and each time her name was stated thereto to be Amanda Underwood. On May 1, 1905, the mother of this child, Alice King, appeared before the Commission to the Five Civilized Tribes and submitted her affidavit as to the birth of said child at which time she refused to give the name of the father of said child.

Applications for Enrollment of Chickasaw Newborn
Act of 1905 Volume VI

You are advised that the enrollment of said child under the name of Amanda Underwood is in strict conformity with the original application for the enrollment of said child and with all proof and evidence subsequently filed in said case. Her name, therefore, can not be changed upon the final roll from Amanda Underwood to Amanda King.

Respectfully,

Acting Commissioner.

Chic. N.B - 501
(Rena McGee
Born December 23, 1903)

BIRTH AFFIDAVIT. No 61

DEPARTMENT OF THE INTERIOR,
COMMISSION TO THE FIVE CIVILIZED TRIBES.

IN RE APPLICATION FOR ENROLLMENT, as a citizen of the Chickasaw Nation, of Rena McGee , born on the 23 day of December , 190 3

Name of Father: Reuben McGee   a citizen of the Chickasaw Nation.
Name of Mother: Lucy McGee   a citizen of the Chickasaw Nation.

Post-Office : Ada I.T.

AFFIDAVIT OF MOTHER.

UNITED STATES OF AMERICA,
INDIAN TERRITORY,
Southern District.

I, Lucy McGee , on oath state that I am about 27 years of age and a citizen by blood , of the Chickasaw Nation; that I am the lawful wife of Reuben McGee , who is a citizen, by blood of the Chickasaw Nation; that a female child was born to me on the 23 day of Dec , 190 3, that said child has been named Rena McGee , and is now living.

                    her
                Lucy x McGee

WITNESSES TO MARK: mark
   Jno. P. Crawford
   JW Bolen

Applications for Enrollment of Chickasaw Newborn
Act of 1905   Volume VI

Subscribed and sworn to before me this   10   day of   January   , 1905.

Jno. P. Crawford
NOTARY PUBLIC.

AFFIDAVIT OF ATTENDING PHYSICIAN OR MID-WIFE.

UNITED STATES OF AMERICA, }
INDIAN TERRITORY,
Southern   District.

I,   Jane Fulsom   , a   midwife   , on oath state that I attended on Mrs.   Lucy McGee   , wife of   Reuben McGee   on the   23   day of Dec, 190 3; that there was born to her on said date a   female   child; that said child is now living and is said to have been named   Rena McGee

                                      her
                          Jane x Fulsom
WITNESSES TO MARK: mark
{ Jno. P. Crawford
{ JW Bolen

Subscribed and sworn to before me this   10   day of   January   , 1905.

Jno. P. Crawford
NOTARY PUBLIC.

BIRTH AFFIDAVIT.
DEPARTMENT OF THE INTERIOR.
COMMISSION TO THE FIVE CIVILIZED TRIBES.

IN RE APPLICATION FOR ENROLLMENT, as a citizen of the   Chickasaw   Nation, of   Rena McGee   , born on the 23^d   day of Dec , 1903

Name of Father: Reubin McGee   a citizen of the   Chickasaw   Nation.
Name of Mother: Lucy McGee   a citizen of the   Chickasaw   Nation.

Postoffice   Ada I.T.

Applications for Enrollment of Chickasaw Newborn
Act of 1905 Volume VI

AFFIDAVIT OF MOTHER.

UNITED STATES OF AMERICA, Indian Territory, }
Southern DISTRICT.

I, Lucy McGee, on oath state that I am 27 years of age and a citizen by blood, of the Chickasaw Nation; that I am the lawful wife of Reubin McGee, who is a citizen, by blood of the Chickasaw Nation; that a female child was born to me on 23^d day of December, 1903; that said child has been named Rena McGee, and was living March 4, 1905.

                          her
                      Lucy x McGee
Witnesses To Mark: mark
{ Johnson Porter
{ Nelson Hawkins

Subscribed and sworn to before me this 12 day of July, 1905

                      WA Guest
                      Notary Public.

AFFIDAVIT OF ATTENDING PHYSICIAN OR MID-WIFE.

UNITED STATES OF AMERICA, Indian Territory, }
Southern DISTRICT.

I, Jane Fulsom, a midwife, on oath state that I attended on Mrs. Lucy McGee, wife of Reubin McGee on the 23^d day of Dec, 1903; that there was born to her on said date a female child; that said child was living March 4, 1905, and is said to have been named Rena McGee

                      her
                  Jane x Fulsom
Witnesses To Mark: mark
{ Johnson Porter
{ Nelson Hawkins

Subscribed and sworn to before me this 12 day of July, 1905

                      WA Guest
                      Notary Public.

Applications for Enrollment of Chickasaw Newborn
Act of 1905   Volume VI

9-NB-501

Muskogee, Indian Territory, July 6, 1905.

Reubin McGee,
    Ada, Indian Territory.

Dear Sir:

    There is inclosed you herewith for execution application for the enrollment of your infant child, Rena McGee born December 23, 1903.

    The application heretofore filed in this office for the enrollment of Rena McGee show that she was living on January 10, 1905,,[sic] in order that said child may be enrolled it is necessary that she was living on March 4, 1905. Please have the inclosed affidavits properly executed and return to this office.

    This matter should receive your immediate attention as no further action can be taken relative to the enrollment of said child, until the evidence requested is supplied.

                                 Respectfully,

LM 6-3   Commissioner.

9-NB-501

Muskogee, Indian Territory, July 18, 1905.

Reuben McGee,
    Ada, Indian Territory.

Dear Sir:

    Receipt is hereby acknowledged of the affidavits of Lucy McGee and Jane Fulsom to the birth of Rena McGee daughter of Reubin and Lucy McGee, December 23, 1903, and the same have been filed with the records of this office in the matter of the enrollment of said child.

                                 Respectfully,

                                 Commissioner.

Applications for Enrollment of Chickasaw Newborn
Act of 1905   Volume VI

7[sic]-NB-501

Muskogee, Indian Territory, September 14, 1905.

John P. Crawford,
    Attorney at Law,
        Ada, Indian Territory.

Dear Sir:

    Replying to your letter of September 11th, you are advised that on August 26, 1905, the Commissioner to the Five Civilized Tribes transmitted for the approval of the Secretary of the Interior a schedule of new-born citizens by blood of the Chickasaw Nation, the name of Rena McGee appearing upon said schedule opposite number 545.

    When the schedule has been approved by the Secretary of the Interior, Reuben McGee will be notified thereof. Until the approval of the enrollment of Rena McGee by the Secretary of the Interior, no allotment can be selected for her.

                  Respectfully,

                  Acting Commissioner.

9-NB-501

Muskogee, Indian Territory, September 22, 1905

Reubin McGee,
    Ada, Indian Territory.

Dear Sir:

    Receipt is hereby acknowledged of your letter of September 13, 1905, addressed to the United States Indian Agent which letter has been by him referred to this office for appropriate action. Therein you request to be advised relative to the enrollment of your minor children, Rena McGee, born December 23, 1903, and Joseph McGee, born July 11, 1905.

    You are advised that the name of Rena McGee has been placed upon a partial roll of new born citizens by blood of the Chickasaw Nation opposite number 545 which roll has been forwarded the Secretary of the Interior for approval. As soon as the enrollment of said child is approved by the Secretary of the Interior you will be duly notified.

    You are further advised, in reply to that part of your letter referring to your infant son Joseph McGee, born July 11, 1905, that no child of a Choctaw or Chickasaw citizen

Applications for Enrollment of Chickasaw Newborn
Act of 1905   Volume VI

born subsequent to March 3, 1905 can be finally enrolled under the privision[sic] of the Act of Congress approved March 3, 1905.

        Respectfully,

              Acting Commissioner.

Chic. N.B - 502
  (Thyra Fay Cravens
  Born November 1, 1903)

BIRTH AFFIDAVIT.   *#143*

      DEPARTMENT OF THE INTERIOR.
    COMMISSION TO THE FIVE CIVILIZED TRIBES.

  IN RE APPLICATION FOR ENROLLMENT, as a citizen of the   Chickasaw   Nation, of   Thyra Fay   , born on the   1   day of   November   , 1903

Name of Father: Charls Thommus[sic] Cravens   a citizen of the   Chickasaw   Nation.
Name of Mother: Willie Cravens   a citizen of the   Chickasaw   Nation.

       Postoffice   Yarnuby[sic]

      AFFIDAVIT OF MOTHER.

UNITED STATES OF AMERICA, Indian Territory,
 Central   **DISTRICT.**

  I,   Willie Cravins[sic]   , on oath state that I am   20   years of age and a citizen by   Intermarry   , of the   Chickasaw   Nation; that I am the lawful wife of   Charls Thommus Cavins[sic]   , who is a citizen, by   blood   of the Chickasaw   Nation; that a   female   child was born to me on   1   day of November   , 1903, that said child has been named   Thyra Fay   , and is now living.

        Willie Cravens

Witnesses To Mark:
  { Tullas Thaxton
    Rosa E Thaxton

Applications for Enrollment of Chickasaw Newborn
Act of 1905   Volume VI

Subscribed and sworn to before me this 20 day of February, 1905.

                S M Mead
                Notary Public.

AFFIDAVIT OF ATTENDING PHYSICIAN OR MID-WIFE.

UNITED STATES OF AMERICA, Indian Territory,
   Central   DISTRICT.

I, Marey[sic] Cravins, a midwife, on oath state that I attended on Mrs. Willie Cravins, wife of Charls Thomas Cravins on the 1 day of November, 1903; that there was born to her on said date a female child; that said child is now living and is said to have been named Thyra Fay

                Mary Cravens

Witnesses To Mark:
   Tullas Thaxton
   Rosa E Thaxton

Subscribed and sworn to before me this 20 day of February, 1905.

                S M Mead
                Notary Public.

BIRTH AFFIDAVIT.
DEPARTMENT OF THE INTERIOR.
COMMISSION TO THE FIVE CIVILIZED TRIBES.

IN RE APPLICATION FOR ENROLLMENT, as a citizen of the Chickasaw Nation, of Thyra Fay Cravens, born on the 1st day of Nov, 1903

Name of Father: Charles Thomas Cravens   a citizen of the Chickasaw Nation.
Name of Mother: Willie Cravens   a citizen of the Chickasaw Nation.

            Postoffice   Yarnaby I.T.

AFFIDAVIT OF MOTHER.

UNITED STATES OF AMERICA, Indian Territory,
   Central   DISTRICT.

I, Willie Cravens, on oath state that I am 19 years of age and a citizen by Intermarriage, of the Chickasaw Nation; that I am the lawful wife of

Applications for Enrollment of Chickasaw Newborn
Act of 1905 Volume VI

Charles Thomas Cravens , who is a citizen, by Blood of the Chickasaw Nation; that a female child was born to me on first day of November , 1903; that said child has been named Thyra Fay Cravens , and was living March 4, 1905.

                                              Willie Cravens

Witnesses To Mark:

    Subscribed and sworn to before me this 22 day of April , 1905

                                                W.T. Thaxton
                                                Notary Public.

AFFIDAVIT OF ATTENDING PHYSICIAN OR MID-WIFE.

UNITED STATES OF AMERICA, Indian Territory,
    Central   DISTRICT.

    I, Mary Cravens , a midwife , on oath state that I attended on Mrs. Willie Cravens , wife of Charles Thomas Cravens on the first day of November , 1903; that there was born to her on said date a female child; that said child was living March 4, 1905, and is said to have been named Thyra Fay Cravens

                                          Mary x Cravens

Witnesses To Mark:
    Tom Hamilton
    (Name Illegible)

    Subscribed and sworn to before me this 27 day of April , 1905

                                                W.T. Thaxton
                                                Notary Public.

                                                          9-NB-502.

                      Muskogee, Indian Territory, June 10, 1905.

Charles T. Cravens,
    Yuba, Indian Territory.

Dear Sir:

    Receipt is hereby acknowledged of your letter of June 5, asking relative to the enrollment of your child, Thyra Fay Cravens.

Applications for Enrollment of Chickasaw Newborn
Act of 1905 Volume VI

In reply to your letter you are advised that the affidavits heretofore forwarded to the birth of your child, Thyra Fay Cravens, have been filed with our records as an application for her enrollment, and you will be informed if further evidence is necessary to enable us to determine her right to enrollment.

Respectfully,

Chairman.

Chic. N.B - 503
(O William Bee
Born August 21, 1904)

BIRTH AFFIDAVIT.

DEPARTMENT OF THE INTERIOR.
COMMISSION TO THE FIVE CIVILIZED TRIBES.

IN RE APPLICATION FOR ENROLLMENT, as a citizen of the Chickasaw Nation, of O William Bee, born on the 21st day of August, 1904

Name of Father: William Bee   a citizen of the Choctaw Nation.
Name of Mother: Nancy Bee   a citizen of the Chickasaw Nation.

Postoffice   Lone Grove, I.T.

AFFIDAVIT OF MOTHER.

UNITED STATES OF AMERICA, Indian Territory,
Southern   **DISTRICT.**

I, Nancy Bee, on oath state that I am 24 years of age and a citizen by blood, of the Chickasaw Nation; that I am the lawful wife of William Bee, who is a citizen, by blood of the Chickasaw Nation; that a male child was born to me on 21st day of August, 1904; that said child has been named O William Bee, and was living March 4, 1905.

Nancy Bee

Witnesses To Mark:

Applications for Enrollment of Chickasaw Newborn
Act of 1905 Volume VI

Subscribed and sworn to before me this 1st day of May , 1905

T.L. Kelley
Notary Public.

AFFIDAVIT OF ATTENDING PHYSICIAN OR MID-WIFE.

UNITED STATES OF AMERICA, Indian Territory,
.... DISTRICT.

See note attached

I, ..., a ...., on oath state that I attended on Mrs. ...., wife of .... on the .... day of ...., 1......; that there was born to her on said date a .... child; that said child was living March 4, 1905, and is said to have been named ....

Witnesses To Mark:
{ ....
  .... }

Subscribed and sworn to before me this .... day of ...., 1905.

Notary Public.

BIRTH AFFIDAVIT.

DEPARTMENT OF THE INTERIOR.
COMMISSION TO THE FIVE CIVILIZED TRIBES.

IN RE APPLICATION FOR ENROLLMENT, as a citizen of the   Chickasaw   Nation, of   O William Bee   , born on the   21   day of   Aug , 1904

Name of Father: William Bee   a citizen of the   Choc   Nation.
Name of Mother: Nancy Bee   a citizen of the   Chick   Nation.

Postoffice   Lone Grove, I.T.

Applications for Enrollment of Chickasaw Newborn
Act of 1905   Volume VI

AFFIDAVIT OF MOTHER.

UNITED STATES OF AMERICA, Indian Territory, }
.... DISTRICT. }

I, ..., on oath state that I am .... years of age and a citizen by ...., of the .... Nation; that I am the lawful wife of ...., who is a citizen, by .... of the .... Nation; that a .... child was born to me on .... day of ...., 1......, that said child has been named .... and was living March 4, 1905.

Witnesses To Mark:
{ ....
  .... }

Subscribed and sworn to before me this .... day of ...., 1905.

....
Notary Public.

AFFIDAVIT OF ATTENDING PHYSICIAN OR MID-WIFE.

UNITED STATES OF AMERICA, Indian Territory, }
Southern   DISTRICT. }

I, Ann Threat   , a midwife   , on oath state that I attended on Mrs. Nancy Bee , wife of Wm Bee   on the 21 day of August   , 1904; that there was born to her on said date a   male   child; that said child was living March 4, 1905, and is said to have been named O William Bee

             her
           Ann x Threat
Witnesses To Mark: mark
{ CR Brinkman
  Dora C Johnson

Subscribed and sworn to before me this 27th day of May   , 1905

         Wm. J. Hulsey
         Notary Public.

Applications for Enrollment of Chickasaw Newborn
Act of 1905 Volume VI

AFFIDAVIT OF ATTENDING PHYSICIAN OR MIDWIFE

UNITED STATES OF AMERICA
INDIAN TERRITORY
Central   DISTRICT

I, Ann Threat   a   midwife on oath state that I attended on Mrs. Nancy Bee (nee Camp)   , wife of   William Bee   , on the 21st day of   August   , 1904, that there was born to her on said date a   male   child, that said child is now living, and is said to have been named   O. William Bee (Jr.)

Witnesses to mark
JD Chastain
Thoms Black

her
Ann x Threat
   mark

$m. D.$

Subscribed and sworn to before me this, the 16th day of   Jan   1905

WITNESSETH:

Must be two witnesses who are citizens { JD Chastain
Thoms Black

Wm J Hulsey   Notary Public.

We hereby certify that we are well acquainted with   Ann Threat   a   Midwife   and know   her   to be reputable and of good standing in the community.

J D Chastain

Thoms Black

NEW-BORN AFFIDAVIT.

Number............

Chickasaw

...~~CHOCTAW~~ ENROLLING COMMISSION...

IN THE MATTER OF THE APPLICATION FOR ENROLLMENT, as a citizen of the Chickasaw   Nation, of   O. William Bee (Jr)

born on the 21st day of   August   1904

Name of father   William Bee   a citizen of   Choctaw
Nation final enrollment No.   9136
Name of mother   Nancy Bee (Nee Camp)   a citizen of   Chickasaw
Nation final enrollment No.   2057

Applications for Enrollment of Chickasaw Newborn
Act of 1905 Volume VI

Postoffice Hartshorne, I.T.

AFFIDAVIT OF MOTHER.

UNITED STATES OF AMERICA
INDIAN TERRITORY
Central DISTRICT

I Nancy Bee (nee Camp) , on oath state that I am 23 years of age and a citizen by blood of the Chickasaw Nation, and as such have been placed upon the final roll of the Chickasaw Nation, by the Honorable Secretary of the Interior my final enrollment number being 2057 ; that I am the lawful wife of William Bee , who is a citizen of the Choctaw Nation, and as such has been placed upon the final roll of said Nation by the Honorable Secretary of the Interior, his final enrollment number being 9136 and that a male child was born to me on the 21st day of August 190 4; that said child has been named O. William Bee (Jr) , and is now living.

Nancy Bee

Witnesseth.
Must be two
Witnesses who
are Citizens.

J D Chastain

Thoms Black

Subscribed and sworn to before me this 16th day of Jan 190 5

Wm. J. Hulsey
Notary Public.

My commission expires: 1908

United States of America,
Indian Territory, Southern District:

Be it remembered that on this the ------ day of June, 19o5, personally appeared before me the undersigned, a Notary Public, duly commissioned and acting within and for said District and Territory, William Bee, and Nancy Bee, his wife, and after being first duly sworn by me; states that they desire to have there[sic] infant child O. William Bee, placed upon the Chickasaw roll.

Witness our hands this the ---7- day of June A. D. 19o5,

William Bee
Nancy Bee

Subscribed and sworn to before me this the -----7 day of June, 19o5.

J.D. Mullen
Notary Public.

Applications for Enrollment of Chickasaw Newborn
Act of 1905   Volume VI

DEPARTMENT OF THE INTERIOR
COMMISSION TO THE FIVE CIVILIZED TRIBES

IN RE Chickasaw Application for the enrollment of O William Bee as a citizen by blood of the ~~Choctaw~~ Nation.

Statement of Mother.

The affidavit of the physician who attended me on the birth of my child, O William Bee, will be furnished the Dawes Commission in a few days. It is impossible at this date to secure same before the rolls close and I now make application, intending to make proof of birth complete later.

Nancy Bee

9-NB-503.

Muskogee, Indian Territory, May 18, 1905.

William Bee,
Lone Grove, Indian Territory.

Dear Sir:

Referring to the application for the enrollment of your infant child, O. William Bee, it appears that you are a citizen by blood of the Choctaw Nation, while your wife is a citizen by blood of the Chickasaw Nation.

Your attention is called to the provision of the Act of Congress approved June 28, 1898, as follows:

The several tribes may, by agreement, determine the right of persons who for any reason may claim citizenship in two or more tribes, and to allotment of lands and distribution of moneys belonging to each tribe; but if no such agreement be made, then such claimant shall be entitled to such rights in one tribe only, and may elect in which tribe he will take such right; but if he fail or refuse to make such selection in due time, he shall be enrolled in the tribe with whom he has resided, and there be given such allotment and distributions, and not elsewhere.

It will therefore be necessary for you and your wife to appear before a Notary Public or other officer authorized to administer oaths and by affidavit elect in which nation you desire to have said child enrolled, forwarding same, when properly executed, to the Commission.

Respectfully,

Chairman.

Applications for Enrollment of Chickasaw Newborn
Act of 1905   Volume VI

9-NB-503.

Muskogee, Indian Territory, June 10, 1905.

William Bee,
    Lone Grove, Indian Territory.

Dear Sir:

    Receipt is hereby acknowledged of the joint affidavit of yourself and your wife, Nancy Bee, electing to have your child, O. William Bee, enrolled as a citizen of the Chickasaw Nation, and the same has been filed with the record in the matter of the enrollment of said child.

        Respectfully,

                Chairman.

Chic. N.B - 504
    (Samuel Pickens Wright
    Born January 7, 1904)

BIRTH AFFIDAVIT.

DEPARTMENT OF THE INTERIOR.
COMMISSION TO THE FIVE CIVILIZED TRIBES.

    IN RE APPLICATION FOR ENROLLMENT, as a citizen of the   Chickasaw   Nation, of   Samuel Pickens Wright   , born on the   7th day of   January   , 1904

Name of Father: Sam B. Wright   a citizen of the   Chickasaw   Nation.
Name of Mother: Nettie E. Wright   a citizen of the   Chickasaw   Nation.

Child present.

                Postoffice   Antlers, Ind. Ter

AFFIDAVIT OF MOTHER.

UNITED STATES OF AMERICA, Indian Territory,
    Central   DISTRICT.

    I,   Sam B. Wright   , on oath state that I am   34   years of age and a citizen by   blood   , of the   Chickasaw   Nation; that I am the lawful ~~wife~~ husband of   Nettie E Wright   , who is a citizen, by   marriage   of the   Chickasaw   Nation; that a

Applications for Enrollment of Chickasaw Newborn
Act of 1905   Volume VI

male   child was born to ~~me~~ us on   7th   day of   January   , 1904; that said child has been named   Samuel Pickens Wright   , and was living March 4, 1905.

                                  Sam B. Wright

Witnesses To Mark:
{

    Subscribed and sworn to before me this   1st   day of   May   , 1905

                                  Wirt Franklin
                                  Notary Public.

AFFIDAVIT OF ATTENDING PHYSICIAN OR MID-WIFE.

UNITED STATES OF AMERICA, Indian Territory, }
    Central   DISTRICT.

    I,   Cornelia E. Mullins   , a   mid-wife   , on oath state that I attended on Mrs.   Nettie E. Wright   , wife of   Sam B. Wright   on the 7th   day of January, 1904; that there was born to her on said date a   male   child; that said child was living March 4, 1905, and is said to have been named   Samuel Pickens Wright

                                  Cornelia E Mullins

Witnesses To Mark:
{

    Subscribed and sworn to before me this   1st   day of   May   , 1905

                                  Wirt Franklin
                                  Notary Public.

Chic. N.B - 505
    (Samuel Richard Oliphint
    Born January 19, 1904)

Applications for Enrollment of Chickasaw Newborn
Act of 1905 Volume VI

BIRTH AFFIDAVIT.

DEPARTMENT OF THE INTERIOR.
COMMISSION TO THE FIVE CIVILIZED TRIBES.

IN RE APPLICATION FOR ENROLLMENT, as a citizen of the Chickasaw Nation, of Samuel Richard Oliphint, born on the 19 day of January, 1904

Name of Father: Samuel R. Oliphint   a citizen of the U.S. Nation.
Name of Mother: Jennie Oliphint   a citizen of the Chickasaw Nation.

Postoffice Wynnewood I.Ty.

AFFIDAVIT OF MOTHER.

UNITED STATES OF AMERICA, Indian Territory,
Southern DISTRICT.

I, Jennie Oliphint, on oath state that I am 38 years of age and a citizen by blood, of the Chickasaw Nation; that I am the lawful wife of Samuel R. Oliphint, who is a citizen, by intermarriage of the Chickasaw Nation; that a male child was born to me on 19th day of January, 1904; that said child has been named Samuel Richard Oliphint, and was living March 4, 1905.

Jennie Oliphint

Witnesses To Mark:

Subscribed and sworn to before me this 28 day of April, 1905

Roy E. Burks
Notary Public.

AFFIDAVIT OF ATTENDING PHYSICIAN OR MID-WIFE.

UNITED STATES OF AMERICA, Indian Territory,
Southern DISTRICT.

I, A.W. Gray, a doctor, on oath state that I attended on Mrs. Jennie Oliphint, wife of Samuel R. Oliphint on the 19 day of January, 1904; that there was born to her on said date a male child; that said child was living March 4, 1905, and is said to have been named Samuel Richard Oliphint

Alexander W. Gray M.D.

Witnesses To Mark:

Applications for Enrollment of Chickasaw Newborn
Act of 1905 Volume VI

Subscribed and sworn to before me this 28 day of April , 1905

Roy E. Burks
Notary Public.

9-NB-505

Muskogee, Indian Territory, July 28, 1905.

Sam. I[sic]. Oliphant[sic],
    Wynnewood, Indian Territory.

Dear Sir:

    Receipt is hereby acknowledged of your letter of July 18, 1905, asking if your child Samuel Richard Oliphant has been approved.

    In reply to your letter you are advised that the name of your child Samuel Richard Oliphant has been placed upon a schedule of citizens by blood of the Chickasaw Nation which has been forwarded the Secretary of the Interior and you will be notified when his enrollment is approved by the Department.

Respectfully,

Commissioner.

Chic. N.B - 506
    (Henry Charles Preston Hays
    Born February 16, 1905)

Applications for Enrollment of Chickasaw Newborn
Act of 1905   Volume VI

CHICKASAW
NEW BORN
ENROLLMENT

506

Henry Charles Preston Hays
(Born Feb. 16, 1905)

Act of Congress Approved March 3, 1905

Cancelled

No. 1 is son of Daniel Hays on Chickasaw Card No. ~~1826~~, whose enrollment was not approved by Department until November 27, 1905. Enrollment hereon cancelled under Departmental instructions of December 1, 1905, (I.T.D. 15900-1905). The name of this child has been placed on Chickasaw Care No. N.B. 545.

506

Chic. N.B - 507
(Lester Brown
Born October 26, 1904)

BIRTH AFFIDAVIT.

Department of the Interior,
COMMISSION TO THE FIVE CIVILIZED TRIBES.

IN RE APPLICATION FOR ENROLLMENT, as a citizen of the Chickasaw Nation, of   Lester Brown   , born on the   26   day of   Oct.   , 190 4

Name of Father: John Brown   a citizen of the Chickasaw Nation.
Name of Mother: Hattie Brown   a citizen of the Chickasaw Nation.

Post-Office: Sneed I.T.

Applications for Enrollment of Chickasaw Newborn
Act of 1905   Volume VI

AFFIDAVIT OF MOTHER.

UNITED STATES OF AMERICA,
    INDIAN TERRITORY,
Southern (21)   District.

    I, Hattie Brown , on oath state that I am 25 years of age and a citizen by Blood , of the Chickasaw Nation; that I am the lawful wife of John Brown , who is a citizen, by Blood of the Chickasaw Nation; that a male child was born to me on 26 day of Oct. , 190 4, that said child has been named Lester Brown , and is now living.

                                                             her
                                                           Hattie x Brown
WITNESSES TO MARK: mark
{ *(Name Illegible)*
  E.S. Davie

    Subscribed and sworn to before me this 25 day of   Mar. , 190

                                            J.L. Wiggins
                                              Notary Public.

AFFIDAVIT OF ATTENDING PHYSICIAN OR MID-WIFE.

UNITED STATES OF AMERICA,
    INDIAN TERRITORY,
Southern   District.

    I, Dr. A. B. Davis , a Phy. , on oath state that I attended on Mrs. Hattie Brown , wife of John Brown on the 26 day of Oct. , 190 4; that there was born to her on said date a male child; that said child is now living and is said to have been named Lester Brown

                                          A.B. Davis M.D.
WITNESSES TO MARK:
{ J.C. Triplitt
  Bab Hunter

    Subscribed and sworn to before me this 25 day of   Mar   , 190

                                        J.L. Wiggins
                                          Notary Public.

Applications for Enrollment of Chickasaw Newborn
Act of 1905   Volume VI

Muskogee, Indian Territory, April 15, 1905.

John Brown,
    Sneed, Indian Territory.

Dear Sir:

    Receipt is hereby acknowledged of the affidavits of Hattie Brown and A. B. Davis to the birth of Lester Brown, son of John and Hattie Brown, October 26, 1904.

    It is stated in the affidavit of the mother that Hattie Brown and John Brown are both citizens by blood of the Chickasaw Nation. If this is correct you are requested to state the names under which you were enrolled, the names of your parents, and if you have either selected an allotment of the lands of the Choctaw or Chickasaw Nation please give your roll numbers as they appear upon your allotment certificate.

Respectfully,

Chairman.

Muskogee, Indian Territory, April 25, 1905.

Hattie Brown,
    Sneed, Indian Territory.

Dear Madam:

    Receipt is hereby acknowledged of your letter of April 19, 1905, stating that last month you made application for the enrollment of Lester Brown but so far have heard nothing from it.

    In reply to your letter you are advised that the affidavits of Hattie Brown and A. B. Davis to the birth of Lester Brown, son of John and Hattie Brown have been received at this office but the information contained therein is not sufficient to enable us to identify Hattie Brown upon our records and on April 15, 1905, a letter was addressed to John Brown, Sneed, Indian Territory, asking the names under which you and your husband were enrolled, the names of your parents and if you have selected an allotment your roll numbers as they appear upon your allotment certificates. To this no reply has been received, and until the information requested is furnished no disposition can be made of the application for the enrollment of Lester Brown.

Respectfully,

Chairman.

Applications for Enrollment of Chickasaw Newborn
Act of 1905   Volume VI

(The letter below typed as given.)

(COPY)

Connission to 5 Trabes
        Muskogee, I. T.

Sneed, I.T. June the 1, 1905.

Hon. Dass Connission

    Sir   Resipt is hereby acknog of your Letter of April 20 the application which that the mistake that I mate to change it in the Mother of Lester Brown afidavit as it apears that John Brown is a roll sitison By Blood that is all the Mistake was Made so I authorise the Comishion to Mark John Brown a united states sitison an that will bee sane as I had don it My self   it will save time and Great _____ to me   I hope that you will send me a Early reply If you canat chang that Mis take please send the application at _____ Brown to John Brown, Sneed I. T.

Your early reply

    John Brown.

(The letter below typed as given.)

7-NB-507.

(COPY)

Muskogee, I. T.
June 1, 1905.

Commission to 5 Tribes,

Sir, if it was Hattie Brown roll NumBer that you want and her parents Name   that her Mother was Marthy McGee a Chick By Blood and her father was TayLor and not a sitson By Blood
I have answered your   quatis _____ 2 weeks a goo
hope to hear from you soon   Hattie Brown.

Applications for Enrollment of Chickasaw Newborn
Act of 1905   Volume VI

9 NB 507

Muskogee, Indian Territory, June 9, 1905.

John Brown,
    Sneed, Indian Territory.

Dear Sir:

    Receipt is hereby acknowledged of your letter of June 1, 1905, in which you say that a mistake was made in the application for the enrollment of your child Lester Brown in stating that you are a citizen by blood of the Chickasaw Nation and that you desire to correct this error.

    This information has been made a matter of record.

Respectfully,

Chairman.

---

9 NB 507

Muskogee, Indian Territory, June 10, 1905.

Hattie Brown,
    Sneed, Indian Territory.

Dear Madam:

    Receipt is hereby acknowledged of your letter of June 1, 1905, giving the names of your parents and other information relative to your enrollment in the matter of the application for the enrollment of your son Lester Brown.

    In reply to your letter you are advised that this information has been made a matter of record and the affidavits heretofore forwarded to the birth of your child Lester Brown have been filed as an application for his enrollment.

Respectfully,

Chairman.

Applications for Enrollment of Chickasaw Newborn
Act of 1905 Volume VI

Chic. N.B - 508
(Viola Lanham
Born March 3, 1905)

BIRTH AFFIDAVIT.

DEPARTMENT OF THE INTERIOR.
COMMISSION TO THE FIVE CIVILIZED TRIBES.

IN RE APPLICATION FOR ENROLLMENT, as a citizen of the   Chickasaw   Nation, of   Viola Lanham   , born on the 3 day of Mch   , 1905

Name of Father: P G Lanham   a citizen of the Intermarried Chickasaw Nation.
Name of Mother: Mary Jane Lanham   a citizen of the   Chickasaw   Nation.

Postoffice   Center IT

AFFIDAVIT OF MOTHER.

UNITED STATES OF AMERICA, Indian Territory, }
         Southern   DISTRICT. }

I, Mary Jane Lanham   , on oath state that I am   30   years of age and a citizen by   blood   , of the   Chickasaw   Nation; that I am the lawful wife of   P G Lanham   , who is a citizen, by mariage[sic]   of the   Chickasaw Nation; that a   Female   child was born to me on   3   day of   Mch   , 1905; that said child has been named   Viola Lanham   , and was living March 4, 1905.

Mary Jane Lanham

Witnesses To Mark:
{

Subscribed and sworn to before me this 2   day of   May   , 1905

J J Copeland
Notary Public.

AFFIDAVIT OF ATTENDING PHYSICIAN OR MID-WIFE.

UNITED STATES OF AMERICA, Indian Territory, }
         Southern   DISTRICT. }

I,   H S Halloway   , a physician   , on oath state that I attended on Mrs.   Mary Jane Lanham   , wife of   P G Lanham   dont remember exact date on the 3x day of Mch ,

Applications for Enrollment of Chickasaw Newborn
Act of 1905   Volume VI

1905; that there was born to her on said date a   Female   child; that said child was living March 4, 1905, and is said to have been named   Viola Lanham

H.S. Halloway M.D.

Witnesses To Mark:
{

Subscribed and sworn to before me this 2 day of   May   , 1905

J J Copeland
Notary Public.

DEPARTMENT OF THE INTERIOR
COMMISSION TO THE FIVE CIVILIZED TRIBES

IN RE APPLICATION FOR ENROLLMENT?,[sic]

As a citizen of the Chickasaw Nation of Viola Lanham, born on the 3rd, daynof[sic] March, 1905, Name of father Perry G. Lanham a citizen of the Chickasaw Nation. Name of Morther[sic] Mary Jane Lanham a citizen of the Chickasaw Nation.

Postoffice, Center, Indian Territory.

Affidavit of acquaintance.

United States of America
 The Indian Territory
Southern Judicial District.

of Mary Jane Lanham Center I.T.

I,   Lucy Black   an acquaintance ^ on oath state that I was present at the home of Mrs. Mary Jane Lanham wife of Perry G. Lanham on the 3rd, day of March, 1905; that there was born to her on said date a female child, that said child was living on the 4th, day of March, 1905, and is said to have been named Viola Lanham.

I further state that I have no interest in the enrollment of Viola Lanham.

Lucy Black

Subscribed and sworn to before me this sworn to before me this the 12th, day of July, 1905.

(Name Illegible)
Notary public.

Applications for Enrollment of Chickasaw Newborn
Act of 1905 Volume VI

DEPARTMENT OF THE INTERIOR
COMMISSION TO THE FIVE CIVILIZED TRIBES

IN RE APPLICATION FOR ENROLLMENT?,[sic]

As a citizen of the Chickasaw Nation of Viola Lanham, born on the 3rd, daynof[sic] March, 1905, Name of father Perry G. Lanham a citizen of the Chickasaw Nation. Name of Morther[sic] Mary Jane Lanham a citizen of the Chickasaw Nation.

Postoffice, Center, Indian Territory.

Affidavit of acquaintance.

United States of America
The Indian Territory
Southern Judicial District.

of Mary Jane Lanham Center I.T.

I, E L Black an acquaintance ^ on oath state that I was present at the home of Mrs. Mary Jane Lanham wife of Perry G. Lanham on the 3rd, day of March, 1905; that there was born to her on said date a female child, that said child was living on the 4th, day of March, 1905, and is said to have been named Viola Lanham.

I further state that I have no interest in the enrollment of Viola Lanham.

E L Black

Subscribed and sworn to before me this sworn to before me this the 12th, day of July, 1905.

(Name Illegible)
Notary public.

9-NB-508

Muskogee, Indian Territory, July 6, 1905.

Perry G. Lanham,
    Center, Indian Territory.

Dear Sir:

Referring to the application for the enrollment of your infant child, Viola Lanham, it appears in the affidavit of the attending physician that the date of birth of said child is given as March 3, 1905, under which is the following notation, "I dont[sic] remember the exact date."

Applications for Enrollment of Chickasaw Newborn
Act of 1905   Volume VI

In view of this statement of the attending physician you are requested to furnish the affidavits of two disinterested persons who are not related to the applicant and who have actual knowledge of the facts, that the child was born, the exact date of her birth, that she was living on March 4, 1905, and that Mary Jane Lanham is her mother.

In having these affidavits executed care should be exercised to see that all names are written in full, as they appear in the body of the affidavit, and in the event that either of the persons signing the affidavit are unable to write, signatures by mark must be attested by two witnesses. Each affidavit must be executed before a Notary Public and the notarial seal and signature of the officer must be attached to each separate affidavit.

This matter should receive your immediate attention as no further action can be taken relative to the enrollment of said child, until the evidence requested is supplied.

    Respectfully,

    Commissioner.

9-NB-508

    Muskogee, Indian Territory, July 21, 1905.

Webb & Ennis,
    Attorneys at Law,
        Ada, Indian Territory,

Gentlemen:

Receipt is hereby acknowledged of your letter of July 15, 1905, enclosing the affidavits of E. L Black and Lucy Black to the birth of Viola Lanham, daughter of Perry G. and Mary Jane Lanham, March 3, 1905, and the same have been filed with the record in this case.

    Respectfully,

    Commissioner.

Applications for Enrollment of Chickasaw Newborn
Act of 1905   Volume VI

9-NB-508.

Muskogee, Indian Territory, September 30, 1905

Webb & Ennis,
    Ada, Indian Territory.

Gentlemen:

    Receipt is hereby acknowledged of your letter of the 22nd instant in which you request to be advised of the status of the application for the enrollment of Viola Lanham as a citizen by blood of the Chickasaw Nation.

    In reply to your letter you are advised that the name of said child has been placed upon a partial roll of new born citizens by blood of the Chickasaw Nation opposite number 547, which schedule was forwarded the Secretary of the Interior for approval on August 26, 1905. As soon as the same is approved the parents of said child will be duly notified.

                       Respectfully,

                                 Commissioner.

Index

ABBOTT
  J A 107,108
  Lavada 107,108
  Levada 108
  Zona.................................107,108
ALLEN, A L........................... 203
ALLISON
  W H 215,217
  W N 179,199
  Wade H..................................... 216
ANGELL, W H 171
ARNOLD
  J H 172,174
  J H, MD 172
ARNOTE, A J 130
ARPELAR, Lynch.................... 125
ATER, W H..........................1,2,3
BACKUS, Dovie 139,140
BACON, William Jesse............... 58
BALL, E J....................16,194,223,224
BARLOW, L G 229
BARR, W L 95
BARTON, C O 229
BEALL, Wm O 162
BEE
  Nancy ... 250,251,252,253,254,255,256
  O William 250,251,252,254,255,256
  O William (Jr) 253,254
  William 250,251,253,254,255,256
  Wm.. 252
BEELER
  Fred G 2
  Geo R.. 2
BENTON
  Davis 168
  Earnest.. 167,168,169,170,171,172,173
  Ernest..................................171,172,174
  Jewell.... 167,168,169,170,171,172,174
  Louisa 168
  Maggie......................168,169,170,174
  Miggey 168,169
  Miggie M 171,172,174
BIXBY, Tams.......... 16,21,52,53,111,127,
128,129,133,137,174,190,191,211,231
BLACK
  E L 267,268
  Lucy...................................266,268

  Taylor 204
  Thoms...................................253,254
BLUE, Annie............................... 93
BOLEN, J W 242,243
BOOTH
  T S 209,214
  T S, MD..............................209,210
BOSWELL, C............................. 20
BOURLAND
  Lulu Catherine 178
  William Howard 178
BRANUM
  T C.. 34
  T C, MD 34
BREEDLOVE, R T 171,172
BRINKMAN, C R 252
BROWN
  Edna.. 9
  Elsie 153
  Hattie 260,261,262,263,264
  John 260,261,262,263,264
  Lester.................260,261,262,263,264
  Lucy.....................................153,154
BRUCE, J H 125
BURFIELD
  E 95,96,97
  E, MD 95,96
BURKS, Roy E......................258,259
BURRIS, Geo W 43
BUXBEE, J H.............................. 173
BYRD, G F 179
CALLAWAY
  Branum 35
  James R, MD 35
CAMP
  Nancy 253,254
  W B 21
CAMPBELL
  Albert.................................181,182
  C M 21,22,111,112,133,134,135,
  165,211,212,231,232
CAMRON, Mary 16,17,18
CARLOCK, J H.............................. 228
CARNEY
  Adaline 225
  Adeline 226
  Adline 223,224

271

Index

CARSON, T J 144
CART, J L 146
CASS
   Cora 223,224,225,226,227
   L W 227
   Lewis 223,224,225,226,227
   Rhoda 223
   Roda 224,225,226,227
CASTEEL, John 237,238,241
CATLIN
   J D 16,17
   J H 172,173
CAVINS, Charls Thommus 247
CHASTAIN, J D 253,254
CHICK, Carnelia M 24
CHIEK, Cornelia M 21,22,24
CHIGLEY
   Bell 113
   Belle 113,115,117,118
   Lizzie Bell 114,115,116,118,119
   Lizzie Belle 114,115,117
   Ruby 113,114,115,116,117,118,119
   Wyatt 113,114,115,116,117,118,119
CLARBORN, Belle 165,167
CLARK, Amelia 218,219,220,221,222
COFFEY
   Dr O F 216
   O F 215,216
   Oscar F 215
COFFMAN, Joseph S 215
COLBERT
   Abbie 105,106,107
   Charley 105,106,107
   Charlie 217
   Clarance Cadian 13,14
   Clarane Cadian 13
   Ida 13,14
   James B 14
   James Beldon 13,14
   Pauline 106,107
   Puline 105
COLLIE, Sallie 36,37
COLLINS
   Ben C 4,5,6
   Hettie H 4,5,6
   Maude 5
   Vernon 4,5,6

COLUMBUS, Etta .. 193,194,195,197,198
COMBS
   B C 134
   Ben 135
CONNELLY
   Hannah 147,148
   J W 147,148
COPELAND, J J 265,266
CRAIG
   J R 48
   J R, MD 48
   W W 20
CRAVATT
   Fred 98,99,100
   Mary 98,99,100
   Randers H 98,99,100
   Rena 98,99,100
CRAVENS
   Charles T 249
   Charles Thomas 248,249
   Charls Thommus 247
   Mary 249
   Thyra Fay 247,248,249,250
   Willie 247,248,249
CRAVINS
   Charls Thomas 248
   Marey 248
   Mary 248
   Thyra Fay 248
   Willie 247,248
CRAWFORD
   Jno P 230,235,242,243
   John P 246
   Maggie 228
CRAWFORD & BOLEN 241
CROSS
   John H 217,218,219,220
   M E 217,218,219,220
CUFFS, Artie 159
CULLUM, J E 78
CUPPS, Artie 155,158,159,161,162
CURRA, Emma 133,134,138
CURRY, Emma 135
DABNEY, B H 151
DAVIE, E S 261
DAVIS
   A B 262

Index

A B, MD 261
Dr A B 261
Jane 7
DIFENDAFER, Chas T 120
DRAUGHESS, Albert 211,212,213,214
DUCKWORTH
   Berry 149
   Lou 149
DUFFY
   Burris Donaven 47,48,49
   Edith E 48
   Edith Ethel 47,48
   Patrick 47,48,49
DULIN, Simp 114,115,116
DURANT, Mollie 224
DURIGO
   Albert Franklin 208,209,212,213
   Martha Jane 208,209
   Peachie Viola 208,209
DURODERIGO
   Albert F 214
   Albert Franklin ... 209,210,212,213,214
   Martha Jane 209,210,212,213,214
   Peachie Viola 208,209,210,213,214
DURODEROGO, Dr Albert Franklin. 212
EBEY, W H 64
EDINGTON
   Eda Elizabeth 110,112
   J F 112,164,212
EDWARDS
   Joe A 79
   Jos A 78
   Joseph A 79
ELLIS
   A C 39,40
   G H 149,150
   G H, MD 149
FACTOR
   Ishtuky 64
   Stamfioke 63,64
FANNIN, E J 16,17,53,172,173
FILLMORE
   Benjamin Franklin 1,3,4
   Mandy 1,3,4
   Sallie 1,2,3,4
FILMORE
   Benjamin Franklin 1,2,3

Mandy 1,2,3
Sallie 2,3
FORD
   Albert 86,89,90
   B P 84,85,86,87,88,89,90,180,181
   Fanney 84,85,91
   Fannie 83,84,86,91,92
   Gorge 84,87
   Henry H 84,87
   Jewel 83,88,89,91
   Jewell 87,88,89,90,91,92
   Maggie 89,90,91
   Robert 85
   Robert P 83,84,85,86,87,88,89,
   90,91,92
   Salley 84,85,88,89,91
   Sallie 83,84,85,86,87,88,89,90,92
FORREST, S S 218,219
FOWLER, O R 187
FRANKLIN, Wirt 257
FREEMAN, W M 131,135
FRY, T W 122
FULLER, J W 93
FULSOM, Jane 243,244,245
FUSSELL
   Alice M 138,139,140
   James E 138,139,140
   Paul 138,139,140
GADDIS
   Eva 69,70,72
   Evie 72
   George L 70,71,72
   Martha 70,71,72
   Pearl 69,71,72
GAMBLE, Lorena M 81
GARDNER
   R A 207
   R A, MD 207
GARRETT
   Jesse A 104,105
   Lula L 104,105
   Lula Lucretia 104,105
   Uldean 103,104,105
GILMORE
   Conchoella B 81,82,83
   Edwin T 81,82,83
   John T 83

Index

John T, MD 82
Sarah A 81,82,83
GIPSON, William 99,100
GOLDSMITH, Robert J 130
GOODWIN, G W 28,29,30,31
GORDON
   J M 205,206
   Jas M 204
GRAHAN, B G 141
GRAY
   Alexander W, MD 258
   A W 258
GRAYSON
   Elsie 65,66
   Felix 65,66
   A J 78
   Miller Woodson 65,66
GRIFFITH, Dr A 126
GUEST, W A 244
HALLOWAY
   H S 265
   H S, MD 266
   Ola 175,176,177
HAMILTON
   F J 164
   Tom 249
HAMM
   C S 33,34,35
   Mattie L 33,34,35
   Mattie Love 34,35
   Thomas Colville 33,34,35
HAMPTON
   Burnie C 36,37
   J W 36,37
   Mary C 36,37
HANCOCK
   Clarence R 6,7
   Katie 6,7
   Robert 6,7
HANNA
   Dr J M 164,165
   J M 163
   John S 232
HARDY
   Cornelius 44,45
   Dr Walter 176
   Janice Heald 5

W 177
W, MD 176
HARJOE, Lucy 53,57
HARRIS
   Benjamin Franklin 140,141,142
   Claud Laten 140,141
   Ella May 140,141,142
HARRISON, Wm 13
HAVERMALE, A M 238
HAWKINS
   Dicey 128
   Ledicy 127,128
   Nelson 244
HAYES, Bettie 60,61
HAYS
   Bettie 59
   Daniel 260
   Henry Charles Preston 259,260
HIGHTOWER, M M 70,71,72
HOGGARD, C P 67,68,73,74
HOLDERMAN
   C W 14
   Minnie 14
HOOK, H P 17
HULSEY, Wm J 252,253,254
HUNNICUTT, Sallie 1
HUNTER, Bab 261
IMPSON
   A B 13
   Isaac 228
   Isaac J 13
INGRAM, Mollie H 5,6
ISBELL, J H 120,121
JACKSON, Leffy 146
JACOBS, Icia 132,136
JOBE
   Alice 84,85,86,91,92
   Allis 85
   B F 126
   Connie 85
   J T 84
   Lillie 85
   Maggie 88
   Magie 88
   Z Y 87
JOHNS, S T 148,149
JOHNSON

Dora C	252
Francis	181,182
G L	68,69,73,75
G L, MD	67,69,74
Leuise	182
Louisa	178,179,181,182,183,186
Louise	180
Nancy	179,182,183,186
O L	120
Susan	178,179,180,181,182, 183,184,185,186
Thomas	178,179,183
Thompson	180,181,182,183,184, 185,186

JOHNSTON
- Etta 67,68,69
- G L 67
- Joseph E 94,95,96,97
- Kirkland B 94,95,96,97
- Lem 67,68,69
- Leo Curtis 66,67,68,69
- Mary Catherine 94,95,96,97

JONES
- J W 146
- W W 82,181,182

KEEL
- Belle 163,165,166
- Guy 76,77
- Irene 77
- Jesse 163,166,167
- Jessie 164,165
- Lula 76,77
- Lutie Mable 76,77
- Sanders 163,164,165,167
- Sandus 166

KEENER
- Lillie May 154,155,156,158,159, 160,161
- Mauley 155
- Maulsey 154,160,161,162
- Moley 158
- Molsey 155,156,157,159
- Stokes 156,159,161

KELLER, T C 81,195,224,225
KELLEY, T L 251

KENNEDY
- Elizabeth 41

Elizabeth A	38,40
Ida May	37,39,40,41,42
James Hardiman	37,38,40,41,42
John E	38
John W	39,40,41,42
Mary C I	38,39,40,41

KEY, B H 151,152

KING
- Alice 236,237,238,239,240,241
- Amanda 241,242
- Anderson 162
- Hayes 162
- Mack 237,238
- Mulsey 162
- Susan 162

KINNER
- Lillie 162
- Mulsey 162

KIZZIAR, Ollie 111,113

LANHAM
- Mary Jane 265,266,267,268
- P G 265
- Perry G 266,267,268
- Viola 265,266,267,268,269

LEE
- James 168,169
- L L 177
- Robt E 175,176,177

LEWIS
- Gollia 77,78,79
- Martin 78,79
- Nora 78,79

LIGON, M W 65,66
LILLIE, Fannie 85

LOGAN
- Clemeakey 121,123
- Clemia Key 122,124
- Cromer 15,18

LUNA, J H 224
LYLES, H T 200
MADISON, Florence 3
MANSFIELD, MCMURRAY & CORNISH 191
MARSHALL, J C 215

MARTIN
- C B 76,77
- C B, MD 77

Index

J M 22
Wm L 170,171
MASSEY
  G R 28,32
  Gus R 27,28,29,30,31
  Guss R 26
  Jno W 114,115,193
  Joeph Overton 26,27
  John W 142,144
  Joseph Overton 26,27,28,30,31,32
  Juel 142,144
  Mildred Marine 26,28,29,32
  N B 31
  Nancy E 32
  Nancy Elizabeth 27,28,29,30,31
  Nancy Elizibeth 26
  Rachel A 144
  Rubey 142,144
MAYER
  Bruno 214,215,216
  Cornelia 214,215,216
  James Bruno 214,215,216
MCCALIB
  D C 27,28,29,30,31
  D C, MD 28,29,30
MCCARTER
  Jackson 101,102,103
  Sarah 101,102,103
  Somie 101,102,103
MCCARTY, Somie 103
MCCOOLE, John I 50,51,52,53,155,
157,158
MCCOY, N H 134
MCGEE
  Joseph 246
  Lucy 242,243,244,245
  Marthy 263
  Rena 242,243,244,245,246
  Reuben 242,243,245,246
  Reubin 243,244,245,246
MCKEOWN, Tom D 64,155,160
MCKINNEY, A J 5
MCLEOD, Julia 102
MCMILLAN
  Mary 207
  W A 207
  William Jasper 206,207

Wm 207
MEAD
  E L 149
  L L 26,27
  Mrs F E 26,27
  S M 147,188,248
MEEKS, Ardil C 132
MELVILLE
  Frances 60,61
  Francis 59
  Newton 58,59,60,61
  Sam C 61
  Samuel C 59,60,61
MILLER
  H C 143
  Helen C 228
  Henry 168
  Maggie 168
  Miggey 168,169,170,172,173
  Sallie 168
MILLIGAN, Charles 141
MONROE
  Nancy 103
  Roman 103
  Sarah 103
MOONEY, W E 93
MULLEN, J D 254
MULLIN
  Cornelia Eldora 129,130
  Seth J 129,130
  Tams L 129,130
MULLINS, Cornelia E 257
NELSON, Tennessee 126,129
NEWMAN, H O 94,104,105
NICHOLS, J M 68,69
NOLEN, W T 108
NOLEY, W T 108,229
NORTON, Elsie 8,9,151,152,153
NORVELL, M G 21
O'DONBY, W J 36,37
OLIPHANT
  Sam I 259
  Samuel Richard 259
OLIPHINT
  Jennie 258
  Samuel R 258
  Samuel Richard 257,258

Index

OLIVER, Newton 155
OWENS
   Daisy Lee 14,15,18
   Mary J 15,18
   S L 16,17,18
   Solomon 15,18
PATTERSON, Hatie 1
PEDDYCOART
   M E 11
   Mary E 12
PERRY
   Albert 62,63,64,237
   Cicen 62,63,64
   Essie May 10,11,12
   Gwendolene Mintahoyo 228,229, 230,233
   Gwendoline Mintahoya 233
   Gwendoline Mintahoyo 227,228,234
   J M 228,231,233
   James M 227,228,229,233
   Jeff 92,93,94
   Johnson 92,93,94,227
   Josephine 94
   Josiphine Kuctchubby 92,93
   Kittie Peddycoart 10,11,12
   Liley 227
   Minna Lee 228,229,230,233
   Mrs Jeff 93
   Simon 62,63,64
   Thomas J 10,11,12
PETTIGREW
   Benin 202
   Louvena 201
   Louvina 202
   Mose 202
PICKENS
   Eliza 119,120,121,122,123,124
   Gincy 121,122,124
   Henretta 150,151,153,154
   Hylam 150,152,153,154
   Isom 119,120,121,122,123,124
   Jincy 119,120,121,123
   John 111,113
   Johnie 109,110
   Johnnie 112
   Lucy 150,151,152,153,154
   Ollie 109,110,112

Thomas 150,151,152,153
Thompson 109,110,112
Tom 154
Tommie 8,9
PITCHLYNN
   Emma 131,132,136
   Evelyn 131
   George .. 131,132,133,134,135,136,138
   George Ann 132,136
   Georgian 131,136,138
PITTMAN
   J B 8,9,152
   W H 8,9,151,153
PORTER, Johnson 244
PRUITT, C C 37
PYTCHLYN
   Emma 137
   George 137
   Georgian 137
REED
   Jackson 155,157,159,161
   Lillie May 157,158,162
   Maulsey 162
   Molsey 158
RENNER, Lula D 43
RENNIE
   Alexander 46,47
   Alexander, Jr 43,44,45,47
   Helen 42,43,44,45,46,47
   Lula 45,46
   Lula Burris 44
   Lula D 43,47
REYNOLDS
   Carial 187
   Ceral 186,188,189,190,191
   Cerial 190
   Frank 188,189,190,191
   Vina Lee 187,188,189,190
REYONLDS, Ceral 188
RICH, Joe 120,121
RICHARDSON
   Dora 201
   Dore 199,200,202
   Lavenie 202
   Liza 198,199,200,201,202,203
   Louvena 201,202
   Louvenia 202

Index

Lovenie 202
Lovinia 200
Lovinie 199
Nevina 198,199
Sarah 202
Walton 198,199,200,201,202
RICHEY
   S M 50,51,55
   S M, MD 50,51
RIDER
   Geo E 76,77
   George E 77
ROBERTS
   Elsa 217
   Elsie 217,218,219,220,221,222
   Nancy 217,218,219,220,221,222
   Wilson 217,218,219,220,221,222
ROBINSON
   Cansada 87
   Frank L 19
ROGERS, Lora 204,205
ROGGERS, Lora 204
ROSS, C H 110
RUSHING, Lucinda 141
SAMPSON
   G L 107
   G T 106
   G T, MD 106
SAVAGE, Martin 121,122
SCHNEIDER, H 141
SEALEY
   Adam 125,126,128,129
   Gouldy 125,126,128,129
   Ledicy 125,126,129
   Ledisy 126
   Louise Johnson 180
SEALY
   Adam 124,125,127,129
   E B 197
   Gouldy 124,125,127,128
   Henry 125,127
   Laticy 124
   Latisy 124
   Liticy 125
   Litisy 127
   Luticy 127
   Vinnie May 197

SEELY
   E D 196
   Esau 193,194,195,196
   Vinnie May 193,194,195,196,
   197,198
SELF, S F 220
SETTLE
   Dr W E 20
   W E 19,20,23,25
   W E, MD 19
SHANDS, N B 230
SHIELD, Simon 53,57
SHIELDS
   Esau 146
   Henry 180,181
   Manda 145,146
   Simian 145,146
   Simion 146
   Wisie 145,146
SHUMATE, J W 131
SIMPSON
   Joe 109,110,151,152
   Mattie 211,212,213
SKINNER
   Permelia 187,188,189,190
   W L 188,189
SLAUGHTER, D O 106
SMITH
   Cora E 14
   D B 64
   V 33
   W A 96,97
   Zona 107
STANFIELD, J M 48
STATLER
   Gale 99,100
   Price 98,99,100,101,102
STICK, Katie 93
STRAWN, D T 132
STRICKLAND
   Itta Fay 74
   Jettie 73,75
   Malita Fay 73,74,75
   Thos 73
   Tom 73,74,75
STUBBLEFIELD, S L 122
TALLEY, C E 39,40

Index

TAYLOR 263
   Sula E 209,210,212
THAGARD
   W C 70,71,72
   W C, MD 70,72
THAXTON
   Rosa E 247,248
   Tullas 247,248
   W T 249
THOMASON, C H 34,35
THREAT, Ann 252,253
TOMAS, E S 88
TOMSON, H 86,90
TRIPLITT, J C 261
TURNER
   Andrew J 149
   Andrew Jackson 147,148,150
   Everett All 149
   Evert All 150
   Evert Allen 147,148,149
   A J 149,150
   Maud 149
   Maud Miller 147
   Maude 148,149,150
TYE, L L 192
UNDERWOOD
   Alice 234,235,237,238,239,240
   Amanda 234,235,237,238,239, 240,241,242
   Gabrel 239
   Jessie 241
   Lema 198
   Lerna 194,195
   Lernah 195
   Mancy 236
   Mandy 236,240
   Nancy 235,236,238,240
   Rena 99,100
   Sallie Sealy 241
   Suckie 239
   Wesley 241
VANDIVER
   James B 162
   Jas B 235
VANNOY
   W W 43,44,47,104,105
   W W, MD 43,104

VAUGHN, John 10,11,12
VICTOR
   Emmet L 203,204,205
   Emmett 206
   Hazel 203,204,205,206
   Lee 203,204,205
WADE
   Geo 49,50,51,53
   Geo, Jr 51
   George 50,51,52,54,55,56,57,58
   George, Jr 49,51,55,56,57
   Minnie 51,52,57,231,232,233
   Minnie M 49,51
   Minnie May 50,55
   Mrs Geo 50
   Nannie 53
   Richard Perry 49,50,52,53,55,56, 57,58
WAGNER, J D 35
WALDREN, Minnie 53,54,56
WALKER
   Isaac D 130
   Isaac D, MD 130
   T C 97
WALMER
   Florence M 25
   Robert 24,25
WALNER
   Cornelia M 20,25
   Florence 23
   Florence M 18,19,20,23,24,25
   May 18,19,23,24
   Robert 18,19,20,23,24,25
   W R 21,22,24
WALTREP
   P M 4
   P M, MD 3
   P W, MD 2
WALTRIP
   Ollie 3
   P M 3
WARREN
   Marguerite N 192
   Marguerite Nancy 193
   Nannie B 192
   William F 192
   Wm F 192

Index

WATKINS
   Henry Furman................... 175,176,177
   Lou Catherine 175,176,177
   Lula Catherine 178
   Lulu Catherine 178
   R 176
   Ruby 175
   Ruby Isabelle 175,176,177
   W R 175,176,177
   W R, Jr. 178
WEBB, James E 60,61
WEBB & ENNIS 268,269
WEIMER, W G 126
WELCH, J S 77
WELLS
   Florence E 80,81
   Lizzie 177
   Lula C 80,81
   Willard W 80,81
WESSON, E A 232
WHITE
   J E 38,39,40,41,139
   J M 7
WHITFIELD
   James 114,115,117,192,193
   James, MD 114
WIGGINS, J L 261
WILLIAMS
   E G 79
   J E 15,45,62,63,65,66,108,
   156,236,237
   Richard 54
WILSON, L 88
WOLTREP, P M 3
WOOLEY, Sam 125
WRIGHT
   Nettie E 256,257
   Rosey 85,89
   Sam B 256,257
   Samuel Pickens 256,257
   Sophey 85,89
YOUNG
   Adaline 117
   Granville W 117
   Lizzie Bell 115,116,118,119
   Lizzie Belle 117
YOUNG & NEWMAN 105

YOUNGBLOOD
   Edna 8,9
   Juneta 8,9,10
   Junetta 8
   L C 8,9

www.ingramcontent.com/pod-product-compliance
Lightning Source LLC
Chambersburg PA
CBHW020247030426
42336CB00010B/657